IGNITE YOUR ADVENTUROUS SOUL
WITH TRAVELLING TALES FROM
AROUND OUR WORLD

dust in my pack

NANCY O'HARE

DUST IN MY PACK

by Nancy O'Hare

Published by Nancy O'Hare
First published: 2017
bynancyohare.com
Editor: Susan Fitzgerald
Proofreader: Stacey Atkinson
Cover & interior design: Bright Wing Books
Ebook design development: Bright Wing Books
Photography: Chad O'Hare
© 2017 by Nancy O'Hare

The information in this book is true and complete to the best of the author's knowledge. All recommendations are made without guarantee on the part of the author. The author disclaims any liability in connection to the use of this information. None of the establishments or services mentioned or reviewed in this book have provided compensation to the author.

CONTENTS

ACKNOWLEDGEMENTS 5

PREFACE 7

INTRODUCTION 9

CHAPTER ONE: BOAT TRIPS 11

    Antarctica — The MV *Antarctica Dream* 12

    Australia — Sailing 16

    Botswana — Mokoro 18

    Chile — The Navimag *Evangelistas* 22

    Egypt — Felucca 25

    Laos — Héua Hǎhng Nyáo 28

    Malawi — The MV *Ilala* 31

CHAPTER TWO: MULTI-DAY TREKS 35

    Australia — Cradle Mountain 36

    Bhutan — Jomolhari 39

    China — Mount Kailash in Tibet 42

    Laos — Nam Ha National Protected Area 47

    Malawi — Mount Mulanje 51

    Uganda — Rwenzori 55

CHAPTER THREE: DAY HIKES 59

    Argentina & Chile — Patagonia 60

    Australia — Bay of Fires 67

    Nicaragua — Volcán San Cristóbal 70

    Nicaragua — Volcán Maderas 73

    Nicaragua — Coffee Country Highlands 75

    Switzerland — Grindelwald 81

CHAPTER FOUR: TEMPLES AND FORTS 85

Cambodia — Temple of Preah Vihear 86
India — Ajanta Caves 92
Indonesia — Temple of Borobudur 95
Laos — Wat Phu Temple 99
Oman — Nizwa Fort 103
Mozambique — Fort of São João 107

CHAPTER FIVE: ANCIENT CITIES 111

Guatemala & Honduras — Tikal, Yaxhá and Copán 113
Jordan — Petra 121
Morocco — Aït Benhaddou 125
Peru — Ollantaytambo 128
Turkey — Ephesus 131
Yemen — Old Sana'a and Kawkaban 134

CHAPTER SIX: GETAWAY ADVENTURES 139

Australia — Bodysurfing 140
Australia — Caving 142
Oman — Diving 145
Switzerland & France — Skiing 148
Switzerland — Snowshoeing 150
Vietnam — Kayaking 152
Zimbabwe — White-Water Rafting 155

CHAPTER SEVEN: SERENE SCENES 159

Bhutan — Kurjey Lhakhang 160
Laos — Si Phan Don Archipelago 164
Namibia — Sossusvlei 168
Oman — Sultan Qaboos Grand Mosque 171
Switzerland — Collonge-Bellerive to Hermance 174

CHAPTER EIGHT: ANIMAL ENCOUNTERS 177

Malawi — Liwonde National Park 179
Rwanda — Volcanoes National Park. 181
South Africa — Kruger National Park 183
South Africa — Sabi Sands Reserve 185
Zambia — South Luangwa National Park 188
Zambia — Near the Lower Zambezi National Park 191

CHAPTER NINE: UNFORGETTABLE ACCOMMODATIONS 193

Argentina — Bohemia Hotel Boutique 194
Cambodia — Rainbow Lodge. 195
Cambodia — Chi Phat Community Tourism Village. 197
Indonesia — Melanting Cottages 200
Morocco — Riad W 202
Mozambique — Nkwichi Lodge. .204
Oman — Shangri-La Barr al Jissah Resort & Spa 208
Switzerland — Hotel Caprice 210
Vietnam — Lien Hiep Thanh Resort 212

ABOUT THE AUTHOR 217

ENDNOTES 219

BIBLIOGRAPHY 223

ACKNOWLEDGEMENTS

I could not have written this book without my partner's equal love of travel, which has enabled our adventures together. Chad's sense of intrigue for remote destinations and his personal philosophy to challenge ourselves have truly elevated our exploits together. This book would not have been possible without his unwavering support through it all. Chad's brilliant eye also captured all the photos presented throughout **Dust in My Pack**. If you want to see more of his photography, visit his Instagram account @flatearthnomad.

As a first-time author, I relied heavily on my editor's literary acumen. I would like to thank Susan Fitzgerald for taking the time, not only to correct and edit my writing, but also to offer much-appreciated rationale and guidance.

A few people close to my heart have endured hours of reviewing sections from my earlier drafts. Nancy McNair, a good friend who also shares a love of foreign culture, provided poignant analytical tips on contextual considerations and messaging, which I have carried throughout my writing.

My parents, Brian and Millie Veale, took time out of their overseas vacation to read numerous sections. They provided helpful pointers to maintain the flow and readability while offering endless positive encouragement and feedback.

Thank you all for your unending support; I will always be grateful.

Travelling feels like part of my DNA. My father describes this call as our gypsy gene. For me, it was first ignited at the age of twelve, when I was fortunate enough to take part in a two-week field trip to Europe. Upon my return, I promptly forewarned my parents that, at some point, I would move overseas. Years later, my choice to become a chartered accountant was partially influenced by the knowledge that all companies, in all countries, need accountants. My plan slowly took shape. Since 1998, when I nabbed a transfer to Australia, my path has led me to some remarkable destinations, even though its course has not always seemed clear.

This book is a compilation of enduring memories from living on five continents and travelling across sixty-three countries. Tales range from adrenalin-inducing exploits to awe-inspiring sites. These favourite adventures are broadly grouped into chapters by type of travel experience. I have not ranked them, as to do so would diminish the very diversity and unique qualities that each imparted.

Throughout my travels, one consistent message has shone clearly. People across the globe are connected by a common quality, no matter their country of origin, economic status or religious leaning. Folks everywhere seem to have an instinct to help their families and those near to them. Compassion unites us.

This compelling pattern became visible to me as I travelled for work and on the occasional five- to twelve-month sabbatical, when I ventured through remote regions of the world. My husband and I came across so many helpful and welcoming individuals, often when least expected. For instance, a staff member at a family guesthouse in an isolated Malaysian village balanced my husband and me on the back of his motorbike for an hour-long ride to the nearest hospital to take a malaria test. Thankfully, the test came back negative. The same theme was reflected by my Omani colleagues, a mix of Sunni and Shiite Muslims, as we developed a camaraderie like that of a second family. Perhaps the clincher was in 2014, at the height of the Ebola outbreak, when our Nigerian steward used his vacation to educate every family in his home village. He walked door to door to advise people on how to protect themselves against the virus.

I have witnessed countless comparable situations. If there is one takeaway from this book, it is a call to respect people of all cultures and races. Differences are not something to be afraid of. Embrace them.

Is your travel bug feeling dejected and faded? Have you chosen a holiday destination, but fear you might be missing out on something special? Well, in either case, this book is intended for you. I have distilled years of travelling across our globe into these accounts of my most memorable encounters. This is not a traditional travel guidebook; instead, these tales aim to relay a sense of the experience. After all, it is the memories of the people we met and our unexpected insights that stay with us long after a journey ends.

These exploits are grouped into chapters according to broad travel categories, such as boat rides or multi-day treks, and then by country. You might choose to reinspire your lust to explore by reading the book cover to cover, or you might prefer to focus on those topics or locations that appeal to your current travel quest. I have included practical guidance about each destination in every section.

I hope that this book inspires the traveller inside you.

Travelling across water brings a certain mystique to a journey. Although people have used watercraft for thousands of years, boat rides still evoke an emotional tug of war inside me. The dread of what the murky depths conceal conflicts with the peaceful bliss of floating past rough overland routes. In my mind, the ambiguity of the unforgiving waters below, which could twist my fate in an instant, is paired with the appearance of calm control when gliding along the water's surface. Boat trips seem to ground the soul in their simple purity. Board, relax and observe the world.

It all sounds so lovely, but in reality the tales in this chapter were not so straightforward. Yet they left a discernible impression on me. Images of these trips easily come to the surface, all bundled with my original sentiments and rounded out with a reminiscent smile. Each of these boat rides is a unique example of a traditional mode of transport still relevant in today's fast-paced world. Entrepreneurial locals have shared their culture by offering their crafts to intrepid foreigners in search of authentic encounters.

The Basics

Synopsis: Enjoy an opportunity to discover one of the least-visited continents on our planet, and catch a glimpse of what a place looks like with virtually no human interference.

Most useful item to pack: Warm and waterproof gloves

For further travel information: Contact Ushuaia Turismo at ushuaia-turismoevt.com.ar. Be sure to check their last-minute specials.

The Experience

Antarctica is a special place. It does not bear the flag of any one nation, but is rather like a great-great-grandparent cherished by fifty-three countries. Twelve of these nations first signed the Antarctic Treaty back in 1959, and since then the treaty countries have ensured that its expansive geography is used solely for peaceful purposes. Under the treaty's shelter, scientific cooperation and ground-breaking studies have flourished across its icy terrain, despite the excessively miserable conditions. After all, those same conditions have won Antarctica the elite title of the driest, coldest, windiest and highest of all the continents.

If you are not one of the few lucky scientists travelling on a frigid assignment, ships welcome visitors on voyages that depart from New Zealand, South Africa and Argentina. Originally, we had not envisioned adding such a journey southward through frosty waters. Rather, we were in Ushuaia, Argentina's most southerly city, as a convenient base to hike its surrounding and stunning island of Tierra del Fuego ("Land of Fire"). However, the charm of Ushuaia's opportune location ignited our desire to push on to even-more-remote regions. An attractive 40 percent last-minute discount also seemed too good to pass up. Oddly, I find that such impulsive trips, made without expectations, often end up being the most memorable. This ten-day expedition grabbed our hearts and topped our list of the most intoxicating experiences of our year-long around-the-world adventure. Quite an impressive coup for a wildcard destination.

After ten months of nomadic wandering and living out of our packs, we cringed at the enormous, generic cruise packages on offer. We sought something unique. Surely such an astonishing continent as Antarctica, with its iconic isolation, would be frequented by an equally atypical vessel. A vacant cabin aboard the MV *Antarctica Dream* answered our call. It was a Chilean navy icebreaker commissioned in 1959 and dedicated to servicing science stations housed in

Antarctica's icy belt. The eighty-three-metre vessel was later decommissioned from the navy and, in the early twenty-first century, recommissioned as an expedition ship for passengers.[1] Its past meant that the ship was lean yet resilient, and in our minds it earned points for its authentic and sturdy nature. Although the ship held only seventy-eight passengers plus crew, our group was even smaller, making for a truly intimate excursion. The trip also attracted a more intrepid type of traveller, which resulted in a like-minded mélange of passengers, despite differing ages, nationalities and backgrounds.

The mere act of reaching Antarctica's shores is an unparalleled venture. The renowned Drake Passage torments travellers in a style all its own. It can often take two days or more to sail through these rough waters where the Atlantic and Pacific Oceans collide into a milky froth. This boisterous bottleneck has come to represent a rite of passage, the obligatory nausea before laying eyes on the White Continent. As the stars aligned for our voyage, swells stayed relatively calm at four metres, well below their most potent power.

Nevertheless, the ship's relatively docile surge was enough to prompt queasiness. Luckily, the doctor on board stocked an ample supply of seasickness medication to mute our discomfort. The crew attempted to distract passengers with informative presentations aimed at enhancing our appreciation of our destination. From biologists to avid photographers, they taught us about some of Antarctica's curious attributes. If educational talks were insufficient to divert our attention, a professional chef and his team regularly served up perfectly prepared, locally inspired cuisine. Of a similar standard, the rooms were elegant, with plush carpet and private bathrooms, and were fully equipped with conveniences such as a television, a porthole and a writing area. The only amenity absent was access to the internet—but it was not missed.

Outside the vessel's windows, massive seabirds captivated us as they soared above the sea's mist. Cape petrels, southern giant petrels and wandering albatross all took turns hovering over the ship's wake. The wingspan of the incredible wandering albatross can reach more than 3.5 metres. These master gliders often stay adrift for months or even years before returning to land to breed. Their speckled feathers seemed like armour that repelled the chilly breeze, which never stopped blowing.

Our first step back onto land was at latitude sixty-two degrees south, where Barrientos Island poked through the arctic waters. It felt surreal to finally touch the land that was home to gentoo and chinstrap penguins. Throughout this journey, we came within metres of their colonies, or rookeries, as well as those belonging to the Adélie penguin. Adélies captivated us with their mesmerizing azure eyes. Chinstrap penguins sported their namesake thin line of black feathers below their beaks, whereas gentoos had a black feathered head marked by a white eye mask. Mother penguins of all three types huddled over their fuzzy babies while remaining alert enough to ward off meddling neighbours. Nearby residents frequented each other's nests in search of a precious stone to pilfer. Apparently, survival instincts overrode neighbourly etiquette.

Well-trodden pathways extended beyond the close-quartered nests of the colonies. Penguins hobbled back and forth along these trails as if their knees were fused together, before suddenly choosing to take the easy route: chin up, belly down and slide. They often let their vibrant personalities shine. The scene played out like a daytime drama as they chattered and foiled suspect visitors. Often, the knee-high birds ventured towards us to inspect the bright red jackets the tour company had given to all the guests. But they soon got bored and returned to their daily activities, usually in search of a prize stone. As we sailed farther south, the ship stopped alongside several isolated islands, where distinctive raspberry-coloured rings could be seen surrounding the penguins' rookeries, uncloaking any pretence of anonymity. The mysterious pink snow was easily explained. Their diet of seemingly innocuous krill triggered a dazzling yet pungent side effect. It bequeathed its pinkish hue in the inevitable splats on the snow, which tainted the penguins' tracks.

Besides becoming familiar with penguins, we also became adept at distinguishing the various varieties of seals: elephant, Weddell, crabeater, leopard and Antarctic fur seal, commonly referred to as a sea lion. Groups of these seals could be caught lounging on an ice pack or stretched out onshore, cuddled close yet snarling in annoyance at one another, like siblings squeezed into the back seat of the family vehicle for a long drive.

We reached our most southerly point at latitude sixty-five degrees and fourteen minutes south, soon after passing through Lemaire Channel. This eleven-kilometre stretch is often referred to as Kodak Gap. True to its name, it was chock full of photogenic moments showcasing bizarrely formed icebergs, rocky crags and growling bergy bits. Bergy bits are small breakaway chunks of icebergs; they would often drift alongside the ship, their icy bodies rubbing so forcefully against the hull that they let out a creaky growl for all those aboard to hear.

Late one evening, we first landed on continental Antarctica with a short Zodiac ride to shore. It was eleven o'clock in Neko Harbour. After an uphill hike along the Rudolph Glacier, we admired views of glassy gunmetal waters and blue snow ridges. Nighttime was nothing like the day. Instead, a hushed mood commandeered the moonlit expanse. Birds fell silent. Seals gave up frolicking. Only the harp-like wind blew its moody chords. Screams of ice torn away from their familiar glacier interrupted the wind's wistful ballad and echoed their sorrows. Their icy sheath had represented the only family known to the fallen shards before they plunged into the dark ocean. There they became floating ice sculptures: not the giant icebergs you often imagine, but smaller nondescript pieces of a greater collective. They were left to slowly melt into a decrepit splinter, eventually swallowed by the ocean. This represented the berg's inevitable aging process—ice to water, earth to ashes.

The MV *Antarctica Dream*'s red-and-white steel glowed in the moonlight where it floated just offshore. Upon our return to the ship, the crew served sparkling wine so we could toast our successful landing on the mainland. It was truly serendipitous being deck-top at midnight with bubbly in hand and surrounded by oddly formed ice silhouettes. Distant rumbles echoed through the air as calving icebergs flipped and the fractured ice chunks crashed into the water at the glacier's edge. Throughout this journey, we were left satiated by so many of these extraordinary moments.

While exploring on land, we could wander alone and take in Antarctica's unique landscape. Its ambience was captivating. Breathe in, breathe out. The air was crisp yet amazingly fresh. Searing wind tentacles would swirl in a frenzied dance as if in search of vulnerable gaps in clothing or exposed fragile skin. In the distance, perpetual sheets of ice merged into the hazy horizon. At first glance, this landscape appeared vast and empty, devoid of any human interference, just land and sky. But it was far from barren.

Penguins rambled here and there and trustfully waddled close. Cries from gulls echoed from every direction. Ominous skuas squawked as they circled overhead in search of a lone chick or an unprotected egg. Soon a seal sputtered and barked. An almost imperceptible splash disguised a black-and-white flash of a penguin diving into icy waters. Inspecting a nearby exposed rock, we saw tiny auburn lichen splayed across the scarred grey surface. Their delicately curled fringe lingered patiently in an attempt to absorb any hint of sunshine. Antarctica was a place beyond isolation—one of pure, self-sufficient existence.

Beneath this desolate land's harsh exterior lay an inconceivable persona with a strangely synchronized ebb and flow. The lack of human settlement has left the terrain unlike any place we had ever visited. It was hard not to contemplate how the world would differ without humankind's intrusion, free from bisecting power lines and heavy clouds of traffic haze. Nature may be harsh, but its state of balance is enduring.

The Basics

Synopsis: Discover hidden coves and squeaky white sand while snorkelling off the side of your sailboat in the secluded waters of the Coral Sea.

Most useful item to pack: Motion-sickness medication

For further travel information: Generally, sailboats depart from the town of Airlie Beach, which can be reached from Brisbane by driving north for twelve hours. For those less keen on a rambling road trip, two nearby airports will gladly welcome your arrival: Proserpine's Whitsunday Coast Airport and Hamilton Island's Great Barrier Reef Airport. For further information, refer to whitsunday.qld.gov.au/153/Airports-and-Aerodromes and hamiltonisland.com.au/getting-here/airport.

The Experience

These memories of sailing among the Whitsunday Islands of northern Queensland are a throwback to my younger years. The trip was a December getaway in the late 1990s, back in the days before digital cameras and social media dominated our communications. Most people could thoroughly disconnect from their jobs' obligations to decompress properly, at least more readily than they can in 2017. The pure waters and flawless beaches of the Whitsunday Islands took the edge off any lingering stress that might have been gnawing upon my mind. The relaxed vibe activated my imagination of a simpler life and helped to ease into vacation mode. These were moments to find clarity, to prioritize what was essential and regroup mentally in order to forge forward once back to the inevitable demands of daily life.

The Whitsunday Islands were not always coloured by lush tropical forests or framed by blindingly white sands. They originally came into existence tens of thousands of years ago from ancient volcanoes, which spewed forth quite a mess. As it often does, time healed these wounds. Waters rose, leaving only the knobs of volcanoes that remain today as islands, unkempt and full of exotic plants and trees. Over time, the Ngaro Aboriginal people discovered not only the islands' beauty, but plenty of fish, fruit and all the necessities of life around the shores. They settled down and ultimately became impressively adept ocean navigators. In the eighteenth century, Lieutenant James Cook from England stumbled across the islands during his explorations aboard the HMB *Endeavour* in an early attempt to map the South Pacific Ocean.[2] Indeed, these islands occupy a primeval niche of our planet's geology and history.

There is a lot more to these islands' mystique than just a pretty beach. In fact, I had never experienced such a strange phenomenon as the squeaky sands along Whitsunday's shorelines. The perfect combination of quartz deposits and extremely fine sand granules produced a distinctive squeal with each footstep.[3] But for those interested in something other than beaches, there were a range of sailing options, from private yachts to group tours supported by a full crew. The opportunity to learn to sail in relatively calm waters, protected by the Great Barrier Reef, alongside other novices was an appealing proposition.

For three days, my partner, fellow travellers and I naively tried to learn the basics of sailing while floating across ridiculously clear blue waters. The crew welcomed passengers to take the wheel or hoist the sails. This all-hands-on-deck approach expeditiously built camaraderie across the group, which was only strengthened as we prepared communal meals in the tiny galley below deck.

Today, flashbacks from this trip play across my mind to a Crowded House soundtrack, taking me back to listless days on deck while the band's tracks played in the background. It is odd how music can epitomize the essence of a moment. When I hear "Weather with You," a vision of our group reclining on the deck in the salty wind inherently springs to mind.

Days progressed easily. We alternated between soaring across the water and pausing for a snorkel beside some anonymous reef. It was exhilarating to dip my face into the water, the world above the waterline falling silent. I had snorkelled only a handful of times previously, so I still felt a rush of excitement when submerging my face into an entirely different world. Enormous groupers eased through the water while orange-and-white bursts of colour darted among the coral. Time disappeared as we floated across the ocean and observed life below.

In the evenings, the boat would anchor in an isolated and sheltered cove. Those of us who were interested swam ashore to explore the deserted island. At night we wrapped ourselves up in comfortably cozy beds. The gentle roll of the boat ensured a peaceful sleep—as long as I had remembered to take an anti-seasickness tablet. How could these days spent with a group of adventurous people from all over the world not be memorable?

The Whitsunday enclave is mostly uninhabited and unspoiled. However, as its appeal grows in the tourism industry, its pristine solitude will be challenged. Before planning a trip there, it would be worthwhile to check recent travellers' blogs for up-to-date advice about tour operators who offer trips on less-travelled routes. The ability to explore the hidden beaches and secluded areas without feeling compressed by gawking tourists grappling for a peek at the same spot is well worth the effort.

The Basics

Synopsis: Relish heart-fluttering encounters with massive yet adorable hippos while surrounded by wispy papyrus stalks.

Most useful item to pack: Driza-Bone wide-brimmed hat

For further travel information: We travelled with Geckos Adventures, a tour company that catered to small groups of young travellers who wanted a camping-based adventure. Current information can be found at geckosadventures.com. Many higher-end tour companies offer more comfortable lodging options. Check with your favourite tour company.

The Experience

The Okavango Delta is somewhat of an enigma among Africa's wetland systems. UNESCO inscribed it as the one-thousandth site on their World Heritage List in 2014 due to its peculiar qualities. Typically, Africa's parched earth is replenished during the rainy season's fierce thunder and rainstorms. But flooding in the Okavango Delta occurs during the annual **dry** season. Such a paradox offers a reprieve for wildlife at a time when water holes and streams are characteristically desiccated. As a result, biological cycles of both plants and animals have adapted to this contradictory water flow to create a complex ecosystem. Perhaps Mother Nature used a touch of her magic. The good witch's mark can be spied from high above: the Okavango Delta is shaped much like a broomstick.

Another oddity is that the Okavango Delta is positioned in the landlocked country of Botswana, so its waters do not drain into an ocean or sea as most deltas do. Instead, the Okavango Delta empties into the Kalahari Basin's sandy expanse.[4] Only a small proportion of the Okavango River's water ultimately reaches the Kalahari Basin, as plants in the delta absorb 60 percent and a further 35 percent evaporates.[5] However, the volume is still sufficient to create an oasis-like ecosystem in the Kalahari that attracts a huge variety of animals and birds. Even tight packs of the endangered African wild dog roam freely throughout the delta.[6] We were intrigued by the prospect of exploring such an abstract environment up close among its reeds.

Thick fields of papyrus shoots sprout across the delta. Their broom-like fans, fresh green or dried pale yellow, rise up to a metre above the placid water. Shorter reeds fill any vacant space like a floating shag carpet, with only sporadic breaches exposing open waters. Low mokoro boats are perfectly designed to plunge through the water, creating an arterial web through the greenery. Local boatmen know these tracks intimately despite their random appearance. The continual motion in the water from animals and plant life ensures an ever-changing latticework.

Traditionally, a mokoro, up to six feet in length, was built from a single large old tree trunk, preferably indigenous jackalberry, sausage or mangosteen because of their height. Woodworkers excavated the tree's core using fire. Once burned, the wood was a lot easier to dig out—hence the term **dugout boat**.

However, the number of tourists choosing to experience the Okavango Delta from the vantage point of a mokoro has been mounting in recent years. This demand has put an unsustainable strain on the woodland population. For this reason, expect your tour to be in a fibreglass mokoro built to protect the native forests and mature trees.

Unlike the tips of canoes, the tips of mokoro boats are pointed. Instead of paddles, which would become entangled in the dense foliage, these trough-like boats are propelled using a long pole. This stick acts as a lever to push the mokoro forward through shallow waters, oh so smoothly. Traditionally, the poleman stood at the bow while a second boatman sat at the rear to steer. However, the arrival of tourists has changed this convention. Nowadays, one boatman stands at the stern to both pole and steer, allowing two visitors to relax, their only task to gaze around at the scenery. The driver's double duty certainly makes any tips, in addition to their typically meagre wages, well-earned and greatly appreciated.

These drivers grew up on the delta waters. Their ears are attuned to recognize the sounds of individual bird calls or the gurgle of a plunging hippopotamus above the steady crackle of reeds that sweep against the boat. The possibility of seeing hippos raised both our adrenalin, in hopeful anticipation, and the trepidation that we might unwittingly float too close to their aquatic domain. Although vegetarian, hippos have become Africa's most dangerous mammal. A hippo's massive jaws and unpredictable disposition can turn ugly if it is startled or feels threatened. This is when people get hurt.[7]

For this reason, be sure to book your mokoro trip with a reputable and experienced tour company. Heed your guide's advice on what to do—and **not** to do—when your boat meets a family of hippos munching in the water. We gained an incredible view, silently floating nearby while the hippos leisurely raised their heads and then disappeared once again beneath the murky water. I could almost hear the familiar cartoon bell-like music play as their ears twirled and twitched. **Do-looloolooloo.**

Each time we spotted them, the hippos tended to hover around one section of a marshy pool. However, we could not help peering through the murky water for signs of movement towards our direction. If the boatman perceived any aggression from the animals, he ever so slowly poled us backwards to ensure the hippos did not feel imposed upon. I am sure the locals are bemused by foreigners' rapture with these bloated creatures, which they have sought to evade for centuries. Nonetheless, the guides' polite and gentle demeanour never displayed any hint of discord, only reverence for the great delta's orchestrated harmony. We felt in safe hands; however, I cannot deny that my nerves juddered occasionally.

It was incredible to observe the hippos as they watched over their pudgy little ones, who frolicked underwater and occasionally popped up beside their mothers. The heads of the young calves seemed small in comparison to those of the full-grown hippos but are twice the size of a human's cranium. The young typically remained under the water, with only their eyes, ears and nostrils occasionally emerging from its depths. The liquid acted as a natural sunscreen, for hippos' skin is quite sensitive to the sun. Their buoyancy helped to balance the hippos' enormous bodies, which can reach 1,500 kilograms for a female or 1,800 kilograms for a male. We spotted only one hippo walking on land. Its short legs seemed in danger of being flattened while carrying such a weight. The creature travelled just a short distance along the shoreline, at an unexpectedly swift pace, before he suddenly ducked out of sight behind a thick layer of reeds—likely to dip down into another refreshing pool of water.

Throughout the morning, we drifted along from one vantage point to another, attempting to remain motionless so as not to startle any hippo lurking below. Twenty minutes of motionless gazing upon a pod of foraging hippos seemed to pass as quickly as a couple of minutes. To watch them in person was exhilarating, as the exposed mokoro boat allowed us to be closer than I had anticipated. At times, the hippos twirled their ears. At other moments, the dominant male would yawn widely, showing off a jigsaw puzzle of fist-sized yellowed teeth set inside his gigantic jaw. Admittedly, there are remarkable nature programs that capture these moments up close. However, they are hardly a match for the intoxicating experience of floating atop the very liquid that these hippos are living and frolicking beneath only metres away.

After we had satisfied our fascination with these beautiful animals, the mokoro gently pushed through more reeds and pathways. Birds balanced atop papyrus, displaying their often burnt-umber plumage, which matched the dried golden reeds. An African fish eagle perched on a wizened tree stump. Its brilliant white head rested atop a darker body, startlingly similar to the North American bald eagle. The bird was staring out and across the delta, its wings ready to take flight once it caught sight of a desirable midday snack. Farther along, a Goliath heron balanced on a luscious tree branch. Its long copper-toned neck curved smoothly into an elongated head that ended with piercing yellow eyes and a grey beak.

The daily challenges faced by wildlife in constant search of food were brought to life as we quietly moved through the reeds at water's height. It felt as if we were inside a viewfinder, a new sphere of activity exposed by every bend as we glided through the vast Okavango Delta. If our mokoro had not taken a given turn, that anonymous piece of the world would have carried on as usual, unseen by human eyes. This boat ride was truly an enlightening experience.

The Basics

Synopsis: Chill out cruising through fjords where the mountains and South Pacific Ocean dominate.

Most useful item to pack: Wind-resistant wool sweater

For further travel information: Go to navimag.com. Be sure to check the last-minute offers for price reductions of up to 20 percent on specific routes.

The Experience

The Patagonia region of Chile and Argentina is a huge and spectacular area. It is a mecca for hikers who prefer a rugged and cool climate, similar to that found in the Rocky Mountains of North America. Conveniently, the inverse seasons of the Southern Hemisphere allow hiking-hungry northerners to satisfy their craving for year-round trekking. Because of its massive size, transport legs in the region tend to be long. While flights are available between key centres to save precious holiday time, their speed can be deceptive. Vast swaths of rugged beauty are lost from a plane's vantage. As is so often the case, there is too much to see in far too little time. Ultimately, your travel schedule will dictate this decision.

An alternative mode of transportation between central Chile and its southern glacial reaches departs from the port city of Puerto Montt. If travelling by bus, one must endure thirty-three unforgiving hours to reach the southern town of Puerto Natales, smack in the middle of Southern Patagonia. To be fair, Chilean buses are of high quality and quite comfortable, even to European standards. However, I am not convinced that being cramped inside a confined space for such a long time can be pleasant. For this reason—perhaps spurred on by a glass of smoky Chilean Carménère in one of the superb corner cafés in the San Telmo neighbourhood of Buenos Aires—we found Navimag's last-minute special on a four-day cruise particularly appealing. While longer than the bus ride, its space to wander and its remote panoramic vistas merited serious consideration.

Navimag's *Evangelistas* was built in 1978 as a cargo vessel and has since been adapted to lodge passengers. It has three decks and a capacity for 320 travellers across six levels of accommodation packages. The most swish is an AAA cabin for two people, complete with personal porthole and private ensuite. Alternatively, the most basic room sleeps four, with access to well-kept shared washroom facilities, but without a personal porthole from which to gaze. All options present clean and comfortable accommodations, roughly akin to a good three-star hotel.

Our journey progressed at a relaxed pace, with plenty of time to do exactly as we wished. The upper level's strikingly green deck looked as if it had originally been intended as a tennis court, but in fact it catered to a less energetic crowd. There was ample space to lounge upon benches or partake in a game of standing chess. Of course, the stunning views provided a lovely background for day-dreaming or photography. Rolling hills, curving inlets and distant mountains shrouded in snow seemed to play on an unending reel.

These scenes carried on uninterrupted despite three diversions during our voyage. The *Evangelistas*' smooth passage was first shattered on the second evening as it traversed the infamous Golfo de Penas, translated as Gulf of Sorrows. Several passengers commiserated with sorrows of their own, brought on by the three-metre swells and alleviated by the friendly doctor's motion-sickness tablets. Thankfully, this was the only turbulence during our journey south.

The second and most memorable interjection was a stop alongside the Pio XI glacier, the longest glacier in the Southern Hemisphere excluding Antarctica. Pio XI is no ordinary glacier. It is one of the few glaciers in the world that has actually advanced in recent years, a rather domineering contra-diction to most ice caps worldwide—which have dwindled in scale in the face of climate change—and a mystery to scientists. Measurements indicate that between 1998 and 2014, Pio XI's southern front, the leg we viewed from the *Evangelistas*, advanced 593 metres.[8] The ship was able to navigate reasonably close to the glacier's edge without being in danger from the ice missiles that sporadically plunged from its lip. Pio XI's blue shadows and dirty-white snow protrusions filled the channel. Its prongs resembled an enormous colony of albino seals popping their heads up to look at us. This opportunity to hover alongside the remote glacier with no other boats or onshore bystanders was truly special.

The last interruption occurred on the third day. The *Evangelistas* anchored just offshore from the remote town of Puerto Edén. This was our only sight of civili-zation throughout the journey, isolated between the water's edge and the rocky mountain range. Colourful homes nestled along the shoreline, hugged by scrubby windblown trees and seemingly content to coexist with nature. The stop was brief, as if the town were keen to return to its solitude after the ship had swiftly unloaded the few necessities it delivered. Both sides wished each other well and expeditiously bid goodbye.

On the final morning, the captain navigated through a mind-bogglingly tight squeeze, identified as the Angostura White. This curving passage compressed the water to a width of only eighty metres. Rocky outcrops with low scrub brush rose out of the eerily calm water. Miniature lighthouses, painted white and topped with a cherry-coloured tip, acted as beacons of perilous edges. The passengers lounged on deck and admired nature's tranquility, oblivious to the tense navigation the captain surely endured to avoid the rough banks.

By the time the ship pulled into Puerto Natales, everyone on board was eager to explore more of the region's wilderness. Although a pricier option than the cheap and cheerful bus route, these four days offered a glimpse into Chile's stunning scenery and remote back country—not to mention the opportunity to see a burgeoning glacier—like an aperitif to the splendour of Patagonia.

The Basics

Synopsis: Be transported back in time to when pharaohs ruled the lands and stories were carved in stone to last the ages.

Most useful item to pack: Sarong wrap

For further travel information: A myriad of tour companies offer felucca cruises down the Nile. Typically, this will be part of a larger tour package. We did this trip back in the early 2000s, so we qualified for Geckos Adventures' small tour groups for eighteen- to twenty-nine-year-olds. Details can be found at geckosadventures.com. Alternatively, intrepid travellers can charter their own boat with a little help from fellow travel bloggers or travel guides such as **Lonely Planet**.

The Experience

The blueprint for modern fibreglass sailboats was essentially pioneered thousands of years ago on the banks of the Nile River. Imagine only slight modifications from modern sailboats by reverting to wood materials and reducing the mast to balance only a single cotton lateen sail. The result is a felucca, a vessel in which the Egyptians have cruised the Nile for centuries.

Originally, the felucca offered an alternative to the smaller and rather unstable reed boat, which was cumbersome when hauling much more than a daily catch of fish. Feluccas then became the dominant mode of transport on the Nile River. Nowadays, feluccas have transitioned into the tourist trade, whereas reed boats have faded from regular use. Egypt's commercial shipping is limited to massive freighters that navigate the Suez Canal—and thankfully leave the Nile in a more pristine state for our travelling pleasure.

Our felucca journey allowed us to respect the past while introducing us to some truly adorable and entertaining Egyptians. Anyone who has read Wilbur Smith's book **River God** will recall how Smith brought ancient Egypt to life through his uncanny ability to reincarnate a bygone world. It was the perfect reading material to take on this trip down a portion of Africa's longest river. A glance up from the book revealed a landscape not unlike that described between its pages. The present and past seemed to morph interchangeably throughout the voyage, making it a rather surreal experience. However, the multi-level cruise ships that plied the waters brought us abruptly back to the present day.

The felucca boats sliced silently through the toffee-coloured waters. Feluccas rely solely on wind, or an unfortunate oarsperson if breezes subside. They could ease up to the shoreline, allowing us to investigate a rustle between the reeds—perhaps a native feline on the prowl for a spiny mouse. As we floated past, we witnessed traditional livelihoods and serene pastoral farms, always with a passing wave and an easy smile. We sailed by clumps of papyrus reeds, which are still plucked and pounded into flat sheets of paper as they have been for thousands of years. Farmers worked on irrigated rectangular fields, often tilled by hand, to grow necessities such as cotton, rice or sugar cane. Hand-knotted rugs in patterns of crimson, saffron and indigo were shifted from our lounge area to become a bed underlay or rolled up to make way for meals.

Interspersed among functioning villages stood the stones of Egypt's past. The ancient temple complexes of Luxor, Aswan, Karnak and Edfu stood resolute, hidden within curves of the river or cut off from view by the water's mist. When we trod through their corridors, delicate paintings and carved edifices depicted a once-powerful society. Each location conjured a unique persona built from a profound past and imbibed with the panache of its favoured god. A temple's personality might be reflected through etchings on towering obelisks, which stood beside fallen bricks of partially exposed carvings. Perhaps it was veiled amid stories portraying the pharaohs' favourite parables, inscribed into archways of the underworld. Our group of twelve was transported between these renowned sites and traditional towns, nurturing our awareness of the multiple layers of Egyptian culture.

The Old World does not rest, however, as archaeologists continue to prospect at ongoing digs and unearth hidden treasures. In November 2016, BBC reported the discovery of a new city believed to be over five thousand years old.[9] As was customary, the structures were positioned near the Nile's life-giving waters but farther south than our particular route.

In the evenings we were introduced to another of Egypt's traditional customs, the shared shisha water pipe. Conventional practice involves circulating the pipe among old mates, sharing the day's stories over a hubbly bubbly. The pipes consisted of a glass base to hold water and a knobby metallic cylinder that supported a pedestal upon which the tobacco was burned. The bases, often tinted and painted with intricate designs, made these pipes a visual splendour. These parts ultimately connected with the most essential component, a woven tube with a wooden mouthpiece. However, because recent newbies to the practice have raised concerns over the hygiene of sharing a mouthpiece among strangers, individual plastic tips are now available.

We were offered a variety of tobacco flavours, from the almost acidic tang of a honey infusion to a surprisingly soft cappuccino essence. The savoury aroma of a sweet apple tobacco blended with humid smoke was quite tasty even for my non-cigarette-smoker's palate. Do not be tricked, however, as this little pile of sweet tobacco diffused with steam delivers a punch of nicotine complete with traces of carbon monoxide in its innocuous swirls.

On one occasion, we pulled ashore to purchase fuel for the cooking stove. Many people from the town meandered over to meet us—children, elders and even a few donkeys. One of the guys on board our felucca pulled out his guitar, and soon its melody prompted more villagers to join the gathering crowd. While some shuffled and smiled, others attempted to converse without knowing one another's language. We sputtered a few basic Arabic phrases, supplemented with hand gestures and amateur miming. Miraculously, this attempt to communicate, here on the banks of the Nile, resulted in some insightful conversations. When our fuel supply had been replenished and the red sun eased towards indistinct hills, the villagers seemed saddened by our imminent departure. They may not, however, have realized that their delightful hospitality and innocent laughter vividly resonated with our group, not to be forgotten.

The Basics

Synopsis: Float peacefully beneath dense jungle and past villages as you watch traditional daily life transpire along the river's edge.

Most useful items to pack: Sewing kit, headlamp and waterproof cover for your luggage

For further travel information: Head towards the town's boat launch in search of captains and tourist information kiosks, which may or may not be staffed. Formal advance bookings are not usually possible. Guidebooks generally provide information regarding prices, but once on the ground, ask at your hotel for current information and advice. Be sure to bring water-resistant gear if travelling during the rainy season.

The Experience

So many waterways, so little time. The tributaries of Laos' rivers run rampant, like tribes of leafcutter ants foraging along a tropical forest floor. Floating down their cappuccino-coloured water offers a reprieve from the often-cramped shuttle buses that also provide reliable transport around the country. However, instead of plush vehicle seats, a *héua hăhng nyáo* ("longtail boat") typically has slatted wooden benches or simple chairs, so I recommend an hour-long journey as the maximum to endure. Entrepreneurial captains have learned to include seat cushions, which give their boats a distinct advantage and are well worth seeking out for longer trips.

We took two longtail boat voyages in northern Laos: one was a shorter hop to a neighbouring town, and the other was a full day's transit. The initial trip left a stronger impression, perhaps because it was our first experience and we had no preconceptions. It felt like we caught a furtive glimpse into the lives of the far northern Laotians. As we drifted past the thick forests, we saw occasional wooden houses balanced on stilts along the shore. There was always laundry hung to dry, surprisingly colourful and bright for having been washed in these cloudy waters. What was their secret? Kids laughed; parents smiled shyly. Their lives were filled with hard work and pure gratitude. The Laotians were intrinsically kind and gentle—and incredible cooks who created fresh and vibrantly flavourful food.

Nong Khiaw to Muang Ngoi Neua

The route from Nong Khiaw to Muang Ngoi Neua followed the river Nam Ou for about an hour. Some longtail boats had a greatly appreciated wooden roof that provided an element of shade from the blaring sun. Painted sky blue, the roof panels stood in stark contrast to the brownish slurry rushing past. The narrow river seemed a thin wedge sliced out of the steep karst-like mountains that dominated the landscape. The scenery was reminiscent of Vietnam's beautiful Halong Bay but devoid of the masses of tourists and junk boats that have disturbed Vietnam's pristine oasis in recent years. Floating through Nam Ou's narrow avenues of serenity, we felt like all was right with the world, at least in this tiny piece of it for this particular moment.

However, perfection cannot last. Rogue nails tended to wriggle loose on the wooden rigs. There was no need to worry about the boat falling to pieces—just an irritant for loose clothing that is easily snagged. After easing into the rhythm of a twelve-month around-the-world trip, the rear of my light pants, which were intended to last the entire journey, seemed to delight in acting as a target for these hidden surprises. The whoosh of cool river breezes certainly caught me by surprise. Once back on land, I delved deep into my pack for a tiny sewing kit and salvaged my pants with a few stitches.

Our destination played an important role towards making this boat ride particularly special. Few people visited Muang Ngoi Neua. Three Israelis were the only other folks to share our incoming boat, leaving the tranquil town to us—and the locals, of course. There was no power infrastructure beyond a few diesel generators that ran intermittently. Consequently, headlamps came in handy after the sun's light had faded. Accommodation was basic—this was not a place to expect air-conditioned comfort—but it proved to be clean and welcoming. A couple of restaurants cooked fresh and delicious meals, best enjoyed with mango juice while trying to catch a breeze on the restaurant's shaded patio. The setting was ideal for travellers craving simplicity and an indescribable serenity. No schedules, no meetings, simply an appreciation of catching a glimpse into the life of a humble yet purely content village. Children's giggles were the loudest sound—well, besides the occasional grumble from a generator.

Nong Khiaw to Luang Prabang

Longtail boats that supply seat cushions are highly recommended for this voyage, as it takes approximately five hours, depending on the water conditions. This route flowed in the opposite direction from the journey to Muang Ngoi Neua but also started along the Nam Ou River before later merging with the larger Mekong. Captains expected a minimum of ten passengers for this route, so we rounded up other travellers hovering in search of transport.

Five hours may seem like a long time to spend on a smallish wooden boat, but do not despair. The backdrop of tropical green forest and white limestone rock formations made for a picturesque journey. We gained insight into village and family life along the river, where the water remained an integral part of daily life. Naked children splashed and giggled while adults tended to the washing, the cooking and their reliable water buffalos. These were not the fierce black-coated beasts of Africa, but rather a docile bunch, often with pink skin and heavy horns that seemed to pull their heads downward as if they were in solemn prayer. Bells were hung around their necks to ensure the owners knew the animals' where-abouts, reminiscent of Swiss alpine cows.

After we had been lulled by the engine's hum for a few hours, the captain deviated towards one of the rocky cliff faces at the water's edge. As we drew near, ancient artwork of handprints gradually appeared beside outlines of buffalo and cattle. The ochre colour had held its beauty for centuries, emitting an ethereal appeal. Here, somehow, people and nature seemed to dance a slow waltz, each respecting one another and moving forward to time's tempo.

Near the end of the trip, the boat passed by the Pak Ou cave, which shrouds hundreds of small Buddha statues and images. However, hold your expectations, as southbound boats will be fined for stopping at this site. Only those boats headed north, or upriver, usually from Luang Prabang, are permitted access. The logic behind this random rule was unclear to us, yet it was followed nonetheless.

The Basics

Synopsis: Leave any preconceptions at the beach, and you will be in for a truly unique journey.

Most useful items to pack: Patience and humour

For further travel information: Go to malawitourism.com and then navigate to the Ilala and Malawi Shipping Company web page for current information about the official schedule and fares. Fares are paid on board. For the latest real-time information or advance cabin bookings, it is generally recommended to ask at your local hotel a day or two prior to your expected voyage date.

The Experience

Malawi's white sun blazed in the centre of the crimson, charcoal-black and forest-green stripes that adorned the pristine flag of Malawi swaying atop the MV *Ilala*. This proud statement hinted at the essence of the ship, more so than the peeling paint encircling its railings. The patchwork of paint was the result of a long-time partnership between the sun's perpetual rays and the hands of countless passengers gripping the metallic bar's reassuring firmness. How many guests over the years had unobtrusively observed random yet captivating daily occurrences while creating their own mark?

The original SS *Ilala* first plied the waters of Africa's third-largest lake back in the late 1800s. The second generation came to be in 1949 with the MV *Ilala*. This younger breed holds up to 450 passengers across its three decks. Over sixty years have passed, and after many a day in the maintenance yard, the *Ilala* continues to chug from village to village around a 365-kilometre loop of Lake Niassa. In 2013, a few years after the trip described here, the *Ilala* was given an overhaul, its new engines reportedly able to reach a speed of up to ten knots, increasing the pace of the voyage. A smaller, newer vessel, the MV *Chilembwe* typically acts as a replacement when the *Ilala* is incapacitated by repair work so life can continue unfettered. Yet the *Ilala* remains the option preferred by both locals and travellers keen to experience their own journey on its seemingly mythical decks.

Just as developed society relies on an established electricity infrastructure to provide a constant supply of power, life around Lake Niassa relies on the ever-present movements of the *Ilala* ferry. Despite its tendency to be late and the rather muddled boarding and disembarking procedure, people depend on the ferry as an ingrained part of their village livelihood. Viewing it in isolation, one would not likely comprehend the vitality that the *Ilala* brings to Lake Niassa. Beyond mere travel from point A to point B, the ferry proves to be essential in trade and local culture. Although the *Ilala* has its challenges, people and businesses have grown accustomed to its fickle ways and slow pace as it carries necessities and fosters communication between villages.

Our intended itinerary was to travel from Likoma Island to Chipoka, a village on Lake Niassa's southwestern shore. Likoma Island is part of Malawi but sits nearer to Mozambique's shoreline and falls along the northern section of *Ilala's* circular route. The official schedule placed the journey from Likoma Island to Chipoka at twenty-four hours; however, the *Ilala* arrived at Likoma Island already fifteen hours late. Schedules are inevitably rough guides.

The ferry eventually arrived late in the evening. The sun had long set. Awaiting passengers crowded the beach as the boat glowed in the moonlight and dropped anchor. When we boarded, the entire lower economy deck was filled with sacks of corn, ground nuts and other essentials. I walked very tentatively across the tops of these sacks in the dark, carrying an eighteen-kilogram backpack plus a day pack hung on the front of my shoulders. My balance was further tested by the continual flow of people manoeuvering within the same corridor. They were headed in the opposite direction, eager to disembark from the very access point we had just entered. The secret was to give a brief smile to the passing voyagers, momentarily recognizing the challenge and humour in one another's journey, and to offer a hand or sway to the side to help each other pass. We were, quite literally, all in the same boat.

Despite sixty years of plying this route, organized chaos pervaded the boarding process. Climbing over and across bags was only part of it. First we had to climb up a rickety ladder balanced vertically between the *Ilala* and its overcrowded bobbing lifeboat. The lifeboat was well used, not for life-saving purposes, but as a loading shuttle because most destinations lacked a suitable dock. Passengers onshore shifted in a rhythm as they jostled to cram onto the lifeboat, often reaching for a child, bags, boxes or all such necessities. The owner of each sack and its specific destination was rather opaque. Yet in practice, bags were off-loaded, new ones filled their place and at times the entire bottom deck lay bare. It reminded me of a revolving door; each movement seemed small, but in their totality they were quite effective.

Our choice of a cabin was markedly advantageous, as the voyage ultimately took sixty hours—a mere thirty-six hours beyond its scheduled duration—and that excluded the fifteen-hour delay before the ferry even arrived at Likoma Island. Yet, with some planning, it is relatively easy to supplement the basic offerings of the ferry to incorporate a semblance of comfort into the wait. Bring a hammock to sway away the hours or reserve a cabin with two twin beds, a wash basin and a private toilet.

The first mishap became apparent when we headed to the upper deck for breakfast after a restful sleep during our first night aboard. Passengers who had expected to get off at the next stop remained on board lounging in small groups. One British university student readily explained, "Oh, have you not heard? We have turned around and are heading back to Likoma Island; they forgot the captain! It is absolute madness!" While the ship had been anchored at Likoma Island, the captain had gone ashore unbeknownst to his second-in-command. A few hours later, after the passengers had been shuttled on and off the ship and the dark beach was clear of those waiting, the acting captain pulled anchor and carried on with his route. Sometime in the wee hours of the morning, when he was due for a shift change, the deputy captain discovered the captain's absence. Consequently, the engines were slowed, the bow rotated and the *Ilala* slipped back towards Likoma Island.

The second and most noteworthy mishap, due to a lack of fuel, caused a twenty-four-hour unplanned layover at Nkhotakota. We had arranged for our tour guide to meet us at Chipoka to start the next phase of our travels overland across Malawi and Zambia. Travelling without a phone, we could only assume that our guide would be well apprised of the *Ilala*'s delay, as it was a common topic of discussion at its many ports around the lake. Unexpectedly, we were the sole passengers headed for Chipoka. The *Ilala* only carried sufficient fuel to go directly to Monkey Bay, its final port of call, **or** to Chipoka, but not both. This conundrum was likely a direct result of the prior day's doubling back to Likoma Island. Hence, the boat paused longer than planned at Nkhotakota as the crew attempted to resolve this predicament. We only knew the name of our tour company, not the specific guide assigned to our trip. After many conversations, a particularly resolute crew member tracked down the name of our guide, contacted him and rescheduled our pickup to Monkey Bay. The chances of a crew member knowing our guide seemed inexplicably slim, but the problem was solved nonetheless. The *Ilala* carried on towards Monkey Bay where, two days later than originally scheduled, we finally disembarked to appreciate having land beneath our feet once again. True to the revised plan, our guide was ready and waiting for our arrival.

The thought of going on a multi-day trek seems to trigger both keen anticipation and subtle apprehension in me in the days leading up to it. The extra level of planning, mornings of squatting at a pit toilet and the lack of running water add an element of awkwardness to these trips. However, it always seems that once I am out on the trail, these discomforts fade away. No matter how long the trip, my mind seems to decide to get on and deal with any inconveniences, at least up until the last day or two, when visions of warm showers and fresh clothing start to replay in my head far too frequently. Perhaps for my next multi-day trek, I can trick my mind into preparing for a longer duration than the actual itinerary. Maybe this alternative reality will be the secret to fully enjoying every last day.

Beyond these mental games, hiking day after day has allowed me to reach isolated places not often seen by anyone other than those who live in such secluded corners of our planet. Nature flourishes. Residents survive. They overcome challenging conditions despite the lack of basic infrastructure such as roads, electricity and grocery stores that are taken for granted elsewhere. The people we have met have exuded a common sense of resilience and upheld reverence for their environment. These traits have held true no matter which sparsely populated region we have found ourselves in, from the high Himalayas of Asia to broad mountain ranges in Africa.

The freedom to witness such outlying spaces drives my desire to keep trekking. It outweighs any superficial challenge of pulling myself out from a warm sleeping bag each morning into the tent's cold air to slip back into yesterday's clammy hiking clothes. I must admit that the thought makes me both cringe and glow with a smidgen of self-satisfaction. These treks can throw a lot at you, scrunch you up and try to toss you down. After five days of dodging swamps or steady inclines, finding energy to push on can be hard. You learn to focus, clearing your mind of everything but your immediate surroundings. I have flipped between squeezing strength from the depth of my gut in order to reach a gusty summit to relishing how lucky I felt to be in that place minutes later. Forge on and prove something to yourself.

The Basics

Synopsis: Experience eucalyptus forests, boulder-laden mountains and scurrying Tasmanian devils over a six-day trek that covers eighty kilometres, all while carrying an eighteen-kilogram pack. Be rewarded with cheese plates and curry dinners as you recall the day's sights back at camp.

Most useful items to pack: Rain gear and J.B. Fields Expedition Merino wool socks

For further travel information: Tasmanian Expeditions operates an excellent camping itinerary with well-trained guides, impressive catering and high-quality equipment. They are one of the best trekking operators I have experienced to date. For further information, check out their Overland Track at tasmanianexpeditions.com.au.

For a more luxe option, Cradle Huts offers a hut-to-hut experience: cradlehuts.com.au.

The Experience

The Cradle Mountain Overland Track is one of my favourite treks. To date, its sole rival is the Jomolhari trek in Bhutan. Expectations are key. There will be rain. There is a heavy pack to carry—between fifteen and twenty kilograms. You will be in remote regions with the only escape by foot or emergency helicopter. So you must prepare for this trek both mentally and physically. Multi-day expeditions require a different mindset compared to day hikes or hut-to-hut trekking. Soggy socks cannot be thrown in the dryer, nor is there a refreshing shower to ease aching muscles at the end of the day. It was during this walk when the virtues of wool shone true for me. Although I could wring a lovely cocktail of sweaty rain droplets from their fibres, these saturated tubes miraculously kept my feet toasty warm day after day.

I was undeterred by the challenge; rather, it only spurred my enthusiasm. After all, the setting was one of the last temperate rainforests that remain on our planet. UNESCO has recognized this Tasmanian wilderness, where humans have resided for over twenty thousand years, as a region subjected to "severe glaciation."[10] Cradle Mountain, our hiking venue, lies in the northern niche of this World Heritage Site.

On our first day, we covered ten kilometres through a myriad of rocky inclines and boardwalks, which ended paradoxically in lush rainforest. The weather bared its temperamental tendencies with sun, rain, sleet and even some hurtling hail. Soon after all eight of us in the trekking group arrived at camp, our two guides prepared an unexpected cheese platter. The dinner that followed was a warming spaghetti bolognese followed by fruit and custard pavlova. This was the most sumptuous camping dinner I had ever tasted, and the feast alone encouraged happy campsite chatter. Although I was still damp, this delectable concoction was warm in my belly and made tucking into the cool tent much more inviting.

At daybreak, we woke to continued rain, but at least the gale force winds had subsided. The drizzle meant that we had to pack everything under an umbrella of mist. For the remainder of the day, we slogged amid lakes and plateaus. When we arrived at the evening's camp, we enjoyed a few hours of reprieve inside the adjacent Windermere Hut. Its enormous stone hearth was nearly hidden behind socks and boots indiscriminately splayed out to dry. Our group continued to bond over crosswords and card games at a corner table. Even a wee Tasmanian devil crept close to the hut's protective shelter. Shortly after dinner, we returned to our tent. As we eased into our sleeping bags, the wind performed a gentle lullaby.

By the third morning, the group had developed its cohesive groove. The familiarity that comes after pushing past mental hurdles and physical pangs grew as we savoured daily personal accomplishments together. Three days may not seem long, but we were all new to the challenge of multi-day treks with soggy gear and strenuous elevation gains. Small moments such as licking the custard tin pot and shared frights over nightly rustles created a relaxed atmosphere. Our different backgrounds and ages seemed irrelevant as we persevered day by day.

For the remaining three days, we progressed through a mind-boggling variety of eucalyptus forests, misty bogs, raised boardwalks and rocky peaks that showcased 360-degree views. Some forests harboured more moss than trees, making for a very dense walk. Some trees displayed lime-green bark that had peeled into long strips to bare tender saffron-toned underlayers. Strange cobalt-coloured land crustaceans and blazing sanguine-tinged fungus emerged from fallen tree trunks. These were our beacons along the trail.

Although every day was varied and special, there were a couple of distinct moments that stood out. During our fourth day, we were able to climb towards one of the most spectacular viewpoints of the trip. Unfortunately, Tasmania's highest peak, Mount Ossa, at 1,617 metres, was shrouded in clouds. Instead, four of us scrambled up a neighbouring crag, Mount Pelion East. By chance, just as we reached its 1,433-metre castle-like pinnacle, the skies opened to reveal Mount Ossa's boulder-strewn top. This tantalizing landmark was a temptress that not even our aching legs could escape. In an apparent quest for pain, we clamoured back down and up towards Mount Ossa's now clear summit. The lower elevations hosted ghostly grey pencil pines that had perished in a former forest fire. Above the treeline, huge boulders set the stage for the remainder of our three-hour extension. The view and self-satisfaction ultimately proved worthy of the effort.

A second unforgettable experience occurred in one of the many mystical forests. At the request of our guides, everyone walked in silence for ten minutes. We eavesdropped on the woodland community and became absorbed in the moment. Our feet trod softly, allowing birds and tiny nuances to become more noticeable. It was a calming period that imparted an impression of tranquility on the group for hours afterwards.

By the sixth day—thanks to a few continuously sunny days—we had dried out and warmed up, only to awake to a rainy finale. After trudging for a damp nine kilometres, we met the ferry at the Narcissus River. Its small frame transported the group upriver to the shore of Lake St Clair. Tired, muddy, but elated to have succeeded, we lumbered towards the tourist centre's parking lot. I am sure that our less-than-elegant arrival was an incongruous sight for those on a leisurely day trip, otherwise enjoying the scene over a flat white.[11]

The Basics

Synopsis: Holler **"Lha gyalo"** as you conquer howling winds, and tie your prayer flag at the highest pass, Yeli La (at 4,930 metres) during this awe-inspiring nine-day trek across Bhutan's northwestern Himalayan range.

Most useful items to pack: Wet wipes, dry shampoo and broken-in hiking boots

For further travel information: Bhutan may not appear to be the independent traveller's dream, as the government requires all visitors to travel with a tour company and pay a steep minimum day rate. However, do not be dismayed. Private, personalized tours can be arranged for virtually the same price as standard group tours. Details of charges, available discounts and inclusions are clearly laid out on the Tourism Council of Bhutan's website: tourism.gov.bt/plan/minimum-daily-package.

An industrious and energetic Bhutanese woman, Mrs. Sonam Wangmo, founded Rainbow Tours & Treks, which we used upon a friend's referral. They specialize in photography tours but also arrange other custom tours, including our impeccably organized Jomolhari trek. Even after weeks together, we still enjoyed the company and advice of our adventurous guide and diligent driver. For more information, refer to rainbow-bhutan.com.

The Experience

It is worth sharing a sense of the astonishing country of Bhutan before plunging into details of the Jomolhari trek. This is a land that few foreigners have witnessed. After all, Bhutan only opened its borders to tourists in 1974. Apart from the country's well-known measurement of gross national happiness,[12] its intrigue stretches beyond its peaceful population. For one, the Bhutanese are incredibly hard workers. While we were in Ogyen Choling in central Bhutan, neighbours had gathered to build a home, by hand. Wooden planks were anchored in parallel to form a cavity. A mud slurry was then poured between the studs and pounded manually with a huge wooden mallet. Slowly, slowly the layers hardened and formed a cement-like wall, which rose up between the support panels. Villagers arrived to offer food or lend a hand. Everyone was welcome to share in the process. It sure was tedious work. My efforts may have added only one centimetre to their wall, but more memorable were the few hours spent joking and participating in this timeless moment.

Beyond hard work, there is a captivating spirituality intrinsic in Bhutan's local culture. Only in Bab Al Yemen have I seen such intricate architecture that truly defines a place. Do not be surprised to spot a mural of a gigantic phallus spritzing its fertility charms on the face of a village home. Similarly, it is not often that one comes across a temple dedicated to the Divine Madman, as Lama Drukpa Kunley is affectionately known. Other unexpected finds range from Bumthang Valley's Swiss-cheese producer and its local Red Panda Weiss beer to mountain ridges amassed with prayer flags. Each day, such varying delights and soulful people divulged layer after layer of the country's distinctive personality.

A favourite sign I saw along the road before starting the trek read "Don't make Guru Drubchu Dirty." In other words, do not litter—a quirky message aimed at preserving the healing spring water associated with Guru Drubchu. In keeping with this theme, throughout our trek all our garbage was carried out with us, and toilets were dug away from streams. The route remained relatively untouched, as few people beyond indigenous yak herders made this journey.

Yet we were supported by a remarkably large entourage for this nine-day ordeal. Ten horses, two horsemen, two chefs and our guide ensured that we were well directed and fully fed and that our packs arrived at the campsite. One may argue that this level of support is overkill; however, food and supplies for the entire trip had to be carried in. Just as important, our tourist dollars directly benefitted each of these people and their families, making the high day rate more palatable.

This hard-working team was consistently attentive and even offered a touch of luxury. We washed down lunches on the trail with warm tea, tents were assembled for us and there was even a toilet tent for privacy, which was thoroughly appreciated each and every day. By day eight without a shower, wet wipes and dry shampoo topped my list of must-haves. Despite the inevitable rustic simplicity, the experience was made noticeably more pleasant with these few added comforts.

Most days we averaged seventeen kilometres, with five hundred to one thousand metres in net elevation gain or loss. The walk started off along an undulating trail, past rhododendron forests and along the Paro Chhu River valley. The path was clear and easy to follow except for one fork in the road, which our guide had luckily warned us about in advance. Stay to the right or risk walking straight into China. An old stone invasion trail that veered left towards Tremo La had evolved into a well-frequented trade route leading to Tibet's frosty mountain border.

By day three, we reached yak territory. Their bulky bodies dotted grassy areas near the river. Unsurprisingly, we soon passed a couple of huts belonging to nearby herders. The stars aligned as snow appeared only on our fourth day, which was coincidentally a designated acclimatization rest day. Other groups turned back, leery of the treacherous conditions that the snow might have brought to the highest pass, which was yet to come. Serendipitously, all the snow melted by midmorning. We then won our first clear view of Mount Jomolhari—an imposing sight at the height of 7,314 metres, coated with a thick sheet of snow and ice.

After leaving the comfort of our acclimatization camp, we started off strong but struggled to pull ourselves over the Nyile La pass. This was the second-highest pass of the Jomolhari trek, at 4,870 metres. The winds blew fiercely, making it a particularly arduous climb—plus we were taunted by a false summit, like a cloak over our actual target. Slow and steady, we finally reached the narrow, gusty ridge. A collage of faded prayer flags, bashed about by the wind but eternally dispersing their climbers' wishes to the heavens, welcomed us. We yelled the customary summit call, **"Lha gyalo"** ("May the gods be victorious"), and with icy fingers fastened our prayer flag while the wind whipped it around. Through squinted eyes, we caught clear views of Tshering Gang, at 6,789 metres, before dropping down towards the protected valley full of rhododendrons, juniper and cotoneaster. Our only complaint about that evening's camp was the vast amount of horse dung that blanketed the ground. However, perhaps it added some cushioning, as we slept ever so soundly.

The following day we reached our highest pass, the pass over Yeli La, at 4,930 metres. Curiously, it was less snowy and cold compared to Nyile La. But reaching this summit came with its own challenges, requiring us to climb a steep trail cut into the rock. The high altitude sapped our breath. Each step took noticeable energy. Eventually, we made it to the top and sang our **"Lha gyalo."** Exhilarated at achieving this highest point, we descended towards camp. The heavens seemed to share our exhaustion, as they too relaxed their grip and unleashed heavy rains soon after we arrived. On this night, we needed all our layers to stay warm as we huddled in our sleeping bags. Having passed this milestone, it was a relief to enter the homestretch. Just three days remained.

That mental shift worked against us. We found these final days to be more gruelling than the initial climb. But the scenery was calming and soothed our troubles. Some sections were scrubby grassland while others were rocky riverbed. Although our knees wanted the trek to end, the scenery ensured that there was nowhere else we would rather be. Nevertheless, by the last day the thought of a warm, soapy shower was more motivational than any of the pine forests or pretty rhododendrons. Looking back, the exquisite shower has faded in my memory while a sense of pure freedom remains as the essence of those nine days.

The Basics

Synopsis: Partake in a four-day spiritual circumambulation around the sacred Mount Kailash, revered by Jains, Buddhists, Bons and Hindus as the centre of the universe and believed by some to emit a cosmic power.

Most useful items to pack: Down jacket and hiking poles

For further travel information: Roger Pfister, a Swiss Buddhist, operates insightful trips to Tibet and Mount Kailash twice annually through his tour company, Snow Jewel. He has made more than one hundred circuits of the mountain. Further information can be found at snowjewel.com.

Lonely Planet's **Tibet Travel Guide** (see Bibliography) has an excellent chapter on trekking in the region, including the Mount Kailash **kora**. The book describes both physical trekking considerations and religious elements of the route.

The Experience

Hiking around Mount Kailash entails following a fifty-two-kilometre clockwise route along a well-loved pilgrimage trail. This journey is called a **kora**. Some pilgrims make the journey in a series of full-body prostrations; starting from a standing position, they then lie down flat, forehead touching the ground, while reciting a mantra. It takes them weeks to fully circumambulate the mountain. These dedicated souls often tuck their hands into old shoes to help cushion them from the repetitive bows onto the rough ground. Others attempt to complete the entire kora in one day, a full fourteen hours of steady hiking. These are the people whom you walk beside. Their skin is often weathered by the sun and etched with their own personal tales. One kora is thought to cleanse a person of all the sins from their lifetime, whereas 108 koras are believed to bring Enlightenment at the time of death.

In attempting this trek, it is not necessary to be a worshipper of the sacred mountain. However, a certain awareness of the various phases, rituals and internal transformations believed to occur along the kora added a complexity that I had not anticipated. As a very inward-focused trek, replete with self-reflection, it provided a distinct channel to clear our hearts and minds. At a minimum, pilgrims sharing the trail deserved an element of respect along their journey.

Beyond the spiritual aspects, the physical peak of Mount Kailash was startling. Its pyramidal symmetry aligns perfectly with the points of a compass—north, south, east and west. Beneath its rocky exterior springs the source of four main rivers in Asia: Karnali, Sutlej, Indus and Brahmaputra, or, as the last is otherwise known, Yarlung Tsangpo. It was with this impressive backdrop that we commenced our walk in the dusty village of Darchen.

Altitudes were high along this trek. By the first significant prostration point, we had already reached an elevation of 4,730 metres. Towards the southern face of Mount Kailash, also referred to as **lapis lazuli**, pilgrims bowed in a cyclical prostration as they rotated in all four directions. Through this ritual, they silently requested permission to conduct their personal kora. Farther along the dusty Lha Chu Valley, the two-legged Chorten Kangnyi welcomed pilgrims beneath its sturdy columns. We shuffled around and through its squat white cone, donating a strand of hair and a stick of incense, as is customary, to purify ourselves of past sins. The chorten's base was a mass of flat, rust-coloured rocks inscribed with Sanskrit verses. We saw similar chunks of rock with various inscriptions throughout our four days. These sacred slabs often lined the trail or were hidden away in a secluded refuge.

Nearby, the Tarboche flagpole was imperceptible under mounds of bright red, blue and white prayer flags inked with faded black prayers. The flagpole's location was believed by some to represent the centre of the universe. Beyond this flagpole, high upon a rocky cliff, was a sky burial site. Vast views of the valley below could be seen from the cliff edges, but otherwise the site appeared as merely a barren, rocky field. However, because we knew its purpose, the rocks were anything but devoid of feeling; instead they imparted an eerie ambience as we tentatively walked through. A sky burial is a tantric funeral ceremony in which the body is carved into small pieces, which are left for nature to return to the four elements—earth, water, fire and air—while the soul rises to heaven.

We were abruptly shocked out of these musings when, in the valley below, we spotted three wild dogs creeping aggressively close to one of our fellow hikers. While we scrambled down the rocky cliff, she fended off the mongrels with her sturdy hiking poles. Such aggression seemed out of place in the middle of a pilgrimage trail, but with the long distances came large gaps between people.

The landscape along this stretch was stark and barren. From a distance, it was lit up by a speckled trail of pilgrims' bright clothing. Some of the women wore full-length skirts, often handwoven, in red, blue, green and black. Yaks, with their dark obsidian-coloured shaggy coats, hauled piles of white-and-red canvas duffel bags or large blue water jugs. These were skittish creatures, so it was best to stay well away from their heels.

Farther ahead, we could see a smattering of people and yaks alike scattered around a brownish rectangular tent. This was the second prostration point. It was here where devotees sought wisdom and clarity. Comfort was offered inside, sheltering travellers from the gusty wind. Classic Tibetan butter tea, acidic yet punchy, appeared to be the vendor's most popular drink. After a brief rest and wishes of good tidings, we tramped off towards the Dira-puk Monastery. Our trusty yaks pulled up the rear, conveniently hauling our provisions. For a reprieve from the cold, our group huddled inside the dining tent, absorbing the luscious heat that emanated from the attached cooking tent. Across from the monastery, hidden behind blowing snow and dense clouds, stood the whitened north face.

The next morning was no warmer. Piercing winds cut across the valley while snow blanketed everything in a matte white. Thankfully, it was our acclimatization day, and we were free to hunker inside our protective canvas shelter. By late afternoon the wind had subsided, and the north face called. As if in a fantasy world, funky ice spikes rose from its gravel terrain, and prayer flags dappled the snow among random piles of rock. Even a golden trident was plunged between rocks in homage to the mountain.

Day three was a time to die—symbolically. We encountered hints that signalled our arrival at Shiwa Tsal ("Realm of the Dead"). Clusters of incense protruded from boulders; some still smoked. Countless rocks had been hand-piled into little mounds scattered around the plateau. Here at Shiwa Tsal, pilgrims were believed to experience a figurative death in which any misgivings or anguish could be released. The smoke from the incense was believed to carry blessings to ancestors and, in return, to receive their blessing and strength. Perhaps our family was sending a subtle message, as the winds acted as a continual saboteur while we attempted to light a handful of the red essence. Ultimately, persistence triumphed.

With renewed vigour, spurred by a squirt of double latte energy gel, off we set to be reborn. The highest pass, Drolma La, at 5,630 metres, epitomized a place for rebirth. Earlier in the trek, we had written the names of those closest to us or those who had caused us strife onto a personalized prayer flag. As we hung this flag, the pass was already thick with previous travellers' banners, which fluttered in odd directions as the winds swirled around. Prayers were thought to be sent to these individuals, whether to cleanse the relationship or heal old wounds or just as feelings of gratitude. Life could continue, refreshed and clear-minded.

Looking around, I wondered what had brought others on this quest. There was the young Tibetan lady with her baby bundled upon her back, wearing a blue-and-white-striped toque and wrapped close with layer upon layer of thick material. She wore tennis shoes, a shiny purple smock and bright silver earrings.

All the while, her baby slept as contentedly as if at home in a crib. One man approached the pass wearing a cowboy hat. A girl wore bulky layers for warmth. She looked as if she had raided her elder sister's closet, but these garments hid her true devotion. She grasped turquoise prayer beads tightly between her fingers as she dipped to the ground on all fours, deep in prayer. People attempted this trek out of passion, shielded by whatever warm clothes they could gather. It did not matter.

This was not an easy climb. A gentleman from our group even hired a horse to carry him to the top, unsure of the strength of his own legs. The two ultimately approached the summit side by side, more as best friends offering one another encouragement. The ice had been too slippery for him to ride.

On the final day, we awoke to temperatures of minus twelve degrees Celsius, ice clinging to the tent. It was not a time to linger. The trail promptly passed by the rocky Zutul-puk Monastery, situated where a showdown had allegedly occurred between Buddhist and Bon deities. The head and hand of the revered Buddhist yogi Milarepa were thought to be imprinted on a nearby boulder. In the rooms of the monastery, sitting Buddha figures were encircled by butter candles that flickered amid curly tails of smoking incense. I am sure not a day went by when those candles would not be kept burning.

By the time we reached Darchen, I was craving a shower. It had taken days on long dusty roads to even reach Mount Kailash, and most towns en route did not have running water. However, the available shower facility in Darchen required one to balance atop a moderately clean squat toilet, which quickly dispelled my desire to step inside. But despite this superficial inconvenience, the trek around Mount Kailash was certainly memorable. Since our visit in 2010, I understand many of the roads have been paved—and perhaps the facilities have been upgraded.

The Basics

Synopsis: Tramp among remote hills forested by dense jungle while building an unexpected rapport with resident critters.

Most useful item to pack: Hiking poles

For further travel information: Most tours start from the tourist -friendly village of Luang Namtha in northern Laos, which has plenty of accommodation and restaurant options. I have decided not to mention our trekking operator, as the maintenance of the overnight huts was shockingly poor. Instead, check with your guidebook, TripAdvisor.com, your hotel and other travellers for current reviews of the companies before selecting a tour operator.

The Experience

The rainy season had recently begun in Laos. In our experience, this season typically brought heavy showers for a couple of hours each morning, but the skies often cleared for the remainder of the day. We packed decent rain gear and recalled our previous treks in muddy conditions. How bad could it be? In fact, it turned out to be quite a miserable experience. We quickly learned that in Asia, the rainy season resulted in much more than just a wet trail. However, I am convinced that this jungle trek has the potential to be amazing if attempted during the dry or shoulder season. So do not despair—just be prudent when choosing your timing.

Perhaps my hope stems from our first day. It started out with such promise. Our guide met us at our hotel in the northern Laos village of Luang Namtha. The three of us took a forty-minute tuk-tuk ride south. The drive passed villages of bamboo huts raised on stilts, below which small pot-bellied pigs rustled or aged men stretched out in hammocks, taking full advantage of the buildings' shade. The landscape was interspersed with limestone karsts that rose high above fields of rice seedlings just breaking through the earth's surface. Time flew and soon we arrived at our destination, a tiny Khmu tribal village where we would start the trek. The Khmu had migrated to Laos centuries ago but retained their own religion and language separate from those elsewhere in Laos. The town was also, not so coincidentally, home to our assistant guide, who quickly joined our crew. We presumed this must be a new job for the young assistant, as the people from the village good naturedly heckled him as we set off. He smiled shyly.

Our head guide led us through the endless plots of rice towards higher ground. Bamboo shafts rose like bunches of celery across the hills, and it was clearly the preferred material for housing construction. Once we were up in the forest, our guide introduced us to some local secrets. The bark from the medicinal camphor, or "tiger balm," tree could be boiled and used to treat aches or other ailments. He sliced chunks from the rattan, bamboo and galangal trees, which all grew near the trail, so that we could sample their silky edible cores. Bamboo was the mildest, galangal had a peppery flavour and rattan tasted bitter.

After we had spent a few hours of walking uphill in the damp heat, our stomachs growled for more sustenance. However, we did not expect the gourmet lunch that was presented atop freshly cut banana leaves. **Laab gai** melded ground chicken with the sensuous flavours of lemon grass, fresh mint, cilantro, chilies and other savoury spices. It was served alongside mashed bamboo, surprisingly mild raw yak meat and a zesty chili sauce. We dined among the forest leaves, mistakenly convinced that the rest of the three days would prove just as delightful.

The hillside grew animated over the afternoon as the jungle's orchestra serenaded us along our walk: birds chirped, frogs bellowed and a mélange of bugs sang their hearts out. The rains only sprinkled off and on. We finally reached a ridge. The humid greenery seemed like paradise. Soon, a small bungalow on low stilts came into view, along with a new sound, a gentle whirring that gradually became louder as we drew near. We recalled being asked by the trekking company whether either of us was allergic to bees. At the time, we had presumed this query was standard protocol for a jungle trek. However, the question was not so innocent. Hundreds of bees greeted us at our first night's hut. They were a curious family; the little critters crawled across any exposed skin, appendage, bag, clothing or food. Our guide did not flinch and cautioned us not to swat them away for fear they would become agitated. After all, we only needed to share our abode until sundown, when they would return to their hive.

In addition to these gracious hosts, it turned out that the mosquito netting, which was to be provided by the tour company, had been stolen from the hut. So we doused ourselves in yet another spray of DEET and tried to relax while the bees continued their exploration down our arms and across our heads. We were not keen to stray far from the hut because unexploded ordnance, or "UXO," remnants from the Vietnam War were known to lie in the surrounding hills. True to our guide's word, the bees flew off when the sun set. After a shot of local Laos whiskey that left fire pulsating down our throats, we unrolled our sleeping bags along the damp wooden-plank floor. We drew the drawstrings tight around our necks as protection against any other creatures that might—and did—come along. Please, we thought, may sleep come quickly.

The bees were persistent little devils. On cue with the dawn, along they came to wake us ever so gently from our slumber. These bees induced us on our way more effectively than any cup of steaming espresso could. We swiftly packed up and ventured out. For five hours, we savoured leaf-padded pathways through a rain-forest clear of any flying bugs. Things were looking up again. We then reached the lowlands. The atmosphere abruptly changed, and we were each provided with a multicoloured dabber. It was of simple construction: a swatch of material tied around a pile of salt and fastened with an elastic band—leech warfare. The trail quickly faded and was replaced by dense undergrowth in dire need of our guide's machete. After tearing open a walkway, we proceeded down slippery, muddy, steep sections for about three hours. The machete's slashing never ceased. This was what one imagines jungle trekking is like. If the thorns did not grab hold, the leeches would take their turn. Our little dabbers worked incessantly battling the lower front while we prayed that none of the little bloodsuckers had snuck through and made it past our shins.

The foliage opened onto what seemed to be a river's edge. Thick marshy reeds blanketed the ground. There stood, although not so firmly, our second night's hut. The building looked even less inviting than the previous night's abode. The familiar buzzing sound welcomed us as we hopped up onto the cabin's ledge. While bees crawled all over us, we attempted to check for rogue leeches that might have advanced beneath our clothing. After a few uncomfortable tweaks to pluck the vile creatures from concealment, we noticed that the bees were a social bunch, for in this camp they were joined by horseflies and wasps that spun through the air. Looking up through a cloud of insects, we saw that the hut's ceiling had been torn apart, presumably by violent rainstorms. Large holes ripped through the thatch and awaited repair. It became astoundingly clear that this night would bring no reprieve. Please, we thought, may there be no rain tonight.

Unsurprisingly, we were woken once again by the all-too-familiar hum. We were comforted knowing that today would be the last day of our dismal trek. The final day's hike took seven hours; however, only three of those were spent in the leech-ridden muddy hills. But they were painful hours, as our slashed path continued to be as slick and steep as it had been the day before. My knees and hips were strained from sliding while I attempted to get some traction and still move forward. Shots of pain surged through my right hip and slowed my descent. It would have been impossible without the aid of hiking poles—and my husband's supportive shoulders. Luckily, the throb subsided once we reached flat ground.

At last we stumbled upon the final river crossing. The water was too deep to wade, so our guide swam across in search of a boat master. Shortly, two young boys ran out of the trees and dashed out of their clothing. They each grabbed a bamboo pole and headed up river. Without much delay, the kids returned in a low, long flatboat. We were expeditiously shuttled across the muddy waters and felt immediately relieved to be done with this trek. After completing their newfound job, the children returned for a playful swim in the river's coolness.

Eventually a tuk-tuk arrived, and we loaded inside to travel back to Luang Namtha. This time the drive seemed to drag. Once we were back in our hotel lobby, the receptionist solemnly advised us that our reservation had not been held. Our mouths dropped; then he quickly broke into a smile and admitted that he was only joking. Drained, our sense of humour was rather tense at that moment. I am sure a wave of relief washed over our faces when he eventually passed us the room key.

Oh, how we cherished the solid walls, the bed enclosed with untorn mosquito netting and the crisp white sheets. Looking back, there were elements of this walk that were enjoyable. Other travellers have raved about it as one of their best experiences in Laos. So learn from us and please only attempt treks in the Nam Ha National Protected Area outside the rainy season.

The Basics

Synopsis: Escape to the highlands of Malawi for cooler temperatures amid cedar trees and boulder-strewn peaks.

Most useful item to pack: Sleeping bag

For further travel information: Access to the mountain's trails starts from the Likhubula Forestry Office, where guides and porters may also be hired. Multiple routes are available, from one-day to multi-night treks. Be prepared to carry all your supplies in and out. For further details on the huts, refer to http://www.mcm.org.mw/mulanje_huts.php.

We travelled with Barefoot Safaris as part of a longer overland trip across Malawi and Zambia. They coordinated local guides and porters to accompany us on this Mulanje trek. For further details, refer to barefoot-safaris.com.

The Experience

Mount Mulanje rises like a mirage, soaring three thousand metres in Malawi's southeastern corner. Although considered one mountain, it covers six hundred square kilometres with multiple peaks and a variety of landscapes. This diversity kept things interesting throughout our four-day expedition. The first incline, up the Chapaluka Path, jump-started my heart. Clearly, days spent sitting in the Land Rover visiting the many animal parks spread across Malawi and Zambia were not ideal pre-departure training. One particularly pleasant rest stop was most appreciated, not only for the perfect curve on the boulder I eased myself onto, but because it was fortuitously situated across from a pretty waterfall. Thankfully, our walking legs eventually kicked back into gear.

Once we were higher up the mountain, the scenery transformed into rolling hills. The country's national tree, the Mulanje cedar, dotted the landscape, along with ferns and dried grasses. Our destination was Chisepo Hut, not to be confused with the alternative Chambe Hut, which also could have been reached on day one.

We spent our nights in a trio of huts on the mountain. All three provided the basics: a roof, a floor and a much-loved veranda. Chisepo Hut was the social hive of the three, the place to see and be seen. It was also the most rustic, meaning it had no beds, only floor space. Of the nine of us who overnighted at the hut, most were lucky enough to nab an available foam mattress. Those too slow had to negotiate a cuddle or risk a sadly distorted sleep without cushioned bliss. Thuchila Hut, our second abode, seemed luxurious in comparison to the minimalistic Chisepo Hut. This lodge offered three simple rooms and was furnished with one large stone fireplace, a classic wooden table and a standard desk. The raised pieces provided invaluable storage to keep our belongings off the floor. No sooner had we settled in for the evening than a friendly mouse popped out to inspect his new room-mates. He was probably in search of food scraps rather than a social call. As much as the wee rodent's intentions were innocent, neither of us wanted a free rider on our trek.

The final lodging, Sombani Hut, afforded the best view from its veranda, which overlooked an imposing chunk of rock called Namasile Peak. The porch chairs were truly the perfect spot to laze after the day's hike and to play with photos or write one's musings. This little two-roomed shelter was crammed full of personality. Its walls were covered in maps and drawings from the local Mountain Club of Malawi. Bunk beds seemed a lavish bonus, lending to an ever-so-sound third night's sleep. On our final morning, we sat on the veranda with a steaming cup of freshly brewed coffee in hand. This seemed an idyllic way to finish our journey. In fact, it was on this Mulanje trek that we became adept at preparing perfectly potent camp coffee. It was a straightforward, one-pot process. Boil water. Add one part ground coffee to four parts water. Perk the murky goodness for six minutes. We found that the local Chipunga Arabica brand was especially flavourful and robust.

The morning caffeine packed the punch we needed to vacate the comfy patios and fuelled our daily walks. We faced the greatest challenge of the trek on day two. Sapitwa Peak, translated as "unreachable" or "a place people do not go," is Mulanje's highest rocky outcrop, rising to 3,001 metres. It was a boulder-strewn, curious place full of awkward squeezes and burnt soil from a forest fire. A few tufts of courageous grass had begun to regrow, whereas the trees were just ashen silhouettes. Over the four days, we came across many sections of the mountain that had fallen victim to such fires. Whether they were lit by rogue loggers' forays gone bad, hunters' follies or illegal charcoal rustlers was difficult to know for certain. They were devastating nonetheless.

The final section of this peak's climb required some acrobatics. Granite boulders bleached by the sun or fire attempted to block our way. Our adept guide seemed to be familiar with every crevice. We wound higher with each of his relentless turns. As we used hands and feet to grasp the rocks and scrambled up and around the crooks and crannies, I understood how Spiderman must feel. Perhaps this was nature's version of an extreme-sport obstacle course, ready for the next reality television contract. The views from the top were unreal. Rounded rocks protruded at all angles and fluffy clouds filled the voids, obscuring our sense of how high we had actually climbed. However, we knew that the round trip took five hours of steady scrambling from our starting point at Chisepo Hut, and we felt triumphant.

The remaining two days continued through undulating terrain, past ravines, dry riverbeds, plateaus and peaks with funky names such as Nandalanda or Chinzama. Not only were there contrasts in geography, but the colours were striking. The forest fires had created a charred-black soil backdrop. Half-burnt bridges framed gold- and emerald-tinged grass, which sprouted before any other vegetation. The leaves of the bushes alternated between copper and hues of green. It looked like an autumn scene painted with an African twist.

The final day was not overly strenuous. The five-kilometre downhill journey offered panoramic views of the valley below before we arrived at the nondescript Fort Lister Forestry Office. Overall, we covered forty kilometres, with the first day having the longest distance of fifteen kilometres. It was an invigorating time and refreshingly cool compared to the lower regions of Malawi.

This outlier of a trek delivered a unique perspective into a country often considered to be "Africa for beginners." It was frequented enough to offer basic amenities, guides and porters, yet attracted few foreigners to crowd the trails. We felt as one with nature, free to roam at our own pace or scale the highest peak unimpeded. As the dusty tracks curled around the mountain, each turn granted a distinct view. And it was a welcome diversion from the long hours travelling overland between game parks and lakeshore beaches elsewhere in the country.

The Basics

Synopsis: Spend nine days trekking through mind-blowing landscapes, with the goal to summit the third-highest mountain in all of Africa.

Most useful items to pack: Rubber boots and fully waterproof jacket and pants

For further travel information: Flights into Uganda land at Entebbe International Airport, which is in the eastern end of the country and adjacent to Kampala, the capital city. If flying in on a clear day, you can catch glimpses of Lake Victoria, Africa's largest lake, from the plane's windows. I recommend spending at least one night in either Entebbe or Kampala. Many hotel options are available, most of which can provide an airport pickup.

We trekked with the well-run Rwenzori Trekking organization, which was one of the few companies with access rights to trek to Margherita Peak. Transport between Kampala and Kilembe, where the trek began, was coordinated by Rwenzori Trekking. The drive takes approximately six hours, so it is best to do it at least one day before starting your expedition. Further information can be found at rwenzoritrekking.com.

For pre-hike warm-up walks or post-hike pampering, check out Kyaninga Lodge, located conveniently along the main highway between Kilembe and Kampala. Further information can be found at kyaningalodge.com.

The Experience

This trek was intense. Over nine days, we climbed from 1,450 metres in Kilembe to a staggering 5,109 metres at the tip of Margherita Peak—and back again. On the first day alone we had a net elevation gain of 1,146 metres. If I were to do this multi-day trudge again, I would put far more emphasis on upfront training. It was a killer. Another consideration is the wet and mud. I have endured globs of muck on other treks, but these paths reached new heights. We wore rubber boots for seven of the nine days—only on the first day and the summit day did we lace up our hikers. Besides the mud, the track was marshy, boggy and at times transformed into a small stream. We wore waterproof pants day in and day out, taking them off only to sleep.

The intensity and the extreme wet made much of this hike rather unpleasant. However, the scenery was truly spectacular and amazingly diverse. The challenge of summiting the third-highest mountain in Africa, here in a remote region of Uganda, while skirting the nearby border of the Democratic Republic of Congo was truly exhilarating. I am convinced that had I been in better shape leading up to this hike, it would have been far more enjoyable. Still, it was an unparalleled experience, a strange yet extreme vacation. If you need to clear your head, this is the trek to do.

The walk originated in the small village of Kilembe, farther up the valley from the larger town of Kasese. In 2013, only one year prior to our visit, this community had been all but destroyed by a flood. Remnants of the damage remained, but life carried on. We walked past giggling schoolchildren, men and women labouring in the fields and chickens scurrying about in random directions. The adults waved and seemed to share a knowing smile of the tough climb ahead. I am sure they wondered why we would willingly choose to leave the warm lowlands for the cold, harsh peaks. They clearly had enough challenge already in their daily lives.

As we rose high above the town, the hilly farm plots quickly turned to forest. This scenery hinted at one of the most astonishing features of this trek, its unique vegetation. Lichen in various shades blanketed many of the trees in a candy-floss-like moss, seemingly transforming them into a new life form. Vines took on the role of the forest nervous system as they appeared to connect with everything. Higher up, bamboo trees dominated, sprouting upward in solidarity. As we climbed, the bamboo was left behind and replaced by trees of heather. Their gangly bodies draped the land. This was all interspersed with valleys, knolls and frequent waterfalls. The one constant was an abundance of rivers and streams. We attempted to keep our balance while scrambling across broad boulders, mossy and damp. It was less slippery than walking in the river, but not by much. Several waterways were crystal clear, whereas others were tainted by tea-coloured tannins.

Trees had been overtaken by thick beds of moss; I longed to climb into one to curl up and ease my aching calf muscles. By the time we neared three thousand metres, everlasting flowers scattered the ground. Giant lobelias curved up and then hunched over. They looked like massive pineapples that had been stretched, twisted and left to balance themselves in a bizarre yoga position. Others were just shrivelled-up leaves atop a dried pillar. By four thousand metres, the landscape was harsher. Scruffy grass clung to a thin layer of topsoil. Chunks of granite shot up from the hillsides amid placid lakes that reflected all this scenery, doubling its impact.

Our greatest challenge was reaching Mount Margherita's summit on day six. The day kicked off with a chipper four o'clock start. As the sky was still pitch black, we all strapped on headlamps over our woollen toques. Before long, we were scrambling up rocky perches high above our camp. Some sections required ropes and crampons, which our guides ever so patiently helped us into. The lack of sleep certainly did not help my dexterity. It is worth acknowledging the unending fortitude and skills of our guides. They were from the local community and had studied indigenous ecology, first aid and extreme mountaineering. The trekking company sponsored their continual development. The guides' next learning exercise was to be conducted by a Norwegian specialist and held in the Himalayas.

We safely crossed the Stanley and Margherita glaciers, all before sunrise. The Margherita glacier started out with a thirty-degree slope and then threw in some rocky bits to navigate with the help of ropes. We scrambled various precipitous sections and climbed up others—and later back down again. As the elevation was high and the air was thin, each step took all our energy. I was feeling rather ill, which added to my mental battle to keep going. Ten more steps, breathe. Twenty more steps. Inhale, exhale. The fog came rolling in as we neared the summit. This last section was extra steep. My stomach lurched, but I eventually gathered strength and pushed on to the top. My husband waited patiently and insisted we would summit this milestone together. Our guide rewarded us with a Twix chocolate bar to regain some of our energy for the return climb. That day, we hiked for twelve hours, including our climb to the summit, the return trip to the prior night's camp and then onward to that night's camp. It was exhausting, but not even the rain could quell our sense of satisfaction.

During the trek, we spent most nights in basic huts. The first night was the most stylish as we, along with two German hikers, shared a log cabin complete with tin roof and front veranda. The cabin had ample sleeping space, with bunk beds that held up to eight people. The second night was not so posh. We nestled into a permanently pitched, slightly dank canvas tent lined with foam mattresses and sheltered beneath a rocky overhang. The two Germans had become our hiking partners and shared a separate but similar tent. Unfortunately, we lost our companions early on, as they turned back on the third morning due to a stomach ailment. For the rest of the trip, the huts were virtually the same from camp to camp. Some were made using curved poles covered by a green waterproof tarp, often with a metallic thermal liner. Other huts were only slightly sturdier, with a wooden construct and green tin roof. They were all styled in the customary beehive shape. Our final night proved to be the coziest. Near bedtime, our guide placed the spare campfire embers in a metal bucket, and we brought them into our cabin. It was the first toasty night of the eight. I could not take my eyes off the red-hot coals. Perhaps they mesmerized me in the same way that campfires do, or I might have just feared that a spark would take flight inside our snug abode.

When we stumbled back to Kilembe, the townsfolk smiled and welcomed our return as they carried on with their daily activities. Visions of Kyaninga Lodge's stilted huts, with their thatched roofs and gourmet dinners, propelled us onward during that last day. The lodge staff knew that we had just come from summiting Margherita Peak, so upon our arrival they presented a platter of glasses filled with chilled mango juice. Oh so refreshing! We stayed at the lodge for two nights after the trek, although we were too spent to take advantage of its tennis courts or its walk around the perimeter of the volcanic lake. Instead, we lounged on the patio, savoured the warm shower, sorted through photos and looked forward to the next three-course meal.

Few people get to experience this remote region of Uganda. During the entire nine-day tramp, we crossed paths with only a handful of other trekkers. The Rwenzori Mountains provide an isolated, pristine opportunity to glimpse strange yet natural landscapes. One might not associate snow and glaciers with Africa, yet here they exist, waiting to be explored. Just be sure to get in shape beforehand.

Fresh air, untamed trees and well-marked trails are ingredients of a satisfying day hike. After wandering through inspiring scenery, sit down over a warm dinner and then peacefully fall asleep in a comfortable bed—a perfect day. As much as I love the challenge of multi-day treks, I certainly appreciate the ease of returning to a room with a roof and refreshing shower. After all, stuffing your feet into cold boots for a midnight bathroom run is never fun. There are a few gems around the globe that combine a convenient base with accessible walking trails. The following sections describe some of these pristine locations that balance serene comfort and fantastic hiking.

The Basics

Synopsis: Discover a virtual candy store for outdoor enthusiasts, dishing up an assortment of volcanic adventures, isolated islands, rugged forests and monumental peaks.

Most useful items to pack: Multiple layers of clothing to adapt to a variety of climates

For further travel information: The Lonely Planet's excellent **Trekking in the Patagonian Andes** (see Bibliography) covers multi-day treks in the region. The regular Lonely Planet country guidebooks for Chile and Argentina also cover Patagonia's trails, but in less detail.

Useful references for these hikes out of El Chaltén in South Patagonia can be found at the following links:

» Laguna Torre: elchalten.com/eng/actividades/lagunatorre.php

» Laguna de los Tres: elchalten.com/eng/actividades/lagunadelostres.php

» Lomo del Pliegue Tumbado and Laguna Toro: lonelyplanet.com/argentina/parque-nacional-los-glaciares-north/activities/hiking-trekking/lomo-del-pliegue-tumbado-laguna-toro

Our hotel in Pucón was average, so I have not mentioned it here.

In Castro, we stayed at the nature-inspired yet quirky Palafito 1326 Hotel Boutique, which can be found at palafito1326.cl.

While staying in El Chaltén, we settled into a double room with ensuite at the homey Patagonia Travellers' Hostel. Further information can be found at patagoniahostel.com.ar.

In Ushuaia, we stayed at an apartment in the superfriendly La Posta Apart Hostel. Further information can be found at lapostahostel.com.ar/en.

The Experience

The Patagonia region is absolutely mammoth, with over one million square kilometres covering both Argentina's and Chile's southern reaches. The entire expanse is stunning; volcanic peaks, sharp rocky pitches and chunky glacier ice masses extend across its land. This may be one of those treasured destinations that entice you back for more, a sweet treat for outdoor aficionados. Between its scenic backdrop, its boutique lodge accommodations, a temperate climate, robust local wines and amicable people, each visit can offer something new and spectacular. Like a puzzle, its picturesque persona will emerge piece by piece to enlighten your spirit.

From north to south, Patagonia is arranged into five subregions: the Araucanía, Lakes District, Central Patagonia, Southern Patagonia and Tierra del Fuego. The descriptions below follow this division, except for Central Patagonia. For this section we chose not to hike and instead drifted aboard the *Evangelistas* ferry, as described in Chapter One. Based on my personal experience, the more southerly locales seemed to offer more challenging hikes and dramatic scenery relative to their northern brethren. However, all the hikes we tackled are described below to provide a full account and to better differentiate the various locations.

While there are many multi-day treks on offer, my exploits in Patagonia were restricted to day hikes. After ten months and numerous multi-day expeditions, a warm shower and comfy bed post-hike took precedence during our Patagonia travels. Perhaps I was getting soft, but nevertheless, the day hikes were captivating. And, I must admit, a locally brewed pint at the end of the trail was equally gratifying.

The Araucanía—Parque Nacional Villarrica

Southeast of Chile's capital, Santiago, lies Pucón, at the southern frontier of the Araucanía region. This community nestles in the land of volcanoes; some still seethe with noxious gases while others have long lain dormant, capped by rock and crusted with snow. Reaching Pucón required a dreaded eleven-hour overnight bus ride. Oh, how we had tried to avoid such unpleasantries. However, we caved at the reputably comfortable and expeditious Chilean buses. After we had settled into snug recliners and munched on the mandatory road-trip snack, sleep intermittently took hold. The ride was blissfully uneventful beyond random streetside lights that blinked into the darkened bus and our occasional repositioning of ourselves in search of comfort.

After an initial reconnaissance of the town, some seed of familiarity gnawed at the back of my sleepy mind. It was not long before the resemblance darted to the surface. This tiny hiking mecca that attracted thousands of tourists was a mirror image of Banff, Canada, except located in the Southern Hemisphere. Its foundation of tour offerings, adrenalin-sport excursions, souvenir markets and perky serving staff inside timber-adorned cafés mimicked that mountainous northern town. Swap the pine-clad volcanoes for the evergreen-cloaked Rocky Mountains and their similarity was uncanny.

Our principal goal here was to hike Volcán Villarrica. Although I am not typically a fan of excursion outings, attempting to climb its smouldering pinnacle independently would have been foolish. It is one of only five volcanoes worldwide with an active lava lake in its crater, so unless a climber is an accredited and experienced member of a mountaineering club, it is mandatory to have a certified guide who is recognized by the Corporación Nacional Forestal, the Chilean forestry service.[13] Guide knowledge is important not only on the hill, but before the trek even starts. Depending upon the winds, the sulphur content can weigh so heavily that tours may be cancelled due to health concerns. Villarrica's latest relatively major eruption occurred in March 2015. Locals were evacuated to escape the ash and lava that gushed out of its cone and sprayed up to one thousand metres vertically.[14] Reuters published some spectacular photos taken by Cristóbal Saavedra of this eruption.[15]

The hike itself was not particularly demanding, in part due to the aid of a chairlift, which knocked approximately 1,600 metres from the initial incline. Couple this with the near-lethargic pace set by the guides and the climb could be considered effortless by those in decent shape. This made it an easy warm-up for the rest of Patagonia's more challenging tracks. Unlike volcano hikes in Central America, which traverse straight up the slope, this pathway was crammed full of switchbacks. Although easier on the legs, these bends could get congested by groups on their descent or just clogged with other climbers ascending at varying speeds.

Reaching the summit was less a moment to savour than one to merely endure. Even on a moderately calm day such as ours, fumes swirled in thick plumes around the cone's cavity. After the quintessential photo and a rapid wince at the pungent air, we were inspired to swiftly retreat below to fresher air. This anticlimax led nicely into the most entertaining part of the day—the descent. With helmets strapped on tight and ice picks in their ready position to act as brakes, we rode trusty plastic discs along snow channels. It was a little like a huge outdoor waterslide without the water but with all the twists. The only challenge was to set oneself down, ever so glamorously, onto one of these bright little spheres while holding legs and feet well above the ground. This was the perfect opportunity to benefit from countless Pilates core manoeuvres, my go-to exercise for compact hotel rooms.

As it was just a few days before Christmas, this outing's charming snowy atmosphere and lighthearted fun were fitting. The destination is best suited for an easy vacation, but is squarely on the tourist track. Thus, we were keen to move farther south towards more remote territory and autonomous travels.

Lakes District—Parque Nacional Chiloé

Parque Nacional Chiloé comprises much of the northwestern rim of Isla Grande de Chiloé ("Greater Island of Chiloé"), the second-largest island in South America. Few visitors appeared to have made the short ferry voyage to its northern shore, even over the Christmas holiday season. In fact, streets were stealthily quiet, with only a few essential shops open to patrons. True to its reputation, the island offered an authentic depiction of Chile's coastal settlements, untainted by foreign travellers or touristic whims.

Perhaps more renowned than the hiking trails were the aged wooden churches, which have been recognized by UNESCO as "a successful fusion of indigenous and European culture."[16] In fact, one of these designated architectural delights was situated in Castro, our local base town. Picture a typical Catholic church layout, but with the entire structure ensconced in wood panelling: the walls, ceiling, pews, altar, arches, pillars and every nook. Even in this festive season, not a single green bough or piece of silver tinsel distracted from the ever-so-thorough wooden veneer. Personally, I found that a glimpse at just a couple of the sixteen churches of Chiloé specifically recognized by UNESCO was ample to satisfy my curiosity.

The trails were calling much louder. But where were they? After a seventy-five-minute bus ride across the island to the ranger station, which clearly denoted the park's entrance, we vigorously started out on a nearby trail. Initially, it meandered along a wooded pathway, but soon the landscape opened onto coastal vistas and scattered Huilliche indigenous communities. The water was steely grey, bordered by a dark taupe sandy beach and windblown dunes. Greenish-yellow tufts of grass grew in clumps out of the sand as if trying to hold it from blowing away. Blades of grass shot straight up from the silty cliff edges. Overall, the shoreline looked as if it had recently received a giant buzz cut.

Due either to the continuous winds or to a lack of local interest, any sense of a pathway disappeared soon after we entered the grasslands. Beyond a few indifferent cows chewing on the sinewy grass, there were no locals or other walkers from whom to ask directions. So our intrepid hike turned into a casual stroll. We eventually came across a road that took us over a deserted bridge to a few similarly quiet buildings. All in all, the scenery was rugged, but the hiking was short lived.

Southern Patagonia—Fitz Roy Range of Parque Nacional Los Glaciares

For those in pursuit of the perfect wilderness setting, the Cerro Torre of the Fitz Roy Range may just tick all the desired boxes. Behold vistas of mountain peaks that look more like switchblades, lakes the colour of blue opals and glacier fields that creep ever so close to the hiking trail. The nearest town is El Chaltén, a jewel in itself that amplified this near perfect locale. As a baby of a city—the town was founded only in 1985—its streets were like ribbons caught between two boulder-like hills on either side. Quaint lodging, a malty **cervecería**, or microbrewery, and a divine artisanal pizzeria ensured that the day's end was just as anticipated as the hikes themselves. In keeping with these impeccable amenities, even the trailheads were conveniently located within walking distance of the town centre. Both day trails and multi-day tracks with campgrounds en route started from the town, saving the hassle of coordinating drop-off or pickup transport. I would surely return to this undeniably worthy destination.

Our first hike was to Laguna Torre, twenty-four kilometres round trip. Its pinnacle was at the Mirador Maestri lookout point with views over the Cordón Adela range and down onto Glacier Torre's gritty arm of ice. Another stunning viewpoint, at Mirador Laguna Torre, afforded a panoramic vista of Cerro Torre's slivery points among a wider snowy range perched above the chilly Laguna Torre. Only the enormous horseflies that took pleasure in hurtling themselves at our necks could distract us. At least they stayed to the lower elevations, near where the trail followed the Río Fitz Roy bank and temperatures were warmer. This hike reached a net elevation gain of two hundred metres.

On our second day, we awoke to raindrops and an overcast sky. Half-grudgingly, we pulled on rain gear and extra layers so as not to lose a precious hiking day. It was well worth the initial discomfort, as the rain stopped early in our walk. The views on this track were surreal; forests of driftwood lay shrivelled along sandy banks, and it seemed that mountain and desert had morphed into some new entity. Farther along, the crystal-clear waters of Laguna de los Tres glowed in vivid shades of turquoise, in blunt contrast to the rusty-tinged layers of rock that rose in elongated streaks above the lake. Soon we came across yet another startling blue lagoon, Laguna Sucia, which was situated high on a precipice beyond Laguna de los Tres. This hike covered an elevation gain of seven hundred metres.

As our time in El Chaltén came to an end, we were both energized and saddened to arrive at our final day's hike. This ramble took us to the eastern face of Loma del Pliegue Tumbado. It was the steepest climb of the three, rising approximately eight hundred metres above El Chaltén. Rocky scree covered much of the terrain at the higher levels. The tough slog paid off. We enjoyed great views overlooking our first day's hike. The Glacier Torre jutted like a thumb below the impressive Cerro Torre and Fitz Roy peaks. The thought of a dark pint and savoury pizza back in the cozy pizzeria fuelled our return journey.

Tierra del Fuego—Parque Nacional Tierra del Fuego

Our final hiking experience in Patagonia was in the far south Parque Nacional Tierra del Fuego ("Land of Fire"). This region earned its fearsome name when the famed Portuguese explorer Ferdinand Magellan caught sight of numerous fires when cruising the shoreline. Fearing the unknown, which is an unusual trait for an explorer, Magellan concluded that the locals must be planning an ambush on his fleet. In fact, the native Yamana people were actually just trying to stay warm. They were not fond of clothing and instead lathered oils, often from seal blubber, onto their skin. The grease nicely absorbed any warmth radiating from nearby bonfires to keep their bodies toasty.

Luckily for us it was late January with moderate temperatures quite amenable for hiking. The first trail that we tackled was the Costera route along the ocean's shoreline. Its reputation as a popular pathway to observe the local birds was true. Upland geese poked around the lake's edge, nuzzling between tiny white wildflowers and stringy turf. Their whitish-grey colouring was in bold contrast to the aquamarine waters and lush green vegetation. Even rabbits frolicked in a meadow before ducking out of sight. Of most interest to watch was a young chimango caracara falcon. He was preoccupied in finding some tasty seafood delight left hidden under the stones at low tide. This was far easier than spying live prey from high above and attempting a precision dive on fledgling wings. From his screeching, the adolescent must have still associated these shrill sounds with the delivery of food. Either that or it was an effective method to hurry prying visitors along and out of his hunting grounds.

In the second part of our visit to the Parque National Tierra del Fuego, we proceeded to its Lapataia Bay area. Lapataia Bay looked comparable to some of New Zealand's lush coastal landscapes, perhaps because both lands sit at similar southern latitudes, within ten degrees of one another. We started along Paseo de la Isla, which led through the Cormoranes Archipelago and then cut onto a second path that led us to Laguna Negra. This was a modest lake, but with a unique ambience, as it was encircled by a woolly bog in shades of amber and olive. The last trail led us up to Mirador Lapataia, which offered panoramic views over Lapataia Bay. The blues of the water and greens from the lenga forests were vibrant. Lengas are a rugged variety of beech with dark burly bark and unruly leaves, which are often covered in a patchwork of gauzy moss. The entire hike was exceptionally bewitching and just made us happy to be alive in such an invigorating and healthy environment, like swallowing a large dose of vitamin C.

There were not many other people on the trails, so we could savour this setting in its tranquil natural state. Getting there and away was also quite convenient. Local buses connected the nearby town of Ushuaia to the park by a fairly direct twelve-kilometre ride. Ushuaia possessed a quirky charm but without a typical seaport's rough atmosphere. Cute cafés, meandering seaside sidewalks and well-thought-out accommodation options made this friendly centre an excellent base.

The Basics

Synopsis: Roam through gorgeous white sand and golden rocks along some of Australia's idyllic secluded beachfront.

Most useful items to pack: A clear map and a cellphone

For further travel information: There are a few options for hiking this stretch of beach. We opted for a self-guided walk and used Johno's "Quickie" 4WD Tas Tours for pickup and drop-off transport. Our two-day route progressed as follows:

Day One

Starting point: Camp #1 in the Cape Naturaliste area

End point: Eddystone Lighthouse via Stumpys Bay, Cod Bay and Purdon Bay

Walking time: Seven hours

Day Two

Starting point: Policemans Point

End point: The Gardens

Walking time: Five hours

Unfortunately, recent internet searches do not list Johno's services, so he may have since retired. Various tour companies offer guided walks. Most notably, the tempting Bay of Fires Lodge offers a four-day, three-night package based at their uber-deluxe ecolodge. Further information can be found at bayoffires.com.au.

The Experience

We spent two days covering this remote section of Tasmania's northeastern tip. Commonly referred to as the Bay of Fires, this beach earned its name for similar reasons as Argentina's Land of Fire. An early explorer, Tobias Furneaux, sailed close to shore and caught sight of the Aboriginal people's fires; hence the name stuck. As if keeping the tradition alive, when we walked the coastline, there were scattered boulders draped in brilliant orange lichen. The splotches resembled little firepits against the bleached rocks and pearly sand.

Both days' walks generally followed the water's edge. However, the terrain on the second day was somewhat trickier than the flat sandy beaches that we came to enjoy on day one. The second day's tramp turned out to be the most memorable—but not because of the blissful scenery for which the area is famous. Our folly began at the final junction near the end of day two. Following our transport driver's advice, we opted to go inland for the final section to avoid an impassable inlet. The instructions were simple: at the final stony isthmus, or rocky wall that juts into the water, climb up and over it and carry on along a wallaby path to arrive at the designated pickup point. Late in the day's walk, the scene before us seemed to match our driver's description and our simple map. Phew—it had already been a long day, and we were all eager to relax.

However, the track quickly transformed from open rock to dense foliage. No wallaby path appeared. Long fern fronds carpeted the ground, making it all too easy to imagine cantankerous snakes hidden in such inviting shade. After trying to follow the supposed course without any indication of a path, we decided to clamber up a ridge ahead of us. Perhaps our target would become clearer from a higher point. We tingled with unease over possible snake encounters and were keen to break free from the undergrowth. Our concerns were mounting, not only for our own sakes but because we were walking with my parents. As fit seventy-something-year-olds with adventurous spirits and uncannily positive attitudes, they were holding up remarkably well during this less than ideal escapade. So off we all trudged up an arduous hill and beyond. Eventually we converged with a gravel road. This was a good sign. Farther along a farmer's field emerged, where Angus cattle placidly grazed. They were oblivious to our anxiety and barely glanced up when we stumbled past. Thankfully, we finally arrived at our destination without any snakebites and before a search party was launched.

Despite some tense moments, I would still recommend this walk. But be sure to take an impeccably clear map, a GPS device and a local SIM card in your phone. The Bay of Fires coastline is unique in Australia. Not many visitors make the effort to reach this remote corner, even with its expansive azure water set against white-and-orange rocks along soft beaches. During both days, we ran into only one other set of hikers. So if you are looking for pristine nature and want to test your navigational skills, this is a walk to consider. Just be sure to notify your hotel to come searching if you do not return by a specified time—or even easier, hire a guide.

The Basics

Synopsis: Prepare for some heat as you head straight up Nicaragua's highest, perfectly formed volcanic peak leading to views inward of spitting lava or outward to the Pacific Ocean.

Most useful item to pack: Plenty of water

For further travel information: A day trip from León can be arranged through the professional Tierra Tours. At the time of our trip, our leader was the city's only female guide who trekked volcanoes. She proved impressively knowledgeable about the area and its vegetation. For further booking information, refer to tierratour.com.

The Experience

We arranged an early morning pickup for four o'clock. Perhaps our senses had been terribly distorted the day before under León's fierce rays of sun, but we had willingly agreed to such a rude start. Rousing ourselves from our beds in our cozy, air-conditioned hotel room was a strain, but the challenge of hiking Nicaragua's highest volcanic peak stirred our adrenalin. Its 1,745-metre elevation seemed daunting. The only alternative in the town itself was to walk tippytoe across the soft white domes of the Basílica de la Asunción's rooftop. While its second-floor views were unique and the architecture was beautiful, we yearned for something more physically challenging. So we bypassed the snooze button and kept our commitment. In a caffeine-depleted haze, we dragged ourselves downstairs and through the heavy wooden front door. There awaited our dependable driver.

Three similarly sleepy travellers joined us for the day's quest. We all slid into the back of a four-wheel-drive truck. Two long benches ran along the sides in the back, and we settled in for the next ninety minutes with a French-speaking couple from Canada and a woman from France. Between our basic French and their well-spoken English, we chatted sporadically for most of the drive. Everyone except us had previously hiked some of Nicaragua's other volcanoes. San Cristóbal was our first.

The trek started out as a deceivingly enjoyable walk. The Reserva Natural San Cristóbal offered a forest of shade around the base of the volcano. Its thick foliage hid the impending steep and barren incline from view. This blissful setting ended abruptly. After a short ascent, the trees gave way to long grasses that encircled the volcano. They reminded me of a pedestal holding some unidentifiable black triangle. From this level, the ultimate peak was barely visible. More apparent were the white clouds of sulphuric fumes that percolated from the volcano's still-active core.

The trail was clear, straight up through thick scree-like volcanic pebbles. As we began to climb, our guide shared a local secret: step slowly, or risk losing virtually all your momentum. The scree has a way of dragging your feet back down. For the next three hours, we trudged up. Straight up. The incline was nearly fifty-five degrees. Before long, the temperature reached a sweltering thirty-one degrees Celsius. The sun became our nemesis. The black sand wavered. Even the typically cool winds at higher elevations deserted us. Water breaks became our most anticipated event.

Not long ago, Volcán San Cristóbal would have offered a shaded climb. But in September 2012, its lovely pine forest was all but obliterated in an eruption. San Cristóbal's active magma core took on a more ominous personality, spewing ash five kilometres into the air. Over four hundred residents were evacuated.[17] This heat explosion turned the mountain's facade into a petrified forest. Its remains looked more like Cirque du Soleil contortionists than Mother Nature's evergreens. So we tramped past the dismally thin strips of shade. The deadened trees' contrasting russet tones did, however, contribute to more than a few sublime photographs.

Once at the peak's precipice, our efforts proved worthwhile. No caffeine could compare to the hit experienced when peering over the edge into the misty volcanic core. **Gurgle. Splutter. Bloop.** This resting spot created the perfect ambience to enjoy a sandwich and yet another swig of water. Once rejuvenated, we were anxious to turn back, as the decline was the most entertaining. We leapt. We bounded. From this direction, the scree's characteristic slide worked in our favour. The four-hour climb took only an hour in reverse. We sailed across those onyx pebbles and created our own breeze.

As much as this climb was hot, it was also satisfying. Few places offer the opportunity to summit a country's highest peak in one day. Volcán San Cristóbal offered such a rare opportunity. From its peak, the Pacific Ocean, sugar cane crops and peanut fields looked minuscule below. Not only can you reach its apex, but it is humbling to set foot atop one of the more active volcanoes in the region. The pain and the pleasure remain etched in my memory.

The Basics

Synopsis: Challenge yourself to a muddy climb up an ancient volcano where the lava was long ago replaced by a misty, murky lake.

Most useful item to pack: Hiking poles

For further travel information: Totoco was our ecocentric hotel on the green banks of Volcán Maderas. The hotel arranged for our guide, fees and a packed lunch for the climb. Just as worthy was returning to their superb bungalows, which included private patios and swinging chairs. Post-hike, the hanging chair was perfect for kicking back and admiring the view of the adjacent Volcán Concepción. For more information, refer to totoco.com.ni.

The Experience

Two contrasting volcanoes sat on either end of the barbell-shaped Isla de Ometepe. Volcán Concepción consumed the northwestern tip. The barren volcano's perfectly formed cone topped by a smoking pinnacle bore a striking resemblance to Volcán San Cristóbal. Upon seeing this desolate giant, we were instantly reminded of the dreaded climb up Volcán San Cristóbal earlier in our trip (described in the preceding section). In contrast, Volcán Maderas engulfed the southeastern end of the island and was smothered by a tropical forest. Humidity oozed from its leaves. It was as if Maderas and Concepción were two weights resting upon the island's scale. Maderas in her wisdom dared the young Concepción to blow some steam and disrupt their balance.

It was this aged beauty that caught our interest. No longer active, Volcán Maderas was dressed in a cooler cloud forest. This shaded reprieve cinched our decision to climb yet another Nicaraguan volcano. The hike started from Finca Magdalena. Wooden steps directed us through fields of plantain. The route started out dry and contained surprising variety. Petroglyphs decorated rocks with engraved swirls, solar renditions that expressed pre-Columbian reverence towards the sun. We continued to climb. Vegetation turned into a bamboo forest, and streaks of light filtered through its leaves like strands of tinsel strewn on a Christmas tree. Soon enough, we left the clutches of these calm bamboo stalks and briefly passed through a coffee plantation.

Rapidly, the pristine trail transformed. In its place, rivulets trickled over tree roots, and water mingled with the rusty-coloured earth. Our steps turned into a dance as we hopped across roots and twisted around mossy trees. Walking sticks provided some leverage for avoiding knee-deep puddles, as their extended reach often allowed us to reach a prized dry spot. We carried on through this mud for two hours. The dewy forest took on every shade of green and yellow that I could imagine. But I forced myself to concentrate on the slick trail: "Quick, focus back on your feet. Dodge that sticky mess." Cloud forests are synonymous with humidity and gooey mud. Virtually nothing could escape their moist grip. Only a cluster of bats could find a dry refuge. These critters were tucked in the darkness beneath a rotted-out tree trunk, all but invisible except to our guide's darting eyes. They slept, oblivious to our slog.

The final segment was particularly steep. The challenge made it difficult to take in the mystical allure of the surroundings. Vines were thick with dewy moss. Leaves exuded a translucent aura. I half expected to come face to face with a local elf. Instead, vines became handles, while rocks became stable landing sites. Finally, the mud was replaced by reeds. We had arrived at the top where a grassy rim encircled the volcano's core. Long ago the magma had cooled and was filled by the rains, leaving a small caramel-coloured lake to mark its heart. The shore provided a dry resting spot, and its comfortable grass became our table. We did not linger, however, as more people approached leaving the trail to become muckier and muckier under the onslaught of their footsteps.

The return felt more strenuous. Perhaps gravity was testing our strength. My formerly blue boots were now an even shade of brown. Similarly, the black of my pants transformed into a cinnamon hue. However, boots and pants could be cleaned. The mystical Volcán Maderas turned out to be a refreshing hike. Its scenery was exotic and temperatures were comfortable. In comparison to the climb up Volcán San Cristóbal, the landscape was more diverse and temperatures much more amenable.

The Basics

Synopsis: Hike through cloud forests in the cooler highlands of Nicaragua in the morning, and kick back with coffee made from freshly roasted beans in the afternoon.

Most useful items to pack: Waterproof hiking boots and a hankering for bold coffee

For further travel information: We visited three ecolodges, each in a cloud forest located within the Matagalpa region of Nicaragua. Two of the three were fairly remote. Since it was the Christmas season, local buses were jammed full and less than ideal for travelling with our big packs to these secluded locations. Instead, we hired a private driver recommended by the owner of our hotel in Matagalpa. A more flexible but expensive option is to rent a four-wheel-drive vehicle. Further details on each of the lodges can be found at the following links:

> » Selva Negra Ecolodge: selvanegra.com/en
>
> » La Bastilla Ecolodge: bastillaecolodge.com/?lang=en
>
> » La Sombra Ecolodge: lasombraecolodge.com

The Experience

It was nearing the Christmas season of 2015. After weeks in the incredibly hot lowlands of Nicaragua, we craved a cooler climate. Central Nicaragua's highlands around Matagalpa offered just such respite. We tracked down three ecolodges that met our criteria. They all offered hiking options, and equally important, they grew their own coffee. Indulging our taste buds with this black essence was our treat over the holiday season. However, the lodges' personas turned out to be nothing alike. These are their tales.

Selva Negra Ecolodge

Imagine, if you will, Germany's mountain huts blended with Nicaragua's gritty appeal. Remarkably, Selva Negra bridged this dichotomy. Authentic hand-carved German nutcrackers adorned the restaurant's wooden shelves while Nicaraguan folk music played listlessly in the background. Our private bungalow was comfy, allowing a restful sleep between crisp white sheets. The cabin's solar-powered showers triumphed by pumping out hot water despite the endlessly cloudy days.

The lodge attempted to offer everything to everyone. We were there for its accessible, well-marked web of trails. Others were at the conference hall for a family reunion. A couple was married in the on-site Capilla Chapel, and an isolated building offered ideal space for off-site office retreats. Families continually arrived from the town of Matagalpa by the busload—the town was only twelve kilometres from the lodge. The attempted rustic appeal seemed lost in Selva Negra's eclectic assortment of services; even the waiters seemed overwhelmed by the entourage of visitors. The defining aspect of the lodge was its coffee. Selva Negra charged for a cup of their blend, whereas La Bastilla and La Sombra served up their local beans brewed to perfection as a complimentary gesture to guests.

However, Selva Negra did come through with its hiking. Maps were provided at check-in. Trails were clearly marked, even if a few signs contained more moss than paint. Indicators of the level of difficulty mirrored ski hill monikers: black diamonds marked more challenging paths, and green trails were the easy routes. For our first outing, we dived onto the Quetzal path. Sadly, we never spotted a quetzal, which I hear are striking birds, with brilliant green-and-red plumage and a long emerald tail floating in their wake. The Quetzal Trail was considered a black diamond. It started out steep and then tracked a small stream. Soon enough, we were given the option to connect with intersecting trails, and we opted for the Bavaria path. It was moderately difficult while remaining under the cover of the thickly forested hill behind the lodge.

Our second day's hike turned out to be a more strenuous excursion. Initially, we walked from the Atajo pathway, along Romantico and up the Canal Trail. By this part of the track, the mud oozed in full force. The steeper the incline, the slicker the trail became. Small fern fronds delicately curled along the path, wet with dew. Few visitors appeared to have taken this longer route. As we switched onto the Mosquita track, the surrounding roots buttressed our climb. Thankfully, this path was not true to its name, and no mosquitos tormented us during our walk. Instead, by the time we reached a ridge, the clouds had thinned. The sunshine reverberated off cathedral trees and tall bamboo shoots, while ferns and moss blanketed nearly everything else. This was the cloud forest we craved. It was lush. The air was fresh. We had it all to ourselves.

The return trek along Fuente de la Juventud seemed more like a walk down a waterslide than a trail in a cloud forest. Vines and stones offered some resistance to our perpetual slippage. The youthful elixir that the track was named after appeared to be on vacation. Instead, it was replaced by a cranky old man who readily donated a few grey hairs by the time we reached the bottom. At the lower levels, the leaf-covered walkways returned. As we emerged from the forest, a couple stood smiling on the dock, and their photographer knelt down to capture their forever moment. The bride's white wedding dress was in stark contrast to our muddy boots. So we tramped along the rear of the trail as quietly as possible. Once back at our cabana, we cleansed our boots back to their former state under the well-placed outdoor tap. The solar shower ensured that we also sparkled.

Although Selva Negra was by no means a remote retreat, it did offer easy access to its cloud forest. The walks were charming and largely deserted. While the bungalows were pleasant, the restaurant could have been better organized. Although quaint, Selva Negra's medley was the least authentic of the three ecolodges.

La Bastilla Ecolodge—Reserva Natural Datanlí el Diablo

Only twenty-seven kilometres from the rough town of Jinotega, we found our oasis. Thick foliage lined the deep valley. Hillsides overlapped and cut steeply down towards a narrow ravine. Rows of manicured coffee bushes were neatly tucked below aged trees. Among these trees, diversity prevailed. Eighty-one species flourished across this 5,848-hectare reserve.[18] Tiny plants also prospered. The land had become intoxicated by twenty-one species of vibrant orchids. It was among this jumble that our humble cabana sat, perched on the edge a hill. Two wooden chairs beckoned us from its veranda and served up truly gorgeous views.

These vistas only instilled our itchy feet with wanderlust to explore the nearby hillsides. A painted wooden map near the main lodge appeared entirely clear. We just needed to follow a four-wheel-drive track beyond the reception area before veering onto the Sendero el Puma loop. Simple. Just to be safe, we snapped a photo of the map for later reference. After a short distance up the trail, a circular sign indicated that we had reached Mirador Nubes de Apanás, true to the map. Lime-green grass led the way to this spectacular lookout point. Any sight of buildings was obscured by the dense vegetation. We knew that our huts were just below, but it seemed as if they had been absconded by the forest.

Off we set, eager to get started on our intended loop. We veered off on what seemed to be a trail in the same vicinity as that marked on the map. It soon tapered into thick shrubbery, a dead end. So we backtracked and convinced ourselves that we had previously misread the map. The correct turnoff point **must** have been that pathway we had spotted earlier through high grasses. In we slipped. Fingers of mud squished between the ridges of our boots and gradually crept over the laces. We tramped onward. The trail looped around; we even ducked through a barbed-wire fence. We stayed the course, as there was nowhere else to go. Eventually, we ran up against a gravel road with no sight of an onward walking route. Once again, we backtracked. We recalled one other slightly overgrown side deviation along the way. Perhaps it was the elusive Sendero el Puma. Not long into this attempt, the track became less obvious. The grass grew high and tree branches dipped low. As each passing step became more obscured, a thought came to our minds. A hot cup of coffee back at the lodge seemed far more amenable than our current random wanderings. The idea stuck, and for the last time, we backtracked.

Once we were back at the lodge, the staff happily brewed up a pot of their crisp local coffee. There were guides available at the lodge, so had we the time or inclination, we could have returned to prove—or disprove—whether we actually had hiked any of the planned trail. However, for our last day we instead chose to lay low and enjoy the views. Butterflies flitted haphazardly while plantation workers hollered, their voices echoing throughout the valley. The occasional howler monkey chimed in and asserted his dominance over his group's preferred tree. It seemed a happy place, everything synchronized into a technicolour masterpiece.

Not only was the scenery stunning, but the concept behind La Bastilla was ingenious. The valley's Technical Centre for Agriculture and Tourism trained local students from low-income families in the art and science of their new industry. These eager young kids operated the ecolodge and brewed a mean pot of pressed coffee, fresh on demand. Its chocolatey tones led to one of the richest cuppas I had ever tasted. We met some of the welcoming young adults around the lodge—they played a big part in our desire to hang around the centre for our last day—while others toiled among the trees. Not a bad setting in which to be schooled. They were taught agriculture skills to maintain the idyllic coffee plantation and tend to the local farm. The garden's vegetables were a regular accompaniment to the dining options, always fresh and tasty. This not-for-profit, sustainable enterprise had transformed the valley's households by providing a future for their children—a true success story. It blended a peaceful setting, helpful staff, low carbon footprint and educational development to create a most appealing stay. If I were to select one of the three ecolodges not to be missed, La Bastilla would certainly win this title.

La Sombra Ecolodge—Reserva Natural Macizos de Peñas Blancas

The last of our triad demonstrated elements from each of the first two locations. In terms of its bustling ambience and accessibility, La Sombra's style lay somewhere between that of La Bastilla and that of Selva Negra. The smallish sedan that we had hired nearly got stuck en route. When we left La Bastilla, the road started out smooth and paved. Then, just as we had relaxed into the drive, the course detoured off the paved road onto a rather rough route. At one point, the road was immersed under a small stream. The resulting sludge and soft gravel clung to the car's tires, requiring an extra push to help the vehicle continue. The driver was not impressed. His little Toyota was his only livelihood. Luckily, no damage was done after more than a few tense moments, and in the end, we agreed to a generous tip for his troubles.

It seemed that we had run out of luck on the transport side of our plans. The driver who had driven us from Granada to Matagalpa had originally agreed to drive us back as well. He should not be confused with the local Matagalpa-based driver who had taken us between the three ecolodges and persevered through this last muddy foray from La Bastilla to La Sombra. Our Granada-based driver also indicated concerns about accessibility to La Sombra from his end. He had heard that its connector road was under construction, so he reneged on our agreed pickup, and we were temporarily stranded. Fortunately, when travelling there is always a Plan B; one just needs an inquisitive mind and persistence. The staff at La Sombra were attentive and attempted to source a private taxi through their own connections. Then the stars aligned. A fellow Canadian couple staying at La Sombra had the freedom of their own vehicle. They were heading back through Managua the next day to stay at a plush hotel on the edge of the city. After a few phone calls, we were able to grab the same deal for a room and travelled back together. Although we lost a day at La Sombra, we were indeed ready for a change after already spending eight days at ecolodges.

From an excursion perspective, La Sombra offered various daily walks, tours of their coffee finca (coffee farm) and entrance to their butterfly enclosure. All outings were included with the day rate, as were meals and free-flowing coffee. We opted for a morning hike. Out through the plantation we tramped with a local guide. Finca staff were busy plucking bright red coffee beans from the lustrous bushes. Heaps of the little nuggets filled their woven baskets. They were full of smiles and waved as we walked past. Of course, the trails were mucky, and our boots would need another cleaning once we were back at the lodge. This was my biggest annoyance of travelling between destinations on a frequent basis—these filthy boots had to go back inside the pack on a near daily basis.

The best part of this hike was the wildlife. It is not often that one gets to see a sloth in the wild. Even rarer is the opportunity to watch two sloths lolling about, both in the same morning. The first hairy mound was nearly twenty feet above us, balanced between tree branches. If it had not been for our guide's savvy vision,

I would have walked on past, unaware of what lay overhead. This animal barely moved as we gaped at its body covered in long hair, a perfect colour match to the adjacent tree trunk. About ten minutes after we had left the first sloth to carry on with his nap, the guide spotted yet another. This second sloth appeared friskier, as its arm actually moved, albeit ever so slowly. It might have been reaching to pull itself up but then ran out of steam and slouched back onto its bed of branches. We glimpsed three chisel-like protrusions extending from its hand: the sloth's telltale fingernails. Beyond this activity, the sloth appeared content to lay low. So we carried on through the coffee fields and the surrounding rolling hills.

Although not a strenuous walk, it did allow us to appreciate La Sombra's coffee plantation and the pretty Reserva Natural Macizos de Peñas Blancas. The geography appeared less intense than the precipitous forests around La Bastilla. From my perspective, La Sombra conveyed a family-oriented slant, offering night walks to spot nocturnal animals and informative tours to explain the workings of a coffee finca. We were at La Sombra over New Year's Eve, and the staff took extra care to make it a special evening. Glasses of champagne were served around a campfire while a neighbourhood mariachi band performed with vigour. Not everyone is a fan of mariachi jingles, but the sloth sightings alone made this trip worthwhile.

The Basics

Synopsis: Hike in any direction up intense scrambles and across mountain meadows to the tune of distant cowbells.

Most useful item to pack: Water bladder filled with crisp mountain tap water

For further travel information: When we visited Grindelwald, free hiking maps were readily available and easy to follow. The trails were well maintained and clearly marked by regular signposts.

For a high-level map of the hiking area and lifts around Grindelwald, refer to mappery.com/map-of/Jungfrau-Grindelwald-region-summer-map.

Useful maps of trails around Männlichen can be found at maennlichen. ch/en/downloads.html.

Minimal information is available online regarding the guided moonlight walks from Schynige Platte to First except during July and August. First is not much more than a gondola station above the village of Grindelwald. From Grindelwald, take a train to Wilderswil. At the Wilderswil station, transfer to the quirky little nineteenth-century cogwheel train that chugs up the mountainside to Schynige Platte. There you can find the well-marked trailhead. The best point of contact that I am aware of is the Hotel Schynige Platte: hotelschynigeplatte.ch/en/walking.

For a post-hike pizza and wine, you cannot go wrong with the homestyle Onkel Tom's Hütte. For further details, check out their website at onkel-toms.ch/en.

The Experience

When we lived in Geneva, Switzerland, our favourite summer road trip was to the beloved town of Grindelwald. The drive took less than three hours from Geneva, passing mountain ranges and pretty lakeside towns. Grindelwald offered a variety of hotels, a handful of restaurants and, most importantly, a gorgeous valley setting. Arguably, the competition is tough, as most Swiss valleys look as if they were lifted from a glossy postcard. Grindelwald sits in a basin surrounded by a mix of green pastures and rocky cliff faces. The three famous neighbouring mountains are the Eiger, Mönch and Jungfrau, which translated means the Ogre,

Monk and Maiden. Wooden houses were adorned with flower boxes overflowing with purple, red or white blossoms.

Grab a map of walking trails from your hotel and pick any direction, as pathways run nearly everywhere. It is hard to go wrong on the trails; all are well maintained with gorgeous views. I have described some of my favourite walks below.

Grindelwald to Wengen (via the Eiger Trail and return via Männlichen)

We spread this hike across two days by staying overnight in Wengen. Our first day started from Grindelwald and headed generally west towards the ridge beyond Wengen. If one is feeling lazy, this entire excursion can be done by riding a cable car and a gondola via Männlichen. Wengen can also be reached by cogwheel trains that interchange at Kleine Scheidegg. Instead, we chose to hike and carried a small overnight backpack. We conveniently stored our main bag in the left-luggage compartment of our hotel in Grindelwald, where it awaited our return the following night. Check Chapter Nine for more details on our unforgettable hotel in Wengen.

The trail guided us through Grindelwald-Grund, which is virtually an extension of the town of Grindelwald. From there, we followed the Eiger Trail signposts that led towards Alpiglen and then on to Kleine Scheidegg. The pathway skirted the Eiger Mountain along the edge of the tree line. The Eiger's peak is a tough chunk of rock, a challenge even for advanced climbers. Its domineering mass of stone exuded its prestigious reputation. We could understand the appeal for rock climbers eager to pull themselves above its 1,600-metre vertical drop in an attempt to summit the gruelling peak. A map posted along the trail indicated the route up the north face to reach the Eiger's 3,973-metre peak. It was first successfully climbed by Anderl Heckmair in 1938. This vertical ascent was not, however, our goal. We carried on below the rock face, enjoying the contrast of grassy meadows and mountain flowers on one side and granite boulders on the other.

By the time we reached Kleine Scheidegg, we had climbed a net elevation of 1,027 metres in just a few hours. There was little beyond the train station, hotel and restaurant at this ridge. Striking views of the snow-covered peaks rose above green grassy slopes, making it a suitable stop for a coffee and tasty apple pastry. Such indulgence was necessary purely for energy, of course. The remaining hour-and-a-half walk was a fairly steep descent that zigzagged towards Wengen. At last we came to a gravel road that led the remainder of the way into town. We reached our hotel, relieved to have completed the day's hike. I craved a hot shower to ease my leg muscles and whisk away the day's salty scent.

Wengen is a cute village, accessible only by cable car, by cogwheel train or on foot. This meant that no automobiles whizzed along its streets beyond a few electric cars. Their engines' low purring was as smooth as a lullaby. The town seemed wholly dependent on tourists, as most businesses were hotels, restaurants or gift shops. As our timing was outside the busy season, we found the Swiss style felt more quaint than kitsch.

On our return journey, we hiked from Wengen to Männlichen before dropping back down to Grindelwald. The initial two-hour trek to Männlichen covered a brutal section of switchbacks that weaved between permanent snow barriers. We climbed 951 metres in elevation alone in this first leg. Brown metal fences crossed the steep valley about every thirty feet. Just above the highest fence jutted a rough pointed rock, our target—the Männlichen ridge. We were hiking in September, and early morning frost had left a crust on top of the green grass, almost glowing against the cloudless blue sky. The views made the effort worthwhile, as we could look down onto the steep cliffs below Gimmelwald, another town accessible only by cable car. The rocks shone like white opals against the dark green forest and bright blue sky.

A little higher along the ridge, a sign confirmed that we had reached an elevation of 2,342.6 metres, measured with Swiss precision. By then, a few clouds had appeared above grassy patches still damp with melted frost. Shards of rock skewered the ground as if making a point to remind us that we were, indeed, on a mountain top, although, our position was clear from the panoramic view of snow-capped jewels and rocky pinnacles that rose all around us.

The remainder of our return hike to Grindelwald was mostly downhill, but at a gentle slope. We passed mountain chalets, munching cows and grazing sheep that seemed to enjoy their meadow vista. Once settled back into our hotel in Grindelwald, we promptly headed over to Onkel Tom's Hütte for a far too delicious **alla diavola** wood-fire-baked pizza. This treat was the perfect end to a perfect day.

Moonlight hike from Schynige Platte to First

The hike from the small cogwheel railway station of Schynige Platte took us six hours through shadowed treetops and vaguely silhouetted peaks. This moonlight hike through the Swiss Alps was too enticing to turn down. Otherwise, the mystique of a midnight trek would have haunted us as we wondered what we might have missed. The pseudo-guided walk was offered only in July and August.

By midnight, my husband, two friends and I sat with approximately forty other trekkers enjoying a hot tea in the restaurant of the Hotel Schynige Platte.

Earlier in the evening, we had taken a short train ride from Grindelwald to Wilderswil and then transferred to a classic cogwheel train that shuttled us to our starting point at Schynige Platte. By the time we disembarked, the night sky had turned black. The nearby hotel was eagerly awaiting our group's arrival to sell pre-departure beverages and snacks. After about forty-five minutes of idling in the restaurant, the leader gathered a few people and headed to the trailhead. The remainder of the group followed, and from there we were all free to walk at our own pace.

The trail started out through patchy forest with boulders and mossy splotches. It looked like an elf's wonderland shaded in darkness. We then walked under the stars and caught glimpses of a few peaks that glowed overhead. The trail undulated, climbing close to one thousand metres and falling nearly the same distance. The occasional cowbell could be heard somewhere beyond our trail. By five forty-five, we had spent the night hiking sixteen kilometres through what I could only assume was some of the most spectacular scenery in the Bernese Oberland. At this point, we were seriously questioning our judgement for choosing to do this walk at night. The downfall was not having the benefit of a full moon, so instead of the dramatic contours we had expected, the scenery appeared rather muted. Everyone experienced either sore knees or sore ankles by the final descent. The path eventually wound down to a cafeteria-style restaurant at the top of the gondola station at First. The sun began to rise, spreading its tentacles to expose the beautiful scenery that we had just trudged past.

The following summer, we returned to redo the trail, but in the daylight. Admittedly, this second time around proved to be a much more enjoyable hike. The vistas lived up to their reputation. The route's challenging trail and vibrant scenery make it one of my favourite day hikes in Switzerland.

A common spark links some of the most incredible monuments on earth. Love spawned religion, and love drove wars—love for good and love of power. Spiritual faith challenged architectural norms and through artistic design created awe-inspiring temples of worship. Stories became legends after they were passed fkeyrom generation to generation and were etched in stone, remembered for eternity. Twist that same emotion, and a quest for power and control erupted. Creativity flourished under such extreme pressure, and fortresses with advanced defensive mechanisms were conceived. People needed to protect themselves and their loved ones. The ancient relics that remain today remind us of such fierce warfare. A fine balance exists between power and religion; a sway of either element can induce war or unite allies.

One consolation is that out of such passion, great temples and formidable forts now wait to be explored. I found it fascinating to delve into some of these historical sites in an attempt to understand a deeper narrative. Repetitive themes screamed out to be remembered. Excessive power and self-righteousness tended to collapse over time. Dynasties rose and fell. Religious rule dominated and then faded. Perhaps history is attempting to teach us moderation and tolerance. Will we listen?

The Basics

Synopsis: Escape the crowds at Siem Reap to discover Khmer architecture in solitude, loftily balanced upon a cliff in the isolated Dangrek Mountains.

Most useful item to pack: Small local currency for snacks and tips.

For further travel information: For further information on the site, refer to cambodia.org/Preah_Vihear/?history=A+Khmer+Heritage.

Due to ongoing and fluid military activity, be sure to look into the current security situation before heading out. Check with your hotel, recent travellers' experiences and your home country's security travel advisories.

The Experience

As fans of Indiana Jones and obscure adventures, we struck gold with the opportunity to visit the eleventh-century Khmer Prasat Preah Vihear ("Temple of Preah Vihear"). This reputed masterpiece of Khmer architecture lies on a jungle-covered ridge of disputed land along the Cambodian–Thai border. Cambodia and Thailand have been squabbling over ownership of this precious land for ages. When we visited in 2010, the situation was relatively calm. However, we checked in advance with many sources as to the security of the site, including the Government of Canada's Travel Advice and Advisories, recent visitors' blog posts, comments on TripAdvisor.com and local advice from staff at our hotel in Siem Reap.

The temple itself is at the crux of the conflict. Its stone walkways have seen frequent skirmishes between the two countries' militaries. Even a ruling by the International Court of Justice in 1962 that favoured Cambodia did not settle the issue. Instead it has continued to percolate over the years. In 2008, UNESCO recognized the Temple of Preah Vihear as a World Heritage Site.[19] They allotted this prestige to Cambodia, which twisted an already searing thorn in Thailand's ego. In 2015, the International Court of Justice ruling was revisited, and once again the court confirmed that Cambodia's sovereign claim to the lands was indeed valid. The judgement reiterated Thailand's responsibility to remove its military from the area.[20]

The temple's remote location merely increased its allure to us. We were enticed by the obscureness of this isolated work of art, compared to Angkor Wat's easily accessible esplanades. The territory had received its first paved road only within the last ten years. This distant frontier was shrouded in heavy greenery that draped across the entire Dangrek Mountain range. Calling these sandstone slabs "mountains" might have been a stretch, as the highest peak was less than 2,500 metres. I would argue that a rolling miscellany of bluffs and lowlands would be a more apt description. From the air, it would have appeared as if the land had been taken over by an overzealous broccoli farmer. At ground level, these florets transformed into plump, full-grown trees with leaves spreading in a circle as if trying to nuzzle up against the neighbouring trees.

Our first challenge was getting to the site. The **Lonely Planet** guidebook described the roads as a muddy slog, especially in the rainy season when we were there. Public transport seemed a poor option to take to such a remote area, given the questionable connections during the wet season. Instead, we hired a car and driver for two days. Our driver had been in the army, based at the Preah Vihear station, so he knew the route well. The temple could be visited as a long day trip from Siem Reap. However, we wanted to stop at the ruins of Koh Ker and Beng Mealea on our return journey. These spectacular sites were part of the Angkor Wat complex, but they lay far from the main centre. They provided the perfect stopoff point for our return route.

We set off early in the morning, leaving the mayhem of central Siem Reap to turn into a quickly fading memory. Country folks pedalled earnestly to get to work in the city. The bikes were simple, single-shift contraptions built for function over comfort or speed. After an hour of driving, the city's congestion dissolved. The remainder of the drive passed by rice fields immersed in water. Most of the intermittent stilted houses were hubs of activity; women hung laundry and old men lounged in hammocks while pigs and chickens rummaged in the dirt. Along the roadside, ladies walked with lengthy bamboo rods balanced across their shoulders. Typically, a basket of food or some essential merchandise hung from each end of the pole. Other people worked in the fields, shin deep in water and muck. Their backs must have ached with all the bending, day after day.

As we neared our destination, a dusty, formerly white pickup truck roared alongside our vehicle. It was crowded with local men, all yelling and motioning for our driver to pull his car to the side of the road. This was not the welcome we had anticipated. This area was so rarely visited by foreigners that we immediately stood out, even from inside our car. The men in the truck assumed that we must be headed towards Prasat Preah Vihear—after all, why else would one come to this isolated frontier? I could not help but wonder if someone passing us earlier had spotted our unfamiliar faces and telephoned their friends with news of a potential deal. The business proposition concerned transportation. From our target town of Kor Muy, a steep five-kilometre drive wound to the temple entrance at the top of an escarpment. A typical car engine was not sufficient for this climb, so we needed separate transport for this final leg. The good men in the white truck asked for forty American dollars in exchange for a ride in the back of their truck for this five-minute drive, nonnegotiable. Unfortunately for the men, we had done our homework and bid them goodbye.

Within a few minutes, we arrived at the centre of Kor Muy. There are small towns, and then there are small towns. Kor Muy was the latter. Beyond a handful of roadside market stalls and a couple of empty restaurants and basic guesthouses, there seemed little to warrant a stop except for access to the temple. Our driver rolled the car to a stop a few metres from a cluster of motorcycles. Within seconds, at least eight faces appeared outside our car's windows, accompanied by wildly waving hands. We could only assume that they were the moto drivers, eager to earn some much-needed cash. We sensed a potential scam might be brewing, so to divert attention from our predicament, which felt more like an ambush, we explained to the driver that we would first grab a snack at the restaurant. As our Khmer language skills were nonexistent, he proceeded to explain our move to the moto drivers. They remained where they stood, watching with inquisitive eyes. As we walked inside the restaurant, the moto drivers followed, and the formerly empty space was filled with the two of us, our driver and eight moto drivers, who lined up along the back wall. We were not hungry, but appreciated the table's width of space.

The concept of snacks was rather difficult to translate. When you can afford to eat, you are expected to eat a full meal. It took some back and forth with the help of our driver to calm the waiter when we placed one order of noodles to share between my husband and me. The attendant was obviously hoping for a larger profit from us strangers. But with a few basic words in Khmer and creative hand gestures, he eventually warmed to us. The moto drivers waited with restraint in the back of the restaurant. Not long after the dish was served, their patience waned. The next phase can only be described as a pseudo-auction. The drivers voiced their prices, either thirty dollars for a seat in a pickup truck or eight dollars per person to ride double on the back of a moto. Our driver's advice was to take the pickup, rationalizing that the road was far too scary to ride on the back of a bike. Realistically, he just wanted a free ride for himself as part of the truck deal. We bantered back and forth with the aid of our driver-cum-interpreter. Eventually, everyone settled down as we landed on a six-dollar-per-person moto ride, including a third moto for our driver. The supposedly hairy five-hundred-metre lane turned out to be a smoothly paved route with a few twists that the scooters easily glided around.

Promptly, the next entourage came upon us. As the motos pulled into the temple's parking area, several children ran to greet us. The kids lived in a small town made up of military families who had formed a community around the temple after years of fighting with Thailand over this borderland. Across the valley, we could spot similar Thai officers monitoring their posts. It turned out that the kids were less interested in welcoming us and more focused on collecting a donation for the soldiers. The charity they requested was not in the form of money, food or clothing, which would have directly benefitted their entire family. Instead, the children's offer was counterintuitive, for they asked us to buy packs of cigarettes to donate to the soldiers. The kids' pleading and outstretched arms only reinforced the unfortunate predicament life had presented them. We were convinced that any ill effects from the cigarettes would only incapacitate their fathers' good intentions, cutting off any source of income from the government's already dry coffers. Their mothers would surely receive no benefit from the tobacco-filled boxes, no aid to feed or clothe their precious little ones. As much as these kids deserved help, funding their parents' carcinogenic addiction was not in their best interest, at least in our view.

Our driver was not impressed, as he was eager to facilitate a few smokes for his long-time friends from the army. He followed along our walk through the site for about twenty minutes, stopping frequently to chat with a former colleague or front-line friend. Most of the soldiers had a machine gun slung over their shoulders or balanced on their hips, ready if the need arose but unlikely to be required on this day, judging by their relaxed demeanour. Some kept an eye on their counterparts across the border through binoculars. The armed Thais appeared similarly docile in the distance. Before long, our driver offered a feeble excuse of being tired and hung back to let us explore while he continued to visit. We preferred this, as we had grown tired of his seemingly distorted intentions.

We followed dug-out trenches and cement barricades topped with spirals of barbed-wire fencing to reach the stony ruins. Tin-roofed shelters acting as homes practically touched the side of the sandbagged walkways. Their walls were made of either a loose thatch or a canvas tarp. The surrounding hills had supposedly been cleared of land mines; however, a soldier had been killed in 2009 when a UXO detonated not far off the well-used walking tracks. Consequently, we dared not deviate from the trodden trails. We ran across one lady, presumably the wife of one of the soldiers along the path. She smiled widely under a brimmed straw hat secured by a red string tied tightly into a bow. The lady emitted a warm style despite the rough circumstances. She stood next to a five-foot-tall wire fence, its barbs a tangle of spiky loops intended to keep any stray Thai forces well away.

Farther along, we came to a wooden army hut. Soldiers appeared relaxed; one sat reading on a hammock while another played with some leaves in a bored attempt to keep his focus. They all wore flip-flops in various shades of blue and turquoise. Rows of sandbags encircled the building, lying a few feet from its walls and serving the dual purposes of protective barrier and elevated walkway. We then met two young boys who attempted to act as our guides. One was fully kitted in military fatigues while the other was less camouflaged with bright red soccer shorts and a matching T-shirt. Both children ran around in bare feet for much of our walk and occasionally pointed out a temple scene. We figured that their efforts deserved an unsolicited tip at the end of our walk, far more so than the earlier cigarette-touting crew.

A sequence of sanctuaries and temples flowed from an eight-hundred-metre-long central staircase. Pillars, ornate archways and teetering rectangular steps squeezed into their allotted space. The temple site appeared weathered, like a seaman who had survived the perfect storm ten times over. Grooves were blackened. The tops of most columns had been lobbed off or tipped over, or at the very least, they still stood but lurched precariously askew. It was unclear whether a stone on the left held its neighbouring rock in place or the block on the right was wedged just so to ensure the pile did not crumble into a mass of rubble. In fact, it was not uncommon to see a jumble of assorted rocks beside a partially standing building, like a reverse waterfall that supported the very mountainside from which it poured.

Leading towards the glorified stairway, various temples lay dormant but still radiated grandeur. On one particularly lavish doorway, geometric stone pieces remained fully intact. However, the grooves connecting them divulged weakened seams that were cracked or missing chunks. The stone was carved into swirling contours. Within this design and etched with lifelike detail, the Hindu god Shiva propped one knee atop a fiery-mouthed deity. The stone itself was the colour of fire, with crimson splashes and cantaloupe-coloured smudges across its facade. It was difficult to tell whether this tinge was part of the sandstone itself or some side effect that came with age. Regardless, the brilliant entrance was stunning against the rest of the rock that remained in varying tones of grey.

The staircase at the end of our walk was actually the entrance to the temple. It was built between the ninth and twelfth centuries in reverence to Shiva. I found the structure somewhat anticlimactic after the details and colours of the carvings leading up to this passage. Multiple flights of stairs and landings led down the hillside. The floor rocks remained in place, albeit somewhat bumpy, as to be expected after hundreds of years of use. The sides were enclosed by an unadorned bannister of thick cement shaped like a long serpent. A carving of the head of a naga, a seven-headed snake, was positioned at the end of each landing to oversee the next flight of steps. Their fourteen stone eyes glowered towards the view beyond. Their gaping mouths seemed to salivate for a morsel of sacred offering. By the base of the stairs, a ramshackle market marked the end of our temple meanderings. Thankfully, when we retraced our steps, the moto drivers were patiently waiting, and we received no further interceptions. It was time to leave the army men to their posts.

The Basics

Synopsis: Meander through hillside caves that hid delicate Buddhist carvings undetected for centuries.

Most useful item to pack: Comfortable walking shoes

For further travel information: No advance booking is necessary. An entrance fee is charged at the gate plus an additional charge for cameras, which can only be used without a flash. For more information, refer to maharashtratourism.gov.in/treasures/cave/ajanta.

The Experience

The Ajanta Caves were a highlight of my first extended around-the-world trip. My then-boyfriend (now husband) and I decided to take the long route back to Canada from Australia, where our earliest overseas contract had wrapped up just as the 2000 Olympics ended. The lead up to this expedition included a lot of planning, but through the process I learned an important lesson: a little effort and an earnest goal can lead to surprising results. This was when I bought into the value of budgeting and trip planning. Decisions to make lunches instead of eating out before the trip or to swap a gym membership for outdoor running were easy to make. After all, being able to afford one more day of travel far outweighed a fleeting hour of superficial pleasures, at least in my view.

We spent the second month of this five-month adventure in India. Because it is such a big country, even one month was insufficient to see the many sights on offer. We started in the city of Mumbai. Walking the streets, I felt like a cosmic outburst had erupted upon my senses. The unfamiliarity of everything was both refreshing and intoxicating. Cows roamed the busy streets while tuk-tuk drivers adeptly navigated around the sauntering beasts. Fresh chapattis were toasted at roadside grills. The scent of spices coalesced between simmering mulligan aromas seeping through kitchen windows and raw sacks of the seasonings piled at street stalls and offered for sale. The perfect mounds reminded me of snow cones, or perhaps I was just craving a cool treat. Then there was the architecture; new, old and everything in between, it kept my eyes wandering in all directions, continually captivated. After taking a few days to settle into our new country, we left the metropolitan area for outlying regions. Away from the manic city streets, we sought a different type of magnetism.

Imagine a place adorned in statues and framed by carved reliefs decorating overhead archways. Surround these monuments with hand paintings across the ceiling and murals that wrapped around walls, illustrating tales handed down across generations. Sprinkle images of peacocks, elephants and other exotic creatures in the vacant spaces. Now envision this mélange crammed into thirty caves halfway up a cliff face with the interiors only partially lit by the odd lamp. This was certainly no modern-day museum, but the coveted Ajanta Caves.

UNESCO considers these caves "masterpieces of Buddhist religious art."[21] They were built from 200 to 100 BC and were used for Buddhist practices until around AD 500. Thereafter, the caves were abandoned and eventually concealed by forest growth, lost for centuries. It was not until the early 1800s that they were rediscovered by a British officer while he was out hunting for tigers in the woods.[22] Initially, the captain spotted a darkened enclosure above some random trees, the perfect hideaway for his target. After a short scramble up a rocky wall, he brushed aside a few branches and must have gasped at the ancient relics that stared back at him. The forgotten rocky cliff had camouflaged the caverns while protecting the artifacts inside for centuries. I believe that such a find may lead one to reconsider hunting animals and turn instead to treasure hunting.

On the morning that we arrived, few other visitors roamed the walkways. After passing through the entrance gates, we climbed high above the parking area along a gravel trail. The horseshoe-shaped valley hugged the Wangorah River; its banks were barely visible through the foliage. A granite arc cut through the forest and extended in a semicircle around the middle of the slope. If I had had an aerial view, the rocky row of caves would have looked like an eyebrow smack in the middle of an emerald landscape. The styles of the many openings varied from double-storied pillars to curved archways to a single row of columns. Not knowing where to start, we selected at random and stepped inside the darkness.

Long shadows draped the interior corridors while an almost ethereal breeze exhaled across the valley. An occasional light bulb illuminated large statues of seated or reclining Buddhas with hands held in symbolic positions. One oblong temple was lined with pillars disguised by all their detailed carvings. The ceiling formed an archway, with more etched colonnades perched above the lower level. Between the two zones, a string of engraved figures filled the panel as if it were an antiquated cartoon strip. Traces of paint remained, a streak of black or fleck of red. The simplicity of colour seemed to highlight the silhouettes in the room.

We ventured back outdoors where the main walkway had started to fill with people. People ducked in and out of dim caverns, looking as if they were participating in Monty Python's "100 yards for people with no sense of direction" Silly Olympics event.[23] We passed through another arch into a room encircled by pillars and domes. Every crevice was coloured with Buddhist-themed pictorials. Dark turquoise and black-brown colours had endured better than had the lighter tones, yet there were also hints of crimson and white if you looked closely. An impressively maintained sitting Buddha statue filled one niche. One open hand faced upward while the tips of the other hand's index finger and thumb touched to form a circle. As we walked out and crossed into another cave, we found rows of carved Buddhas resting along a wall. A line of yellow spotlights along the floor revealed the statues' contours. Each Buddha within an alcove was intended for a specific prayer and offering. It was overwhelming how many different designs had been created and entwined throughout the dim caves. Sometimes the ceilings bore exceptional workmanship. In other cavities, niches along the walls were the focal point. By just turning a corner, we went from a darkened space concealing a roughly etched statue to witnessing vibrantly painted strips illustrating detailed narratives from Buddha's teachings.

We spent the entire morning wandering through the Ajanta Caves. The emotion that radiated from this place was mesmerizing. Our visit was many years ago, yet the caverns still jump to my mind when I think of India. Although remote, the caves were definitely worth the effort to visit.

The Basics

Synopsis: Listen to Islamic calls to worship in the distance while treading blackened stone corridors through this Buddhist temple that winds up nine terraces towards the realm of Enlightenment.

Most useful item to pack: A guidebook to explain the many moralistic tales of Buddha

For further travel information: Borobudur is forty kilometres north of Yogyakarta, the nearest city with an airport on the island of Java. A three-hour bus ride provided easy transit from Yogyakarta to the town of Borobudur. For more information on the site, refer to borobudurpark. com.

The Experience

We discovered Indonesia's Candi Borobudur ("Temple of Borobudur") while perusing a friend's coffee-table travel book a few years before our trip. The book challenged readers to visit the lesser known Temple of Borobudur as an alternative to the widely popular Angkor Wat in Cambodia or Bagan in Myanmar. From the time we saw the book, the delights of this Buddhist temple tempted us with their obscurity. It should be noted that Borobudur is a single temple, whereas Angkor Wat and Bagan each offer numerous temples across a vast landscape. So the sites are not identical. But the detail and style exhibited at the Temple of Borobudur were remarkable, while its isolation amplified its breathtaking backdrop.

The temple was both imposing in its construction and illuminating through its storytelling. Sixteen million blocks of andesite, a volcanic rock, were hauled here between AD 780 to 833 to erect this edifice. Tales emerged from carvings across this volume of rock. Consider the impact of messages emanating from 2,500 metres of stone covered with narrative reliefs and decorative panels. People were taught lessons through storytelling. The depth of meaning was overwhelming.

The concept behind the temple's design was to recreate the path to Enlightenment in order to teach followers how they too could attain this higher state. For eons, humans have tended to accumulate tangible things, deriving their personal identity from this stuff. This has changed little today. Under Buddhist teachings, the state of Enlightenment can be reached by letting go of fruitless feelings of desire and attachment and a sense of self or ego. Borobudur was constructed many hundreds of years ago based on this same basic premise. The temple's levels progressed skyward towards its pinnacle, the Enlightened phase. Siddhartha Gautama was the first person to find Enlightenment, and he became known as Buddha, or "the Awakened One," in the sixth century BC. Stories from his journey are conveyed along the temple walls.

We entered at the base level, considered to be Borobudur's hidden foot, where the first lesson was one of karma. Cause and effect were portrayed through numerous carved tales. Ill-willed actions led to punishment while virtuous deeds received praise and reward. This entry level signified the lower realm of the universe and depicted humans' greedy nature. It was like a slap to the face. Here was an ancient block of rock that had stood for ages across innumerable generations, and yet we had not changed. Our world was still plagued by an obsession for excess: bigger houses, fancier clothes and greater power.

The next five levels represented the sphere of forms. At this phase, people had improved themselves to a certain extent. They had let go of desires but remained attached to things or objects. The temple bore an uncanny ability to convey this message. The corridors were dominated by high walls that manifested a sense of claustrophobia. Hundreds of etched panels covered their surface, often across three or four rows. Detailed narratives drove the message home. Wealthy merchants rode in carts, shaded by parasols held by poorer folks. In effect, the enclosure explained how our reliance on physical possessions has constrained us, as if we are unable to truly experience freedom. The depictions were intricate and included facial expressions and ornate jewellery. Even individual leaves hung from tree branches in the carvings. Birds sang from trees as old men and women sat beneath the branches. A balance scale showed a bird on one side to be equal in weight to an empty pan on the other—perhaps this bird represented Buddha, free from the weight of human desires. There were stories upon stories, each with its own significance. The level of detail, step after step, was astounding.

Some panels conveyed local bands playing age-old instruments. Carved figurines beat drums slung over their shoulders, blew into flutes and strummed ancient stringed instruments. The musicians' heads were adorned in what looked like piles of beads or perhaps a fancy hairstyle. In another scene, an old man with a long, pointed beard walked, hunched over his walking stick. Stories of animals also filled the corridors. Elephants walked alongside cows and deer towards a temple. Even boats were carved in such detail that their wood planks were clearly visible. Individual sails blew in the wind and seas sloshed turbulently. Most of the panels were in various shades of grey; the paint had faded long ago. However, a few reliefs were constructed on mottled yellowish sandstone. It provided a radiant contrast to the darker colours.

As we rose higher, the final three levels opened before us. The walls became shorter. We could see distant fields and, farther still, mountains covered with jungle. It felt as if we had let go of a dreaded weight; our shoulders seemed to have become perceptibly lighter. Coincidentally, the call to prayer from a nearby mosque reverberated off the stone walls. **"Allah Akbar"** echoed in gradual crescendos that floated through the air. The message seemed to imply that harmony was indeed possible between religions. Buddhists and Muslims had both lived for centuries in this town. It was a special place.

The higher levels contained rows of niches that faced the mountain range. Within each stone alcove sat a Buddha statue with legs crossed and eyes closed in solemn meditation. In total, there were 432 sitting Buddha statues tucked into the walls to watch over the pilgrims of Borobudur. From below, this section looked like a wall of pagodas perfectly placed for Buddha to catch the morning sun's rays. Unfortunately, this place had not always been peaceful. Certain sections had been damaged, and some statues were headless or missing arms.

We climbed higher still and the walls fell away completely. An additional three levels of stupas, bell-shaped domes, surrounded us. Like honeycomb, their structure alternated between solid supports and empty holes that allowed light to enter the interior. A subtly smiling Buddha statue was sheltered inside each stupa. The first of these three levels held thirty-two Buddha stupas, whereas the upper platforms were smaller and contained only sixteen each. These levels reflected the realm of Buddha in timeless meditation. Everywhere we turned, we saw stone domes and Buddha images. The sun was starting to set, creating long, majestic shadows. The effect was bewitching. Other visitors also seemed to sense the calm. Footsteps fell silent.

We returned early the next morning to catch the rising sun's orange reflection. The contrast between a life-size Buddha shaded in black and the hazy auburn rays was like an elusive dream. The imagery of dimmed corridors and expansive rooftop levels played back in our minds over the following days. The purity of the temple reflected a different perception of living one's life. It was an impression worth cherishing.

The Basics

Synopsis: Admire an eclectic array of Khmer empire relics situated between the Mekong River and Phou Kao Mountain, which was believed to be the home of the Hindu god Shiva.

Most useful item to pack: Moisture-wicking short-sleeved shirt

For further travel information: We based ourselves in the town of Champasak, located ten kilometres from the Wat Phu Temple. Bicycles can be rented in town to pedal to and from the temple along a paved road with little traffic.

The Experience

The inconspicuous Wat Phu Temple rests near the town of Champasak in southern Laos. This rarely visited site managed to cram a heap of history into its stony walls. Relics from both the Hindu and the Buddhist faiths adorned the rambling corridors and darkened stairways. UNESCO has recognized the site for its integration of nature and spiritual beliefs because it seamlessly blends the man-made objects with the mountain and the river.[24] The Wat Phu complex of sanctuaries and stone temples cascaded gently from the edge of Phou Kao Mountain towards the Mekong River. Khmers believed that the mountain was the home of Shiva, their Hindu god. They envisioned that the knobby peak of Phou Kao resembled the phallic symbol, or **linga**, associated with Shiva, signalling that he lived underneath its peak. As we approached the site from the river valley, the god's mark peppered the grounds, and rows of stone lingas lined both sides of the main entranceway. A few pillars had crumbled, but the majority stood erect. This remained the land of Shiva.

As we walked along the lengthy corridor approaching the jungle-strewn mountainside, wide empty fields stretched out from either side of the stone pillars. Native grass grew in these former reservoirs, called **barays**, which represented great oceans and were used by worshippers to cleanse themselves. Some archaeologists believe that Wat Phu may have been a mock-up or early blueprint for the Angkor Wat Temple, which has similar expansive cleansing lakes around its perimeter. The earliest sections of Champasak's temple date back to the fifth century, whereas Angkor Wat was constructed much later, in the twelfth century. Proof of communication between the colonies lies with an ancient road leading from the Nandin shrine within Wat Phu through other Khmer temples and may have gone as far as Angkor Wat. Conversely, the similarities may just reflect a natural evolution of architecture styles within the Khmer empire.

As barays symbolized the ocean, temples represented sacred earth. In Wat Phu's case, its main temple represented Mount Meru in Tibet, otherwise known as Mount Kailash. This poignant place is believed by some to be the centre of the universe, the nucleus of all energy. Considering that we had recently trekked around Mount Kailash (see Chapter Two), this association hit close to our hearts. We were keen to see the Khmers' recreation.

Once we had completed our walk through the symbolic oceans, the scene changed dramatically. The open spaces of the baray faded, and we felt as though we were being observed. Seven-headed naga serpents carved into reinforced stone corners stared down at us with stony eyes. Intricate designs crowned the rock face that surrounded their heads while wooden support beams upheld their curved bodies. These ghosts protected two symmetrical palaces, which acted as a transition from the ocean to the sacred earth elements of the complex. The ceilings had long since disintegrated, but the walls of the buildings remained standing, decorated with frontons. Rusty-brown stone blocks formed the sides. The frontons must have been made of a different stone because white and grey lichen covered them, leaving a distinctive light wash across their intricate patterns. As we continued to walk, the lighting changed from the opaque clouds of the lower fields to dappled streaks that pierced an umbrella created by the forest's leaves.

The rocks leading up the hillside had shuffled over time. In some places, all that remained was an irregular mass of blocks. Forlorn lintels lay in the grass with detailed engravings peering up. Proud craftsmanship still seemed to pervade each block. During the thirteenth century, the Theravada Buddhism belief system had taken off within the formerly Hindu-predominant Khmer society. This dichotomy created dual practices in the same space. We saw both Hindu and Buddhist remnants scattered across the site, some of which were still revered by local believers. We found many fresh offerings placed in front of both seated Buddha statues and Hindu relief images. Banana leaves were rolled into cones and sprinkled with bright pink and orange flowers. Incense sticks pointed up to the sky, with a few still burning, their smoke dancing delicately in the still air. These packages of devotion fringed many stone effigies, especially near the upper levels of the complex. One life-sized statue was draped in a shiny red wrap, and rings of flower offerings were looped over its right forearm. A bright pink parasol with a fringe border shaded the statue's entire head.

As we progressed, we could vaguely discern a flight of stairs here or partial layer of steps there. A long walkway composed of rock planks looked like a box of

chocolate wafers that had been shaken before its lid was opened. We continued to pick our way through the tiers of rectangular rock bricks towards the higher levels, sometimes hopping over onto the grassy banks. We knew that we had reached the top of the complex when we approached a three-doored temple. Inside the centre door, a golden cloth covered a Buddha statue. At its base, and nearly obscuring half the statue, rested offerings of smaller statues, flowers and shiny ornaments. This temple had been constructed in the eleventh century and had been the first part of the complex to receive the precious mountain's spring water. The doorways were decorated with swirling pillars, deities carved into niches and slabs of stylistic lintels balanced overhead. Since the temple was of relatively recent construction, the carvings were in distinctly pristine condition; even the wrinkles etched across elephant trunks were still visible. Reliefs dedicated to various Hindu deities could still be identified. Krishna, Indra and Shiva were depicted in scenes from the Ramayana story. Additional clusters of naga curled from stone blocks and were randomly positioned across the sanctuary's grassy spaces.

The site was a jumble of surprises. When we first arrived, the ruins appeared to be no more than a few rocky fragments amid a lush forested hillside. However, Wat Phu slowly revealed its intricate corners hidden within the shade, as if serving a platter of gourmet appetizers to her favourite guests. As we swerved between rocks and slowly climbed the temple grounds, partially standing walls revealed gods, people and aged tales finely carved into their visages. There were sections, as well, with less detail. One boulder taller than me had the outline of an elephant scored onto its corner. The ears splayed outwards as the eyes peered through green moss to check out passersby. Not far away, a slab of rock revealed a life-sized crocodile excavated across its top. It looked as if the reptile had run full force, leapt and fallen in a bellyflop smack on top of the stone block, never to move again.

By the time we bicycled back to our guesthouse, the sun had burned away the morning clouds. It seemed only right to cool off with an iced coffee and crisp green papaya salad.

The Basics

Synopsis: Tread secret corridors and tricky stairwells in a centuries-old Arabian fort.

Most useful item to pack: A lightweight scarf

For further travel information: Four-wheel-drive vehicles can be rented from a number of rental companies. Check TripAdvisor.com and customer reviews for the latest feedback on vehicle quality and company service. When I was there over ten years ago, Mark Tours was a reliable company. For further information, refer to marktoursoman.com.

There is minimal information available on the internet regarding opening hours and entrance fees for the Nizwa Fort. I would advise checking your guidebook or asking at your hotel for the latest information.

The Experience

Oman has a special place in my heart. It is truly a gem of a country. I lived and worked in Muscat, the capital city, for three years in the mid-2000s. Sultan Qaboos bin Said al Said has been in power since 1970, a rare long-time ruler who has ensured that the country's citizens directly benefit from the nation's wealth. Everyone receives education, health care and access to robust infrastructure, including a well-maintained road system. Even most of the tap water was drinkable, although most Omanis and foreigners I saw consumed bottled water. Local Omani men and women worked across all sectors, from grocery store cashiers to senior executives in private and public companies. The country seemed to have found the sweet spot of religious tolerance, as people of Christian, Sunni Muslim, Shiite Muslim and other faiths worked together in relative harmony. I remember Muslim women selling Christmas ornaments and baked goods at a local mall while carols played on the overhead speakers.

Oman was an easy country to travel around independently. My husband took his mother on a road trip when she visited us. Once well out of the city, he felt the tug of a deflated tire. Not minutes after he had pulled to the side of the road, a vehicle full of local guys pulled over behind him. They were youngish, likely in their midtwenties, and immediately offered their help. They had obviously changed tires many times before and appreciated the ease that came with extra hands. Once the task was completed, they shook hands and waved goodbye, and everyone happily carried on to wherever they had originally been headed.

One of my favourite day trips from Muscat was to visit the nearby forts. The well-maintained Highway 15—commonly referred to as the Muscat-Nizwa Highway—unsurprisingly connected Muscat with Nizwa. Bahla, a smaller town, could also be reached by the same highway, just beyond Nizwa. Green road signs in both Arabic and English clearly indicated the road names and turnoff points. It was nearly unnecessary to carry a map; however, having one is advised, just in case.

A colleague accompanied my husband and me on our first trip to the Nizwa Fort. We all piled into my four-wheel-drive vehicle. A shrewdly placed mini-fridge was built in underneath the armrest between the front seats. Water stayed icy fresh so long as the vehicle's ignition was on. Carrying a sufficient stock of water bottles was critical when travelling outside the city, for it was not uncommon for temperatures to reach forty or fifty degrees Celsius.

The highway's tarmac ensured a smooth drive out of the city. We sailed through the Al Hajar mountain range, more frequently referred to as the **jebels**, which is the Arabic word for mountains. The route followed dried riverbeds, or wadis, which were often lined with palm trees. Sumail Gap was one of the first towns that we drove through. Its buildings were no higher than two storeys and were styled in the typical whitewashed plaster or sometimes just left unpainted. The town looked tranquil resting below the jebels. The rocky ridge appeared in a multitude of shades of rust, beige, grey and seemingly every tint in between.

Within an hour and a half, we had reached the town of Nizwa. Oman's distinctive architecture stayed true across this town as well. Low buildings in white and beige tones lined the streets. Before going to the fort, we paused at the market, or **souq**. It was one of the oldest souqs in the country, and its merchandise focused on the essentials. Fruits, vegetables, fish and animals filled the stalls where interested buyers milled about, ready to strike a bargain. In recent years, the market has been extended to cater to tourists. Crafty items, such as hand-stitched rugs and silver jewellery, are now sold there. Nizwa is known for its **khanjars**, traditional tribal daggers stored in cases decorated with threads of silver spun into swirling designs around silver beads.

Soon we tired of the market and were keen to move on to the fort—after a quenching slug of cool water, of course. The fort stood in the middle of town, and its oblong tower was its most distinctive feature. This stronghold's construction took twelve years during the seventeenth century. From inside the tower, its concept appeared simple and functional. But this appearance was deceiving. The original architects, the Ya'rubi, were ingenious at incorporating defensive elements into the building's structure. False doors and secret tunnels foiled attackers. Even the front entrance included multiple doors and random obstacles, which at the very least would slow any advance and force incoming troops to form a narrow convoy. An enclosed stairwell encircling the main watchtower was the only way to get inside. While some soldiers fought outwards with cannon and firepower, others secured the stairwell.

We climbed this cramped staircase. Initially, the deception was not obvious. The steps were built at varying heights to trip up a potential attacker. When we climbed at a walking pace, the irregularity was hardly noticeable. However, imagine running up a dark, unfamiliar stairwell, weighted down in full combat gear, only to stub your toe and fall on your face. Step height is something we naturally assume would be uniform.

The seemingly innocuous date palms that surrounded the fort, in addition to providing a tasty treat for its occupants, also offered a secret weapon. The dates were dumped into large cauldrons and cooked until they turned to a runny syrup. Inside the main open area of the fort, soldiers could tip boiling pots of the bubbling sauce into narrow ducts that connected directly to inconspicuous slots above the stair's door frames. The enemy had to cross through these doors to reach the main defensive tower. The scalding sweetness would be sure to slow unsuspecting assailants with a mighty unpleasant shower. Many similar doors were staged along the entire stairwell. Further defensive mechanisms included trap floorboards located along the same route. If the scorching shower did not stop the onslaught, trap doors would dump the aggressors into Nizwa's dungeon.

The Nizwa Fort held another enviable advantage. The fortification was built above an underground stream of fresh water. Cisterns set in the fort's basement stored this life-giving essence, a critical element for survival in these arid lands. There was even a pulley system to haul fresh water directly to the highest defensive level of the tower.

From this upper level, we looked across the entire town of Nizwa and its surrounding valley. The mountains appeared indistinct through the heat's haze, although the warmth was less discernible inside the fort enclosure. An incredible aspect of Omani forts was their early air-conditioning system. Holes were cut in walls near the ceiling to allow air flow throughout the building. This system functioned well. Temperatures could have reached the midforties when we visited, but we were fairly comfortable walking through the fort's interior rooms.

When we visited the Nizwa Fort, only a few other people toured its many rooms. We could wander the narrow stairwells without having to dodge anyone. Over the years, I believe that Oman has gained a reputation as an enticing place to visit in the Middle East, so the country's forts likely receive more visitors nowadays. Other sites near Nizwa can also be visited in the same day. Jibrin Castle, sometimes spelled as Jibreen, sits in the town of Bahla, thirty minutes farther along Highway 15. Jibrin Castle is more a wealthy residence than a military stronghold. Its interior rooms and living quarters have been restored and tastefully decorated to give a sense of traditional daily life. I have read in recent visitor reviews that an excellent audio guide is now available to accompany the informative signage in each room.

Since I left Oman, a further ancient site has become accessible in the small town of Bahla. The UNESCO-recognized Bahla Fort, a fortified oasis, opened its doors to tourists in 2012.[25] I cannot offer any personal advice about this site; however, given its UNESCO status, I expect that it would be quite impressive.

Besides forts, Bahla is renowned for its clay pots. The traditional style was a teardrop-shaped urn that hung on walls by rope twisted around its neck. Other styles can be placed on the ground and come in a variety of sizes. When we visited, the pots could also be found at Nizwa's market.

The Basics

Synopsis: Wander through a white star-shaped Portuguese fort overlooking the pristine blue Indian Ocean before haggling with residents over your chosen Swahili artistic creation.

Most useful item to pack: Sunscreen

For further travel information: We stayed at the quaint Cinco Portas, a colonial-styled house turned hotel. For further information, refer to cincoportas.com.

Based on our experience of their welcoming restaurant, the Miti Miwiri hotel and restaurant seemed to offer a friendlier atmosphere. For further information, refer to mitimiwiri.com.

We flew to the island at the reasonable price of one hundred American dollars per person. However, I have read that travel options have expanded since we visited in 2010, so it would be worth researching further at your time of travel. Check with your hotel for the latest options or with Kaskazini for charter flights from Pemba. For further information, refer to the Ibo Island page at kaskazini.com.

The Experience

The Fort of São João was wrapped in many historical layers. Imagine looking at it through an enormous telescope. Up close, the outline of the white walls resembled a sheriff's star with freshly painted black iron cannon aligned inside each tip. Zoom back a notch and a town could be seen hugging the Portuguese-styled fort. The village lacked the crisp white punch of the fort walls but held its own mystique. Dialing farther back on the viewfinder would expose Ilha de Ibo ("Ibo Island") within the Quirimbas Archipelago off the northern shores of Mozambique. I rarely hear anyone speak of Mozambique's pristine beauty, which makes the country even more appealing.

We reached the island on a twenty-minute hopper flight from the mainland town of Pemba. The best part of this small plane was its ability to fly low, offering incredible views. For the entire journey, we flew over a mass of turquoise coral reefs, mangrove-lined coastlines and sands that swirled with the waters of the Indian Ocean. Channels appeared to mix with sand, creating various shades from white to blue, like a toy kaleidoscope that had recently been shaken.

Life on Ibo Island operated at a relaxed pace. We strolled around the island's streets, which were just lines of dirt running between buildings, delineated by rows of rocks painted white. The roadways were not bisected by power lines; semireliable electricity was instead transmitted underground by a cable from the mainland. Each of the few tourist hotels owned a generator to ensure a smooth stream of power for their guests. Houses and streets alike were neatly maintained and swept clean, regardless of their residents' wealth. Most of the architecture comprised simple cement structures. Painted patterns added some flair. Often a stripe of bright blue paint outlined a window or framed a doorway. The paint was often aged, darkened with patches of mould and faded by the sun.

Once the sun fell, the streets took on a haunted aura. We quietly padded across the dirt road, the only other noise the soft murmur of families chatting inside their homes. Most houses possessed just one light bulb, which flickered a few shards of light onto the street. The moon was full, and its light bounced across the whitewashed walls as we walked in its velvety glow.

There were three forts on the tiny island, but I found that the Fort of São João, built in 1791, was the most impressive. It was originally designed for defence and could accommodate up to three hundred people. Unfortunately, this virtuous purpose was short lived. By the end of the eighteenth century, the fort was caught up in the slave trade,[26] and many innocent people were forced through its dark underbelly. Thankfully, the fort had since been transformed, and nowadays people wandered freely in and out of its rooms. Ramps led through iron gates up to the fort's perimeter walkway. We passed by a modest chapel with a small white cross sticking up from its roof. The church's front entrance was framed by an arch of limestone-like bricks. Their rough grey texture pierced the smooth whitewashed finish of the rest of the fort.

Once we reached the upper level, the best vantage points were at the corners, where cannon sat dormant. We peered across clear azure waters that eventually merged into the horizon. Soldiers would have surely gained an advantage from this view.

We dragged ourselves from the stunning ocean vistas and returned to the comparably drab main level. As if to compensate, former storage rooms and sleeping quarters had been transformed into alcoves for artisans. A large old tree grew in the centre of the fort's courtyard, offering a shaded area for artists and visitors alike. Resident painters stacked canvases of local scenes against the wall. In other rooms, local Swahili jewellery was crafted in delicate swirls. The processes stayed true to tradition; after all, with no air conditioning or electric tools, the artists had little choice.

We shuffled back towards the town centre. The Catholic church stood at an intersection, prominent with its brilliant white Portuguese-styled facade. A few palm shrubs had been planted with tender care around its grounds, their lime-green leaves a bright contrast to the white walls and dusty soil. We sat in the shade of a large tree and listened while a choir inside the church belted out a chorus. This was the sound of Africa you might imagine: it had depth; it had power. Nearby, a few children were playing along a side street. There were no cars on the island to dodge. The favourite game seemed to be rolling a metal hoop or tossing a ball to knock over an empty soda bottle. We watched the ball game for a while. A bottle perched on a pile of dirt, which acted as a pseudocricket pitch. A girl of about ten wore a ruffled pink skirt with a few pieces torn away, topped by a yellow-and-red-striped soccer T-shirt. Her eyes narrowed in concentration as she set her arm in motion to hurl the well-used baseball. Another girl chuckled and teased, while a much younger girl stood watching it all go down. In this match, the girls ruled.

If one got bored by the streets, there was always activity at the waterfront. Men gathered to help repair a dhow boat. The **Shan Yake** had fished many waters, from the look of its sun-bleached canvas awning, but it looked well cared for. The bottom of the boat was painted in red, criss-crossed with blue lines, as if a Spiderman suit had been stretched around its hull. The boat was constructed in the standard dhow style with one central mast. A row of about fifteen men and boys leaned shoulder to shoulder over the boat's side. Heave! They pushed in unison while trying to flip it over onto the edge of the beach. Eventually our interest in their efforts to rock the **Shan Yake** back and forth waned, and we wandered back to the village.

Our other favoured spot to visit was the local **pastelaria**. Local women sold sweets, typically little bags of cookies or a fried pastry filled with sweet coconut. Two plastic tables with chairs filled the room in front of the bakery display. I believe their specialty was not actually the baking, but their delectable stew infused with local flavours. Each morning, the ladies ensured a pot of freshly prepared seafood chowder simmered on the gas stove. It would be ready to serve for lunch or as an early dinner. Savoury aromas blew through the bakery and hit our nostrils in a fragrant wave when we walked through the doorway. Each bowl was served with a whole crab immersed in its thick broth, for a bargain price of three dollars. The meal turned into a delicious daily routine over the four days that we spent on the island. I have never tasted a more tempting seafood stew than that dished up by the ladies of the pastelaria on Ilha de Ibo. If the fort does not grab your interest, this meal surely will.

Bit by bit, archaeologists have uncovered elements of age-old cities turned to ruins. At some sites, stories were chiselled into rock, painted on walls or inked across scrolls of antiquated paper. It makes me wonder what our cities will look like in a thousand years. Most of our time is spent in the present moment. Cars rush past, data is collected and people work to ensure life as we know it continues to function. However, our lives are not so different from those ancient civilizations that have since turned to rubble. Those cities were also home to thousands of people. The streets were busy. Business was transacted and deals were made. Families separated and tribes united. Young people learned from the masters; they honed their skills and built their trades. Full lives were lived. Over time, cities fell and civilizations faded.

Of the ancient civilizations that I have visited, the Maya lasted the longest, at over three thousand years. Their downfall stemmed from foreign militia that came and conquered. The next most lengthy settlement is still functioning today. Old Sana'a has been inhabited for over 2,500 years, but its endurance is currently being tested by a force similar to that faced by the Maya—foreign invaders, but with a modern twist. Instead of acting on expansionist ambitions, international militaristic interests are attempting to smother internal separatist uprisings. Other civilizations lasted from a few hundred years up to a maximum of just over a thousand years at Ephesus, depending on which historical starting point is used. Ephesus also declined after a destructive invasion in the third century. It seems that humans' innate pursuit of domination is, in effect, destroying our most durable cultures.

Archaeologists can build a historic story to an amazing level of detail. The challenge is akin to completing a massive jigsaw puzzle without the picture on the box as a guide. A triangular chunk of pottery buried under the ground for centuries can tell a story of a once-vibrant civilization. Answers about the type of food eaten, how a dish was cooked, pottery skills and artistic styles surface after the object is tenderly brushed clean. An unearthed altar with traces of animal blood could signify that sacrifices were thought to appease some god. Beliefs and rituals once held by an ancient society can then be pieced together. Structures that took years to construct were somehow perfectly aligned with the summer and winter solstices. Circular sundials allocated time according to the sun's shadows. These ancient technologies shed insight into how crops were managed and festivals were planned.

When exploring such archaic centres, I have felt as if I were looking at the city through cotton gauze, not quite fully clear. Even so, its tangible remnants felt grounded. Perhaps the fragility of time became all too apparent as the present world was revealed as just a tiny sliver in the huge tree of humanity. Our ancestors created some pretty powerful societies long before today's technology was available. If I were thrown back in time several thousand years, I wonder whether I would have the patience to observe the seasons, plot the stars or apply geometry to plan a city. Could we do it all again?

The Basics

Synopsis: Wander jungle-clad temples, and imagine how ancient city streets shimmered long ago before vanishing beneath the forest's grip.

Most useful item to pack: A guidebook to unravel the meaning behind the ruins

For further travel information: We based ourselves in the cute town of Flores in northern Guatemala to visit nearby Tikal and Yaxhá. We visited each site as a separate day trip. Many tour companies, hotels and restaurants are situated in Flores to ensure all your needs are met. Be sure to do some reconnaissance on sites such as TripAdvisor.com for up-to-date information on the transport companies. We have read reports of organized robberies along the drive to or from Tikal with one of the larger companies, so be sure to check the latest reviews.

The town of Copán Ruinas in Honduras is chock full of boutique hotels and restaurants and is a convenient base for visiting the adjacent ruins of Copán. This town is located just twelve kilometres from the Guatemalan border and can be easily reached on shuttle buses, which run daily from Antigua and Guatemala City. Once in Copán, we went on an insightful walking tour with Gerardo, the owner of ViaVia Travel. For further information, stop by their friendly restaurant and hostel or check their website at viavia.world/en/america/copan.

The Experience

Mayan society is intriguing. It can be traced as far back as 2600 BC. The Maya's homeland stretched from the Yucatán in Mexico southward through Guatemala, Belize, Honduras and El Salvador. Secrets uncovered in their settlements' rocky rubble allude to expertise in astronomy, calendars—of which there were many—and enduring stone temple construction. These imposing structures were somehow built without using metal tools.[27] Mayan kingdoms were massive and their cities were dramatic. Yet for some reason, the residents deserted their extensive capitals around AD 900.

The reason for such a drastic downfall remains a mystery to archaeologists. Three theories have been formed, which regrettably mimic some of the same challenges facing our society today. One belief is that the growing population became too much of a burden for the environment to sustain. Fields became fallow and unproductive. In a similar yet more dramatic vein, others propose that a disastrous environmental event occurred. An extended drought may have disrupted water systems from functioning. The third hypothesis is a conflict-driven explanation in which the endless intercity warfare corroded their system of power, and society ultimately collapsed into chaos.[28] We may never know the true cause. Notwithstanding this mystery, many remnants of Mayan cities have withstood time and offer a small glimpse into their remarkable world.

My husband and I explored three such bygone cities. These civilizations rested beneath the jungles of Guatemala and Honduras. Each site displayed common threads while hinting at its own vibe, not unlike today's metropolises. Paris and London both have underground trains and monumental museums, but still exude entirely different personalities. Common characteristics of Mayan cities included pyramidal temples, ball courts, stelae and acropolises. Nobility lived and worked in the prestigious acropolis of each city. Stelae, or carved pillars, stood in honour of every king who ever ruled. Ball courts were as integral then as our sports venues are today, but the ancient games also displayed a darker side. Cities could settle disputes through a match rather than going to war. Some accounts claim that players from the winning or losing team were sacrificed at the whim of the successful team's king.

On a side note, it can be confusing to differentiate between the ancient civilizations of the Aztec, Maya and Inca. Images of stone pyramids may come to mind for all three of these venerable societies. The trick is in their time and place. Maya were the earliest people and tended to stay in the region from southern Mexico down through today's Central American countries as far south as El Salvador. Aztecs came later and remained primarily within the present-day Mexican border. To confuse things, there was some overlap. Trade alliances existed between Aztec and Mayan cities for a period, but they occurred near the end of the Maya' era, early in the Aztec's reign. Incas typically lived farther south. They settled in South America from Colombia down to Chile. Both the Incas and Aztecs were overthrown in the 1500s by the Spanish conquistadors, whereas the Maya' downfall is not completely understood.

Tikal, Guatemala

Entering the thick jungle surrounding the ruins of Tikal, I felt as if we had been transported far from civilization. Howler monkeys screamed from their favourite tree while a lone toucan perched on the branch of a soaring ceiba. A family of coatimundis scurried around the forest floor.[29] Their pliable noses sniffed at seemingly everything they spotted, a mossy rock here and a thicket over there.

Tikal National Park's green abyss stretched for thousands of hectares, covering savannah, wetlands and dense palm forests.

As we walked along the leaf-strewn pathway, the cityscape was camouflaged by wild green foliage. Hillsides appeared to poke up all around us, but in fact these were temples that had succumbed to the forest's tentacles. Long ago, soil blew over the stone pyramids. Their rocky bases were then transformed into a bed for tree root systems. Only a few structures nuzzled out from the undergrowth, resolutely standing their ground to ensure that their story lived on. The rather uninspiringly named Temple V was one of these formidable towers. Its base alone covered 4,200 square metres, while its temple stood fifty-two metres in the air, stretching well above the treetops. It took some creative juices to imagine how this same scene had appeared when the Maya ruled. Across from Temple V stood a field of forest, formerly the base of a grand water reservoir. That huge, calm pool of water reflecting the colossal rock structures must have been a formidable sight.

The modern-day addition of wooden scaffolding and stairs wrapped around one of the tall temples allowed us to climb to its peak. From this vantage, we looked out across the top of the trees. The multi-toned greenery was interrupted by an occasional massive stone temple. These beasts stood higher than the tallest trees. It was odd to view such a thick forest intercepted by the surreal sanctuaries of a once-powerful society. This blend of diverse plant and animal life amid fragments of a time-worn civilization ticked five of UNESCO's criteria to be included in their distinguished list of World Heritage Sites.[30] Four thousand structures have been detected within Tikal's boundaries. It was certainly a prominent city in its day. However, UNESCO regulations, coupled with funding constraints, have restricted excavations to uncover only a fraction of these formations. A huge amount of jungle remains like a veil draped over history. Ironically, the curtain-like forest added a touch of realism as to what the city may have felt like to live in, long before modern conveniences.

Another of the Mayan architectural features lost beneath the vegetation were its majestic walkways. White alabaster once coated what are now broad forest paths—Main Street, Mayan style. These streets would have contrasted against the brilliant temples painted scarlet to represent life. Tikal was a huge cosmopolis. In one temple, a marker of the Aztec city of Teotihuacán was found etched into the stone, illustrating trade relations or a military alliance between the two cities. In Tikal's acropolis, human teeth with iron pyrite fillings were discovered. Dentistry is an impressive skill to have mastered thousands of years ago. It was hard to imagine the extent of this city, including government offices, markets, residences and even a precious water reserve.

Pyramid structures showcased the complexities of the Mayan calendar. An example was the twin-pyramid complex, one of the first structures we came across in Tikal. Its stone alternated between brilliant white and blackened moss, making for a striking facade. The buildings had been a notable discovery and depicted a surprisingly well-thought-out design. Mayan pyramids typically comprised five levels and four sides, each facing precisely north, south, east or west. Stairways centred on every side led straight to the temple's pinnacle. The product of these levels—five times four—equals the twenty days in a Mayan month. There were nine stelae and nine altars at the base of the twin-pyramid complex. The sum of these monuments—nine plus nine—equals the eighteen months in the Mayan solar calendar. When considered together, the twenty days across eighteen months produced a 360-day period. The calendar was then allocated five bonus days, referred to as the Uayeb month, to reconcile it with a 365-day solar year.

The Maya followed more than one calendar. They also used a 260-day sacred calendar, which tracked nine lunar cycles and, not so coincidentally, mirrored a woman's pregnancy term. Beyond this, there was a Long Count calendar to cover periods longer than fifty-two years.[31] The Maya were truly good planners, and my description of their calendars only scratches the surface. The permanence of the stone temples used to track time signifies its importance to the Maya. After all, events ranging from religious ceremonies to farming practices were all centrally coordinated. This complex organization facilitated such a society without the aid of electricity or computers. It makes one wonder whether humans today take for granted what our elders simply figured out through observation. Do we even possess the patience for such a task? I doubt if I could sit and watch the night sky or manually track weather patterns year on year to devise a de facto compass or calendar.

Between early dentistry and the grand water reservoir system, Tikal represented a remarkable piece of human history. The ruins covered such an expansive area that it would be easy to feel overwhelmed or miss intricacies without a guide. Several guides waited near the entrance gate and offered their services to interested visitors. We hired an older gentleman who brought the site to life during our walk. His broad spectrum of knowledge was impressive.

Yaxhá, Guatemala

Yaxhá was also located in northern Guatemala, not too far from Tikal. It also stretched across an immense jungle, thirty-seven thousand hectares in its case. Yet

Yaxhá exuded an entirely different aura. Unlike Tikal, which received hundreds of thousands of visitors each year, Yaxhá was the lesser known sister city.

Our trip to Yaxhá's peaceful setting started off a little more troublesome than expected. The travel agency that we had booked our day trip through had

forgotten to notify the transport company about us. So while we waited patiently in our hotel's lobby, our bus was obliviously driving to the site. After we made a few telephone calls and a visit to the tour company's office, the staff salvaged the situation by arranging a private car to drive us instead. Although we missed out on the guide at the site, we made up for it in solitude.

For much of the drive, rain pelted down. We started to question why we had pushed to go in such dismal weather. However, as we approached the entrance gates, the rain slowed to a gentle mist. It drizzled on and off as we ambled around the ruins, only adding to their serene ambience. Before long, the sun peeped out, and its beams glinted off leaves dripping with humidity. Birds soon reconnected with one another. For at least thirty minutes we wandered alone, up stone stairways and through the second floor of an acropolis overgrown with thick moss. It was not until we reached the farthest temple cluster, Grupo Maler, that we ran into twelve people also exploring the ruins. We figured that they must be our lost tour group. Between our guidebook and information gleaned at Tikal, we were still able to appreciate many of the stories behind Yaxhá's mysteries.

The most memorable views were at one of the site's highest temples, taller than the trees themselves. A wooden staircase allowed access to the upper level. From this viewpoint, we gaped across treetops. In the distance, the occasional whitened stone temple broke through the trees' solid cover. Each tower stood hundreds of metres away. The scene was similar to what we had seen at Tikal but still felt awe-inspiring. It seemed odd that such vast spaces were once covered with rocky sanctuaries and solid stone buildings, but were now nearly engulfed by nature's soft greenery.

One of Yaxhá's quirks was its amazing Greater Astronomical Complex. This ancient construct tracked the sun's trajectory. It made me wonder whether the twenty thousand people who had lived here yielded some special relationship with astrology, more so than those in other Mayan settlements. Was this massive building built for any other purpose? Although the skies played an important role in all Mayan cities, it was curious that this one site possessed such a distinct building purely to monitor the movement of the sun. Perhaps Yaxhá's people oversaw seasonal tracking, like the supreme court of calendric rulings.

The other most memorable spot at Yaxhá was the drably named Structure 216. From its peak, we looked down into a courtyard while the sun set over the not-so-distant Lago Yaxhá. It seemed the perfect way to end our day reminiscing with the lost Maya.

Copán was a pleasure to visit. It may have been because we could walk from the town of Copán Ruinas to the nearby site of Copán. The walk passed by crumbling stelae that seemed to watch over the stone pathway connecting the old with the new. We hired a certified local guide at the main entrance of the Copán site to walk with us through its maze and decipher its codes. Imagine growing up next to Mayan ruins thousands of years old. A mother's instructions to go outside and play take on a whole new meaning when hide-and-go-seek is set among temple relics. It made me wonder if our guide's ancestors or maybe even his neighbours' distant relatives played a role in the ancient town's planning or perhaps carved the side of an elaborate stela for a favoured king.

Approximately 3,450 structures have been discovered across twenty-seven square kilometres in Copán. UNESCO considers Copán to be of critical importance in Mayan civilization.[32] It was here that the intricacies of the stelae shone brightly for me. Kings would commission pillars to be carved in their likeness, including full ceremonial dress. The first king, Mah K'ina Yax K'uk Mo ("Great Sun Lord Quetzal Macaw") was frequently carved dripping in macaw feathers and often wrapped in two-headed serpents and other iconic symbols. Our guide explained the significance of the figures and how each king's story was retold through hieroglyphics on the back of the pillars. As sixteen kings once ruled over Copán, there were more than a few such stelae resting on its grounds.

Most kings' stelae recounted tales of victories and bragging rights, likely embellished somewhat. Sadly, one king's unfortunate fate is now one of the most talked about stories. The king known as Eighteen Rabbit was captured in a military mission turned sour. The unforgiving victor sacrificed Eighteen Rabbit as a show of strength, granting the defeated ruler the infamous title of the only king ever to be sacrificed in Mayan culture. The altars that lay scattered around the stelae were mostly used for animal sacrifices. However, traces of human blood had been found, proving at least the possibility of Eighteen Rabbit's legend. Typically, prisoners of war or luckless ball-game players were thought to land this unfavourable fate.

The most comprehensive storyline was documented in hieroglyphics along the lengthy Escalinata de los Jeroglíficos. This monumental staircase stood three to four storeys high and faced the ball court. A protective tarp covered its detailed etching. Archaeologists had deciphered the hieroglyphics and believed them to describe the entire succession of kings who ever ruled over Copán. Every step was covered in characters that retold the kings' lives.

The ball court was also a spectacular stadium for its time. Beyond the spacious court, changing rooms for both the home and away teams had been constructed. It was easy to imagine a vibrant society cheering in this arena, hundreds of fans filling the stone bleachers while the king watched from his elevated position. The players from each team could run into the court from their respective private enclave.

Personalities seemed exposed here. In fact, one of my favourite carvings was of a cranky old man. He rested nearby, beside Temple Eleven. His chiselled face emerged from a stone block about a metre square in size—with details including a bandana tied around his head, wrinkles, a furrowed brow and a couple of missing teeth. This effigy was aptly named El Anciano ("The Old Man").

In addition to the heavy stonework, I found the level of logistical oversight necessary to construct the city of Copán particularly astounding. This was only increased by what we witnessed in the surrounding hillsides. We spent four hours with a long-time expatriate of Copán in the countryside around the central ruins. The three of us walked through fields and past grazing cows to La Pintada, or, simply, Stela Twelve. It rested in a farmer's field beneath the shade of a tin roof braced by four steel poles. A placard set in stone at its base explained Stela Twelve's story, and our guide's visual narrative brought the tale to life. Across the valley sat a similar pillar named Stela Nineteen. It was out of sight and miles from where we stood, but if one were to attach a piece of string to Stela Twelve and run it over to Stela Nineteen, it would cross exactly through the main temple sanctuary in the Copán ruins, the Grupo Principal. Consider the geometric expertise and precision of measurement required for such a feat, which represented an early city grid system. This knowledge alone made the walk worthwhile, and we had not even reached our target.

We were headed for Los Sapos, which merely means "The Toads." The Maya adored these little amphibians. They could live in water as tadpoles and on land as adults. The Mayan belief system extrapolated that these attributes signified life and fertility. Far off in the adjacent hills, wedged between a dribble of a stream and bushy jungle, sat a stone toad and serpent, each about the size of a wheelbarrow. The grooves of their mouths ran the width of their heads and were filled with a velvety moss. Splotches of lichen in pale yellows and greens covered the critters as if they were plagued by a cluster of timeless warts. Theories varied about the precise use of this site, some more unexpected than others. Beyond the customary feminine fertility explanation, kings were believed to donate their own sacrifice to prompt productive crops. This was not just any prick of blood. The spine of a stingray had to be used to pierce the royal scrotum. Only under these circumstances could the soils receive a droplet of the king's illustrious fluid. Strangely, another rock formation apparently portrayed a man holding his rather enlarged appendage with a huge grin on his face. However, this chap's happy disposition seemed in acute contrast to what the poor king endured. Los Sapos was certainly an unusual site.

The Basics

Synopsis: Absorb Arab hospitality while satisfying your curiosity about ancient societies and Bedouin tradition.

Most useful item to pack: Sunglasses

For further travel information: If travelling in Jordan, be sure to stop at the town of Madaba for its brilliant Byzantine-era mosaic tiles. Madaba offers a smaller base than the congested capital city of Amman and is a convenient stopover when travelling to Petra.

There are daily private tourist buses between Madaba and Petra, which travel along the stunningly curvy King's Highway. Alternatively, a private taxi offers more flexibility over your route. Once in Petra, we stayed at the Crowne Plaza Resort Petra, which is located just a few hundred metres from the Petra Visitor Centre at the entrance to the site. For booking details, refer to crowneplaza.com.

Further details on the evening performance, Petra by Night, can be found at petrabynight.jo.

The Experience

Jordan offers much more than the renowned city of Petra. My two favourite places that we visited on our way to the ancient site made the trip particularly special. Near the capital city of Amman sat Madaba. This smaller centre offered a pleasant base. Its real draw was an intricate patchwork of timeless tiles. The best artwork can be found in the basement of a sixth-century Byzantine church. The ancient cathedral was not obvious from the street, as it has been concealed by the Greek Orthodox Church of St. George. This newer building was built in the 1800s above the original church's foundation, but somehow managed to preserve the lovely tiles. Visitors could now walk amid the historic artistry. Some mosaics depicted animals while others showed trees laden with fruit. An incredibly detailed map formed by these little fragments illustrated how the world was viewed centuries ago. Considering that a building rested over top of the original tiles, the condition of the mosaics was quite astonishing.

From Madaba, we took a private taxi along the King's Highway towards the Dead Sea. The road coiled like a serpent in attack mode. I was travelling with my husband and my parents. We arrived at the Dead Sea's beach, which was less for suntanning and more for lathering on the rejuvenating muds found along the coastline. Once sufficiently smeared, we tentatively stepped into the heavily salted water and slowly eased ourselves in. Like a bodybuilder keen to show his strength, the water quickly buoyed us up. Be warned, however, as it is deceivingly jittery. If we were not careful, the water would quickly flip us over and, in the process, sting our tender eyes with its salinity. We all waded out of the sea with slightly bloodshot eyeballs, some more so than others. At this point, the arid sands of Petra beckoned.

From the Dead Sea, we travelled on a shuttle bus farther south to the site of Petra. I stared out through our vehicle's window at the rough sandstone mountains filling my view. The deep canyon carved long ago from the cliff's edge was now home only to a dry riverbed. I noticed that the sky had taken on a hazy grey, which seemed to meld into the mountainside, only slightly bluer than the beige rock. If it were not for the black bitumen highway that wound through the hills, I bet the scene would be awfully comparable to the view that the Nabataeans had come across a few thousand years earlier. It was easy to picture a train of camels plodding along the gravel, some pulling caravans while others carried the elderly or were laden with supplies. The caravans would have jostled and creaked as they rolled across the stones while shells scrunched underneath. Strange that shells could be so abundant even on the highest ridge of the mountains. They certainly were not carried from the Dead Sea, which was the nearest body of water. Its salted waters housed only the smallest of bacteria, not shell-toting creatures.

After the Nabataeans' caravans had been rolling for days or longer through the dry and hot desert, the protective rock around Petra must have offered an appealing place to pause. Its location was conveniently midway between the Dead Sea and the Gulf of Aqaba. This position offered prime real estate for the Nabataeans, who were a trading people, for the Gulf of Aqaba fed into the Red Sea, which in turn offered relatively easy transport between Africa and the Middle East.

The entrance to the city seemed to be marked by a golden arrow. A narrow fissure had cut eighty metres through yellowish sandstone and left a long, thin crack. This fracture must have appeared like a neon-yellow beacon when sunlight shone through its centre and shadows played off its rocky border. The gap was just wide enough for one caravan. Through this entranceway, the cavity stretched for more than one thousand metres. It zigged and zagged over the entire distance, providing a perfect natural barrier to protect the city. The Nabataeans called this entrance Al Siq.

The great city of Petra was constructed about 2,300 years ago. Travellers needed a place to rest in the harsh desert, while traders wanted people with whom they could transact. The Nabataeans answered this call. They carved temples, chiselled rock tombs and devised an intricate water management system—essential for a desert home. Eventually the Nabataean traders linked up with the Silk Route farther north for access to the markets of the Far East and Europe. They prospered for hundreds of years and grew into a powerful empire. The subsequent downfall of the city of Petra remains a mystery to archaeologists and historians alike. From what they can gather, the residents packed up and left in a slow and organized manner. Few coins or valuables were left, indicating that the people did not vacate in a panic. Perhaps a local economic downturn forced traders to follow business elsewhere. After all, by the fourth century commerce had begun to pick up in Palmyra, Syria. Sadly, for whatever reason, Petra was utterly abandoned. Only local Bedouins knew of the site's existence for centuries afterwards, and it was not until 1812 that a Swiss explorer rediscovered the ancient city.[33]

Remnants of a former dam have been found. Its barrier safeguarded Al Siq from flooding and provided a steady supply of fresh water. Pieces of the stone channel, along with pottery pipes, were detected along the length of Al Siq. These tubes carried fresh water into the city and were even notched with holes, which acted as a filter. After we had walked through Al Siq, the first structure that jumped out at us was a two-storied monument carved into the rocky cliff. The facade was covered with columns, sculptures of goddesses, intricately designed niches and decorative arches. This illustrious backdrop appeared in the movie **Indiana Jones and the Last Crusade** and is commonly referred to as the Treasury.

Truth be told, archaeologists do not actually know the purpose of this structure. Some believe it was a temple, while others think it was used to store documents. To confuse matters even more, a graveyard has been discovered beneath its foundation. This mystery was only the beginning to the city of Petra. Beyond this impressive entrance, the landscape curved, plateaus became exposed and cliff overhangs provided more hidden caverns. Remains of former theatres, colonnaded streets, tombs, a palace, temples, gardens and other places lay waiting for us to explore.

The colonnaded street would have been the activity hub of the city at its peak. This was the marketplace where traders convened and business among the twenty thousand residents took place. There would have been a continual supply of new goods, as historians estimate that the city could hold up to one hundred thousand people.[34] That volume would bring a lot of transient merchants carrying the latest products. Citizens certainly must have made a profitable business of feeding and housing all these visitors. When we walked through, only partial columns remained standing in the market area. Fragments of the stone floor also endured. It was an expansive area, and from here we could appreciate how large Petra had once been. Its stone constructions seemed to go on indefinitely. Most of the sites sat between Al Siq and the Great Temple, covering a distance of four kilometres. Some lined the main track, and side lanes led to additional hidden clefts. We meandered around the site for an entire day. It was also worth venturing beyond the Great Temple to see the Monastery, larger than the Treasury but less ornate.

The city of Petra did not fit within my preconceived image of an archaeological site. There were few stone walls to delineate rooms. Rather, the buildings were constructed right into the cliff face. So when we walked through the valley, stone crags shot straight up beside us, with intricate details carved directly onto their surfaces. Small rectangular openings, usually windows or doors, were scattered across the rock facade. The gaps gave way to larger cavities for storage or living quarters. I recall looking up to where a rectangular niche was cut into the red sandstone cliff. Perhaps it had once been a market stall or a storage vault. There a white donkey stood squarely inside the niche, enjoying the shade. He did not flinch, but remained steadfast, as if caught up in the Mannequin Challenge. These little surprises made it easy to spend the day looking inside rocky caves or scrambling high atop yet another rock-strewn ledge.

Another way to experience Petra was in the dark. Petra by Night tickets were sold separately from the main entrance voucher. The best part was walking down Al Siq while candles lit up the walkway. When we reached the Treasury, Bedouin music played and elderly men, dressed in traditional wear, danced. Admittedly, it was difficult to feel authentic, as the presentation was purely for tourists, but the attendees stayed relatively quiet. The traditional music curled through the night, and candlelight bounced off the rock with a mesmerizing effect.

The Basics

Synopsis: Walk through a traditional Moroccan village of kasbahs, or mud homes, leaning against one another and locked in time.

Most useful item to pack: Fleece jacket

For further travel information: My husband and I visited Aït Benhaddou as part of a tour in December 2008. Only a few days earlier our group had driven through snow in the Atlas Mountains and then camped in the Sahara Desert. It was a trip of contrasts. For more information, refer to geckosadventures.com.

Alternatively, the town of Aït Benhaddou can be visited as a day trip from Marrakesh. For further information, check with your favourite tour company.

The Experience

Aït Benhaddou is the famous site that you never knew that you knew. Not only is this traditional mud village a UNESCO World Heritage Site, but it has been a filming location for movies such as **The Mummy** and **Gladiator**. But somehow the town's population has not been tainted by Hollywood's modern influence. There were no film crews on standby or reams of scaffolding draped in lights when we arrived. In fact, I had to rewatch the films shot in Aït Benhaddou to check that the town we saw was actually the set for these movies. I am not sure how much the town profited by supplying its scenery, but it certainly was not apparent from our casual meanderings through its streets. The mud houses looked well maintained, but no different to those in many of the traditional towns scattered through Morocco's countryside. The interiors appeared as they have for hundreds of years; windows were free of glass, and dirt floors were swept tidy. The Town Planning Division ensured this tradition was maintained, in part to adhere with the criteria required to retain the town's standing with UNESCO.[35]

From a distance, Aït Benhaddou appeared to be a condensed tangle of red mud houses and towers covering the side of a hill. The houses jumbled together, almost pushing one another higher to avoid touching any of the water on the lower ground. The lower valley was left for agriculture. This meant that a fringe of palms and fields encircled the town like a green ring. In the distance, the landscape transformed back to the rolling rust-coloured foothills typically found south of the Atlas Mountain range. Within the green band, low packed-dirt walls outlined small plots of land and doubled as pathways. Locals could continually be seen walking along the dirt rims to visit a neighbour or pop into town.

Once we tramped through the town gates, the streets quietened. Motorized vehicles tended to avoid the community's inner core. Stone and dirt paths curved through the village. A dirt wall towered over the walkways and provided shade. Most of these walls were the sides of houses that butted against the main route. In essence, the street functioned as both a family's front patio and a public thoroughfare.

Residents were clearly accustomed to visitors in their tiny town, a side effect of their fame. They capitalized on this by transforming any vacant street space into a permanent market. Hand-stitched rugs in black and red were strewn across any empty surface. Worn metal pots were stacked on ledges, and large turquoise beaded necklaces hung nearly everywhere. Old wooden doors with brass insignias leaned on an angle. I am not sure that many travellers would have space to pack a clunky full-sized door, but from the number I saw on display, they must have been a popular souvenir. Presumably, local venders were accustomed to shipping the parcels to a buyer's home country. The rugged style would have made for an iconic tabletop.

Between the irregularly shaped stone steps, the twisty streets and an occasional small child running out of a doorway, we kept our eyes focused downward when walking, taking advantage of cleared curbs to step aside and look around. From a distance, all the houses had appeared similar, but up close they differed slightly. One showcased geometric designs carved into the mud around its window holes, whereas the borders around windows of others were painted white. Still other homes had decorative circles cut into their walls. Towers were frequently attached to buildings, as their extra height improved air circulation. In addition to the mud construction, hollow sticks of bamboo or palm stuck out about thirty centimetres at higher points along the walls. During the rains, these eaves ensured that the water drained off the rooftops rather than pooling overhead. Otherwise, the town would have become a mucky mess.

We continued to wind up through the street towards the peak of the hill. Chattering resonated from the houses. There was little privacy, since the buildings opened right onto the street and any open-air area looked directly down onto neighbouring houses. One family invited us inside their home. Everyone from the grandma to the young children smiled as they welcomed us. Their movements flowed in a comfortable style, which grows only after years of living together in close quarters. The kitchen was more a workroom than a social hub. Over time, black smoke had caked the walls, likely from bread baked daily in the charcoal-fuelled clay oven. The stove was made of the same mud cement as the house, but had been fashioned into a dome. An ash-filled arch allowed access into its base, while a triangular tajine pot balanced on top. The earthenware pot possessed the same black tinge as the walls. I had a feeling the grandmother in this household prepared a mean tajine. We circled through to another room where a weaving rack rested against the back wall. White threads hung taught. It was obvious that many rugs and cloths had been woven on this contraption over the years. The edges of the wood gleamed from the oily residue left by the weavers' hands.

The father then led us to the rear of their home, which connected to an open-air animal pen. The air was surprisingly fresh throughout the house, perhaps partially due to the time of year. It was December and cool enough that we wore a light fleece during the day. Throughout the summer, there was likely a fair bit of air flow, as cross breezes would have danced between the scattered windows and open doorways. The animal coop seemed spacious enough for the family's prized possessions. A baby lamb hopped through straw, while two black-and-white sheep foraged through the roughage in search of clover petals. A couple of feet away, a rooster stood tall and a chicken walked along a wooden post lying along the ground. A grey donkey stood calmly in a section of the back corner, cordoned by a low stone wall. The barrier was more superficial than functional, as large gouges distorted sections, but the animals seemed unfussed. They all carried on with their daily scrounging, content in their cozy suite.

We thanked the family for their generosity. They would have received some compensation from the tour company, so it was a fair exchange. Regardless, they seemed quite happy to share their culture. It worked out well for everyone.

We carried on with our upward climb. When we finally arrived at the peak of the town, the view of the valley opened below us. There was little else on the top of the hill; it was mostly just a gravel field. In this case, the journey was more rewarding than the destination. But the view over the town was enlightening. We gained a different perspective from above than we had from walking up or from inside the buildings. The rooftops of some homes had become extended rooms. Pottery jugs lined the entire top of one house. I am not sure what one does with fifty pots. Maybe the owner did not trust the town's irrigation system and collected his own rainwater. More likely, however, they were inventory to ensure the street markets were well stocked. A young man sat on another rooftop. His feet hung over the edge while he peered at something down below, hidden from our view. That sight was probably the most genuine: a typical day in the life of a teenager watching his world go by.

The Basics

Synopsis: Witness crumbling Incan ruins marking the only battle in which the Spanish conquistadors did not triumph.

Most useful item to pack: Spanish–English phrase book

For further travel information: A convenient train offers a great way to travel from Cusco to Ollantaytambo and then onward to Machu Picchu. During the rainy season, the Cusco-to-Ollantaytambo leg is covered by a **collectivo**, or minibus.

Once in Ollantaytambo, we stayed at a quaint little hotel, Sauce Hostal, located between the main square and the ruins. For more information, refer to hostalsauce.com.pe.

The Incan ruins are a five-minute walk down the street from the hotel. For an informative description of the site, refer to theonlyperuguide. com/peru-guide/the-sacred-valley/highlights/ollantaytambo-ruins.

The Experience

It seems impossible to talk about travels in Peru without mentioning the illustrious Machu Picchu. Despite this pinnacle's title as the most visited travel destination in the country, the ruins were only discovered about a hundred years ago. Even Incan records do not speak of it, leaving much about the ancient peak a mystery. My memories are less alluring. Indeed, on the day that we visited this prominent peak, its terraces were shrouded in a thick white fog. There were no jaw-dropping views. Our eyes were instead glued to our steps so as not to slip on a stone slick with rain and moss. Rain lashed out during our travels to reach this mighty mountain and tempered only slightly while we wandered through the excavated wonders. Of our day spent scrambling around the oft-favoured Machu Picchu, the most unique sight was of a bulbous viscacha—a rabbit-like rodent related to the chinchilla. You may wonder what ancient remnant this viscacha epitomized; however, it was no artifact at all. The viscacha was perched sombrely on a stone wall, which had come into view as the fog drifted slightly. The critter posed for one of the mere five photos we captured at Machu Picchu that were not just cloud cover. So, although it was a cute fellow, I am unable to honestly report that this popular site was my favourite Incan ruin.

This takes us a step back into the Sacred Valley. This valley was like a pearl necklace that traced Incan villages along the Urubamba River. The narrowly chiselled ravine started at Cusco, the diva of Incan cities, which offered ancient sites, lush accommodation, eclectic restaurants and a peppy personality. The valley then led through a few other Incan villages until it reached Ollantaytambo. Beyond Ollantaytambo, train tracks extended onward to Aguas Calientes, the drop-off point to visit Machu Picchu. The overall circuit contained an interconnected delight of sights in a relatively compact area. Whereas Aguas Calientes turned out to be touristy, busy and verging on tacky, Ollantaytambo remained as composed as it surely was thousands of years ago.

Ancient Incan storehouses towered over one side of the town, while exposed terraced hills crowned with a grand fortress dominated the opposite side. From a distance, the storage huts looked like a piece of honeycomb stuck to the rocky cliff face. After climbing a narrow, dusty track, we could see that the complex was composed of tiered townhouse-like stone structures. A couple of dogs from town followed us up the narrow and arduous rocky path, familiar with its terrain. They played and wagged their tails for the most part, not noticing the steep ascent. During our return, they proceeded to latch onto the next set of hikers taking the same route. It seemed the dogs had designated themselves as chaperones for anyone climbing to the storehouses.

Expansive views from atop the adjacent terraced hillside exposed the valley beyond. The scene directly below highlighted a maze of ceremonial walls surrounded by the ancient structures from which we had started our climb. In the centre, a strangely familiar Inca Bucks Coffee Shop displayed a neon sign whose lettering imitated an all-too-recognizable green font known to coffee lovers worldwide.

We spent another morning walking alongside the Urubamba River to see an old quarry located six kilometres southeast of town. Little remained except vacant spaces on the rock face. Long ago, heavy boulders had been floated upstream, manually manoeuvered out of the river and then chiselled to engineer the fortress city of Ollantaytambo. An occasional dud stone lingered along the path, apparently unworthy of transporting farther and left where it lay for hundreds of years.

Ollantaytambo was once a hub for the Incas' administrative, agricultural, religious and military activities. It seemed things had changed little in this town over the years. During our visit, farmers still tilled the fields using plows hauled by pairs of oxen. A father directed while his eldest son balanced on a wooden tee fastened to the cows' harness. A younger son walked behind to gently steer the contraption. Ancient stone homes were spun around the town square like a spider's web, yet definitively sturdier. These buildings were once home to ancient Incas and now housed present-day families. Plaster had filled time-worn defects, and new wooden doors updated the entrances. Some panels were freshly painted in a sky blue, while others peeled to reveal layers of faded blue paint curling down to darkened, washed-out wood.

The locals held a tender pride and rightly so. Their home was the sole site where Incas had thwarted the Spanish conquistadors who were attacking villages throughout the valley. Ollantaytambo's ingenious irrigation system not only offered reliable water, but had also saved the city. In 1536, the Incan residents remained safe in their terraced refuge while their leader, Manco Inca, flooded the valley below. The Spanish had not anticipated this sort of warfare and quickly fled. Unfortunately, it was a short-lived reprieve, as the conquistadors swiftly returned. They brought reinforcements and eventually conquered Ollantaytambo's Incan residents.

During the two days we spent around the town, we enjoyed its relaxed vibe. Children tossed balloons along its cobblestone streets. Their mothers sold maize and popcorn snacks from handwoven baskets. We found a favourite café, serving strong coffee and dishing up a perfect vista at the corner of the main square. One day, everyone flowed out from the central church in their best dress, celebrating a local wedding. Buses lined the square to shuttle family and friends to a reception. It seemed that the entire town had joined in to send their best wishes to the bride and groom. On another occasion, two young brothers played along the sidewalk and seemed particularly intrigued by us as we lounged with coffee at our outdoor table. They proceeded to giggle at our limited Spanish. The youngest quickly lost his shyness and tentatively stepped out from behind his elder brother's protective height, all three feet of it. The boys never tired of our teasing, especially a particularly catchy joke of pretending to stretch their noses out from their faces like an elastic band. They provided endless renditions of shocked expressions followed by a giddy laugh when their invisible nose was released and supposedly snapped back to their face.

Ollantaytambo may not enjoy the fame of Machu Picchu, but its ruins were indeed impressive. This setting, coupled with the locals' touch of reality, shed light on what appeared to be an authentic Peruvian community. People worked hard to earn a living, but seemed focused on friends, family and enjoying time together. I got the impression that the locals appreciated the interest and financial support that tourism had brought their town, but they did not let it consume their lives. Normalcy endured.

The Basics

Synopsis: Amble through an enormous ancient Mediterranean city whose endless architectural delights reveal traces of Roman and Greek empires.

Most useful items to pack: Wind-resistant jacket and comfortable shoes

For further travel information: The town of Selçuk provides a convenient base from which to visit the ruins of Ephesus. Check your favourite guidebook or social media site for current recommendations because my referrals from the year 2000 would be sorely out of date.

Dodge the crowds and visit in the winter months. You will be more likely to find your own corner of the site during the shoulder or low seasons, as estimates range between two and three million visitors annually.

The Experience

Ephesus was not your average port city. There was no hint of the grit or roughness often associated with seaports. Streets were lined with white marble slabs and carved columns. The ruins of Ephesus covered a behemoth of an ancient site. We walked for hours, and although we visited seventeen years ago, the memory still stands prominent in my mind. I was taken by the sheer grandeur of the site. An ornate wall of a building on one side was followed by a few hundred metres of palatial colonnaded street. Not far away, tucked into a small rocky area, we found a cordoned-off section with archaeologists actively excavating pottery bits and old walls. Farther afield rested large amphitheatres and the nobility's residences. Some areas of the site looked like a football field but filled with row upon row of stone blocks. Each one varied only slightly. The ruins outlined an image of a bustling ancient city with enough vacant space to inspire your imagination.

One of the oldest sites was a temple dedicated to Ephesus' fertility goddess, Artemis. Confusingly, a Greek goddess held the same name but was a hunter. Little evidence of this majestic temple remained at the site itself because most of its original features resided elsewhere in museums. Despite this lack of visibility, the Temple of Artemis ranks as one of the Seven Wonders of the Ancient World. It was a huge temple in its day. Indications imply the site was initially more shrine than temple. The very earliest sacred site was thought to have been built around a fallen meteorite in the 800s BC. The locals believed the stone that had plunged from the heavens was sacred.

By the seventh century BC, the city had grown into a bustling port town with trained architects. Grand columns and expansive floor stones were constructed around Artemis' tiny shrine, and an enormous sanctuary was created in its place. Over the years, the temple was destroyed by fire, wars, an earthquake and other mishaps. It was always rebuilt, tempting fate before it was once again obliterated. Despite the deconstruction and removal of its remains, Artemis' majestic appeal was still apparent in the area when we visited the temple. Her original statues had long since been removed. In their place, realistic copies stood scattered around the site. To my untrained eye, the copies appeared impressive despite being replicas. Artemis' characteristic image was easily identifiable by the dozen of her signature breasts that swayed uniformly below her shoulders.

When we arrived at the amphitheatre, the Great Theatre, we had the entire place to ourselves. It had been built in the third century BC.[36] My husband talked in a hushed tone from centre stage, and his voice clearly carried to where I lounged in one of the higher rows. The semicircular seating could hold approximately twenty-five thousand people. It was hard to imagine such a large production over a thousand years ago.

The library astounded us. It was absent of old books—and most of its walls, for that matter. But the one remaining wall looked as if someone had been overcome by psychedelic visions while engraving its facade. There were three doorways. Each door frame could fit three or four people standing on each other's shoulders and was protected by two mammoth pillars rising twice as high as the door frame itself. Everything looked to be made of white marble, lightly swirled with the rock's distinctive grey pattern. Between the pillars in each of the four sets stood a sculpture of a goddess. Two were lucky enough to have kept their heads, but the other two had been tragically decapitated. Intricate carvings of decorative leaves, swirls and other fancy designs topped everything like a layer of piped icing. And then there was the second floor. It would take pages to describe the details of this one wall of one building left partially standing on a single street of Ephesus.

Ephesus is a city to experience for yourself. Only in person can you take a deep breath and absorb the atmosphere of the vast marble streets. It felt as if we could almost hear the ancient stories seeping out through the cracks. If you have any interest in the ancient Persians and Romans, Ephesus is a must-see site. Its depth of history and detailed ruins were mind-boggling, even if my memories have romanticized the experience over the years.

The Basics

Synopsis: Meet talented Yemenis who introduce foreigners to their ancient cities, designed with an incomparable artistic flare.

Most useful items to pack: Local currency and bargaining sway for the markets

For further travel information: I travelled to Sana'a from Oman, where I was living at the time. There were no direct flights between Yemen and Oman, but many airlines offered tickets via the United Arab Emirates. Regrettably, at the time of this writing, the conflict in Yemen has made the security situation uncertain and at times virtually impossible for nonessential travels. Check with your home country travel advisories before making any trip plans.

The Experience

It breaks my heart to see the destruction that so many regular Yemeni families have endured with the recent bombings and attacks in their country. On top of war, extreme food shortages and outbreaks of cholera have devastated communities. I visited Yemen both for work and pleasure in the mid-2000s. I found it to be a country full of gifted people. The kindness and enduring spirit of so many individuals touched my heart. Images from those daily interactions run through my head when I recall this lovely country. These memories are reminders of people who intrigued me with their vitality and initiative. Consider the Queen of Sheba, who reigned as a legendary figure across Yemen's sands over three thousand years ago.[37] Sheba is held in high esteem across Christianity, Islam and Judaism, although her story varies somewhat across the texts. For more about her intriguing story, check out Wafaa Abdulaali's article entitled "Echoes of a Legendary Queen" (see Bibliography). Likewise, many compelling women live in modern-day Yemen.

There was a lady in my office's accounting department whose true passion was to play the electric guitar. From her smart phone, she replayed videos of her music for me. She rocked that guitar. I often wonder if she carried on in finance or has since started a band. In the sections described below are other remarkable people I met during my visits. I stayed in Sana'a, but explored its old city, Old Sana'a, and was lucky enough to join a day trip to Kawkaban.

Old Sana'a

Old Sana'a is the oldest and most distinct quarter of Sana'a, the capital city of Yemen. It has a comfortably cool climate due to its elevation of 2,200 metres. It also has a long, resilient history. After all, not many places can claim that they have been inhabited for over 2,500 years and have earned UNESCO's blessing for their architectural oddities.[38] We entered Old Sana'a's ageless centre through a fortified wall, accessible via Bab Al Yemen ("Gate of Yemen"). The clouds of exhaust and piercing horns grew softer from inside this old centre. Its streets were too slender for modern vehicles. Mud-brick buildings lined the streets. These narrow constructs reached up to eight storeys and are thought to represent some of the earliest skyscrapers. Windows looked out like attentive eyes, framed by dazzling white paint in contrast to their brownish brick walls and bearing witness to everything that happened on their watch. Some windows were outlined with just a simple rectangular perimeter of white paint, while others were embellished by more decorative styles including arches, geometric designs or squiggly arrows. Some were moon-shaped stained-glass windows called **qamariya**. Their white borderlines were visible in the daytime, and their coloured streaks reflected onto neighbouring walls under moonlight.[39]

From the top of one building, we peered across a patchwork of square roofs, all built at varying heights. The structures seemed crunched together as if compressed by the surrounding walls. Every house within the 360-degree radius held at least one satellite dish; often multiple spheres dotted the flat plateaus. White water tanks, gently heated by the midday sun, were also scattered across the rooftops. Laundry hung on strings fastened to the brick walls, and metal buckets filled with potted plants balanced on ledges. These likely sprouted a mélange of cooking herbs used to flavour the many exquisite Yemini dishes. The buildings were tied in ribbons of loosely swaying electrical wires, which criss-crossed the streets in a muddle. It was no surprise that generators had become a necessary standby for power. Among this array, my eyes were drawn to one spot where two contented goats rested on a bed of green roughage. Their raised enclosure filled the rooftop of one of the small lower buildings, but the docile animals seemed oblivious of the street activity not far below.

At ground level, the streets were a winding mass of market stalls adorned with coloured tarps. Mounds of spices including chili, corn kernels, garlic and dried beans filled white cotton hampers that stood three feet tall and lined the stone streets. When we first crossed through Bab Al Yemen, a few children bounded towards my husband and me. The kids were filled with smiles and offered to introduce us to their beloved city. Typically, I do not like to support children selling any service, as I would rather they were in school. However, it was the weekend.

As we walked forward, a young boy trailed us closely and soon jumped closer to offer his advice on random stores' merchandise. Inevitably, he eagerly offered to show us to his family's shops, all while explaining interesting local history. As we walked past the dark doorway of a tall building, the boy pointed it out as the grinding tower. Inside, a camel harnessed to a stone mill slowly circled the small room. His leather binding acted as a lever that triggered the stone to grind wheat kernels into a fluffy flour. This traditional method produced the main ingredient for the ever-tasty Yemeni **malawah** bread. The camel seemed all too familiar with his venue and content to be away from the heat of the day. The shadowed room was perhaps a little dusty and the work monotonous, but likely no worse than the conditions faced by many low-income residents on a daily basis. We continued to peruse the streets, stopping at intriguing vendors for some warm-hearted bargaining battles. It was a good day.

Over a year later, I returned to Sana'a to visit my husband while he was based there on rotation. Old Sana'a's charms unsurprisingly enticed us back. No sooner had we entered through Bab Al Yemen than a couple of kids ran our way. One boy started chatting and welcomed us back. My instinct marked him as quite a charmer—spinning stories of recollecting former visitors was quite an entrepreneurial move. He would have encountered countless foreigners since our last visit. But I was in for a shock. This young lad would indeed prove himself, for he recounted the specific items I had bought the year before. He even described the shops where I had bargained for the items. My purchases were not particularly noteworthy, so his precision was extraordinary. If this boy could market his retention skills, he would surely be a rich man.

Kawkaban

By happenstance, another visit coincided with the annual company day trip held by my husband's office in Sana'a. The road trip was scheduled to visit the ancient clifftop town of Kawkaban (pronounced "Cocoban"). The town was known for its school of music back in the fifteenth century. Our group's bus parked at the base of the Kawkaban cliff, in the small rocky town of Shibam. This location should not be confused with the UNESCO-recognized town of Shibam, which is situated in the Hadramaut district of Yemen.

We followed a gravel trail that skirted the 350-metre cliff face and led us straight into Kawkaban's dirt streets. There were a few people rambling about. A young girl, probably about seven years old, latched onto my hand. She asked if I spoke English and where I was from. When she learned that I was Canadian, she quickly asked if I spoke French. Embarrassingly, my French was poor at that time, and she spoke more fluently than I. She went on to explain that she had learned to speak five languages just from talking with visitors in her town. Imagine if your young niece or daughter was exploring your neighbourhood streets and talking with strangers, only to return home speaking five languages. This Yemini girl's ambition was impressive. Keep in mind that Kawkaban was a small town where strangers could be trusted and locals watched out for one another. As foreigners, we were welcomed by the people of this village, who were happy for us to wander their streets. They were also known to offer refuge to citizens from the lower Shibam village in times of trouble.

This girl did not ask for money. She was merely happy to walk and talk as we meandered around town. For some reason, the sandy mud-brick houses, reminiscent of the fascinating Old Sana'a, exerted less of an impression than the indelible mark left by this pint-sized girl. She garnered such potential if only she could be given the opportunity to realize it. The current war's destruction has most likely crushed any such possibility for her hopes to materialize.

This chapter is for the light and airy places. These getaway adventures may not gain attention as the focal point of a trip or have enough substance to warrant hopping on a plane to fly across the world. Yet some travels can get rather repetitive without something to shake things up. Your gut may be begging for a dash of chili to spice up the experience. I suggest you listen to it.

By our fourth cloud forest in Central America, I had surpassed my fill of muddy trekking. Similarly, after perusing the fifth cathedral adorned in intricate stain-glassed windows in France and Italy, my interest began to wane. I mean this as no disrespect to those sites, as they were spectacular in their own right. Admittedly, it is in my nature to crave something more. In my search for new experiences, each place naturally builds my expectations for the thrill around the next corner. This is the opportune time to throw something new into the mix.

Spending an afternoon out of your comfort zone might brighten those glazed eyes. You may just surprise yourself and find that the most memorable moment of your trip jumps out when it is least expected. These are the getaway adventures that I refer to in this chapter. They pack a poignant punch. These little nuggets can revive your day and reenergize your entire trip in the process.

The Basics

Synopsis: Lunge across the surf, and let the waves propel your body with their power.

Most useful item to pack: Bathing suit, or "togs" as they are called in Australia

For further travel information: North Stradbroke Island is just off the coast of Brisbane, Queensland. For information on transport, accommodation and other up-to-date details, refer to stradbrokeisland.com/straddie.

The Experience

I was living and working in Brisbane in the late 1990s when a few friends and I escaped to North Stradbroke Island for the weekend. This destination, a favourite among locals, felt like a different world compared to the city, but it took a ferry ride less than an hour long to reach. Straddie, as the island is commonly referred to, had a dynamic environment. Half of the island is protected under the Naree Budjong Djara National Park's conservation efforts. The other half is a mix of coves, camping areas, the occasional road and small communities. Take your pick of soft sandy beaches framed by gnarly eucalyptus, sand dunes speckled with grey creeping grass or maze-like mangrove forests along the coastline. The island now has its own travel website and is home to a World Junior Surfing Champion, Ethan Ewing. So my memory of it as a hidden treasure seems sorely outdated. Nevertheless, the island's marketing theme is grounded in the familiar holiday concept of slowing down, and its gorgeous scenery lives on.[40]

We landed on Straddie for one central purpose: to learn how to bodysurf. The location made it a compelling proposition. First, a short ferry ride shuttled us across the channel from Brisbane, leaving maximum time of our precious weekend to spend on the island. Second, the shores offered a mélange of beach environments, from pristine white sand to rocky heads and secluded inlets. Lastly, the island boasted a chilled-out vibe. There were no pretentious swimmers or cocky surfers to mock us newbies at the sport. We found a relatively empty beach, free from other swimmers so that we could concentrate on our bodysurfing rather than on dodging people.

We opted to self-instruct. After all, bodysurfing requires no equipment and is not an overly technical sport. It is like regular surfing but without the board.

Nowadays, fins are recommended, and streamlined handplanes are marketed to improve the surfing experience. However, we kept it simple—our bathers and a good Australian friend feeding us some helpful hints. The concept was straightforward: stretch your arm out in front of you, catch the wave with your body, aim towards your fingertips and, if all goes to plan, glide towards shore. If the waves are coming left to right, then you jump towards the right and extend your right arm. Alternatively, if the waves are curving towards the left, then stretch your left arm out and leap leftward. Soon enough, I started to get the hang of the timing. Jump too soon and I was doused by the wave. Too late and I hovered stationary in the water. On the well-timed runs, I was carried close to shore. It felt like gliding across the ocean, a moment of pure freedom.

Our morning of bodysurfing turned into the perfect getaway activity. It forced my mind to focus on the task at hand so stress and random worries niggling in my head quickly evaporated. When I felt tired, the solution was simple. It was just a matter of standing up in the shallow water and taking a few steps to the beach before flopping down on a towel. When the sun's rays felt too hot, it was time to get back in the water. When our stomachs started to growl, a nearby barbecue shack or smoothie bar replenished our bellies. The weekend was an ideal no-fuss getaway with friends, a little exercise and the satisfaction of learning something new.

For me, the fun started to subside when my mind began to play tricks. Thoughts started to whirl through my head: "That wave looks too dark. I think I see a shadow." Despite the incredibly low chance of an accident, my imagination took hold of me, and my enjoyment fizzled. There were no sharks in the area on the day that we were out at the beach. Besides, the risk of a shark attack is extremely low. Excellent lifeguards keep watch over Australia's coastline, and most beaches are cordoned by protective nets. In 2016, there were only twenty-six shark attacks across the entire country, eight of which resulted in no injury whatsoever.[41] I should have been more concerned about getting hurt in a car accident on the drive from the ferry, but this logic did not seem to stick. Regardless, it was still a great weekend. My advice is to try the sport. Most people love it.

Between the warm air and our exertion in the water, it seemed perfect to end the day with a chilled glass of Australia's Hunter Valley Semillon Sauvignon Blanc wine and a plate of barbecued Moreton Bay bugs. These **bugs** were the local specialty, but not insects, as one might initially assume. These crustaceans looked and tasted like a cross between lobster and prawns but with the lightness of crab meat. The tail's edible flesh tasted especially exquisite.

So if you find yourself in Queensland and want to try bodysurfing in an idyllic cerulean ocean setting, consider North Stradbroke Island. Straddie offered the perfect location, with gentle waves and an unoccupied surf.

The Basics

Synopsis: Scramble through tight squeezes and across knobby rocks inside a cave blanketed in a crystal-like motif.

Most useful item to pack: Clothing in a stretchable fabric for crawling and climbing

For further travel information: For information on cave tours, regional accommodations and other visitor information, refer to margaretriver.com/members/ngilgi-cave.

The Experience

We spent a few days in the oceanfront city of Perth before heading southwest towards the wine region around Margaret River. A glut of wineries had opened their doors for visitors to explore their vineyards and sample an array of grape varieties. Many labels were only available from the cellar door and were not sold on the international market. My husband and I happily spent a few days swishing, spitting and becoming closely acquainted with the wines. Eventually, however, our palates begged for a reprieve. The opportunity to spend a morning scrambling through underground caves seemed to offer the perfect diversion.

We selected a three-hour tour through Ngilgi Cave, near the town of Yallingup. There are numerous limestone caves in the region open to climbers, but we opted to visit Ngilgi Cave because it was listed as one of the highlights for the southwest region of Western Australia by Lonely Planet's **Australia Travel Guide** (see Bibliography). The cave was named for an Aboriginal legend about a clash between a good-hearted spirit named Ngilgi and the evil-spirited Wolgine. Ngilgi won the scuffle and earned title to the cave. The cave was an old, cantankerous cavity containing tight squeezes, steep dips and surprise openings connected by interlinking tunnels, which the guides appeared to know intimately. Our small group—my husband, about seven other visitors and I—were keen to get exploring on the morning we met. We all fastened bright orange, blue or red helmets kitted out with individual headlamps over our heads. Soon we were tramping along a short pathway, which veered towards a sunken pocket in the ground.

Inside the cave, the sides, bottom and ceiling were a mass of stalagmites and stalactites. These cones of solidified minerals had formed over hundreds of years as, drop by drop, water seeped along the cave's ridges. Stalagmites rose from the ground, whereas stalactites hung from the ceiling. In between these icicle-like formations, rough crystals in varying tones of amber and orange covered broad slabs. They looked fuzzy, seeming to transform into weird shapes wherever we looked. Some sections of rock were dark brown with white edges, almost as if a fungus had grown across them. On one piece, it appeared as if someone had poured molasses across the tawny rock and left it to harden. Other sections looked like a candy maker had attempted to pull a batch of caramel taffy but had given up and left a swirling mess on the rocks.

The guide then took us deeper into the core of the cave. We stepped off the grated metal walkway, which was open to the public, and headed down a narrow path of dirt and rock. The rock that bordered our trail was damp and steep. It took many twists and odd balancing manoeuvers to descend without scraping ourselves. Water droplets plunked into unseen puddles behind dark boulders. I looked down one vertical five-foot section and wedged my back against the rock. Bit by bit, my hand grasped a groove, and my foot eventually sank onto a toehold for support. Inch by inch, I shuffled downward.

We enjoyed a fun scramble through the dark gaps and short chutes under-ground. Our headlamps became our best friends along these sections. When we reached the bottom, it felt good to jump down onto a dirt floor. The solid flatness was comforting after contorting ourselves around and over jagged rocks. Our guide pointed out some old bones along one side of the cavern. Long ago, animals had picked the bones clean and left them to decompose ever so slowly. We were careful to avoid kicking these skeletal remains as we walked past. They were clearly a talking point that allowed the guides to explain the history and mysteries of the cave. Bones from kangaroos, possums and even a tough little Tasmanian devil lay throughout the cave system. What a dismal place to spend your final days, in this dark rocky abyss.

The climb back up offered a few trickier parts—tight squeezes, as they were called. To get up these little beauties, we slithered one by one through a crevasse made of rough rock at about an eighty-degree angle. The gap was not much wider than our shoulders, and our helmets just scraped through. It was a moment to push any claustrophobic tendencies to the far recesses of my mind. The air seemed to get thicker, and I felt the humidity get denser while I heaved my shoul-ders up through the opening. My hips swivelled and my buttocks ricocheted off the overhead rubble as I slowly raised myself to the next rocky platform. Phew. Somewhere, I had lost a few drops of sweat, which should eventually find their way to a stalagmite and donate whatever salts and minerals I had to give.

After three hours of weaving up, down and around while underground, the sight of sunlight was startling. The exit from the cave inclined gently, and we all casually sauntered out from its mouth. It felt nice to stand upright, but I was sad to have already finished exploring the unusual world below. After the fun of scrambling through fissures and exploring bizarre subterranean formations, being back on the surface felt a little dull. A glass of Mongrel Creek's Cabernet Franc Merlot seemed back in play for a post-caving dinner.

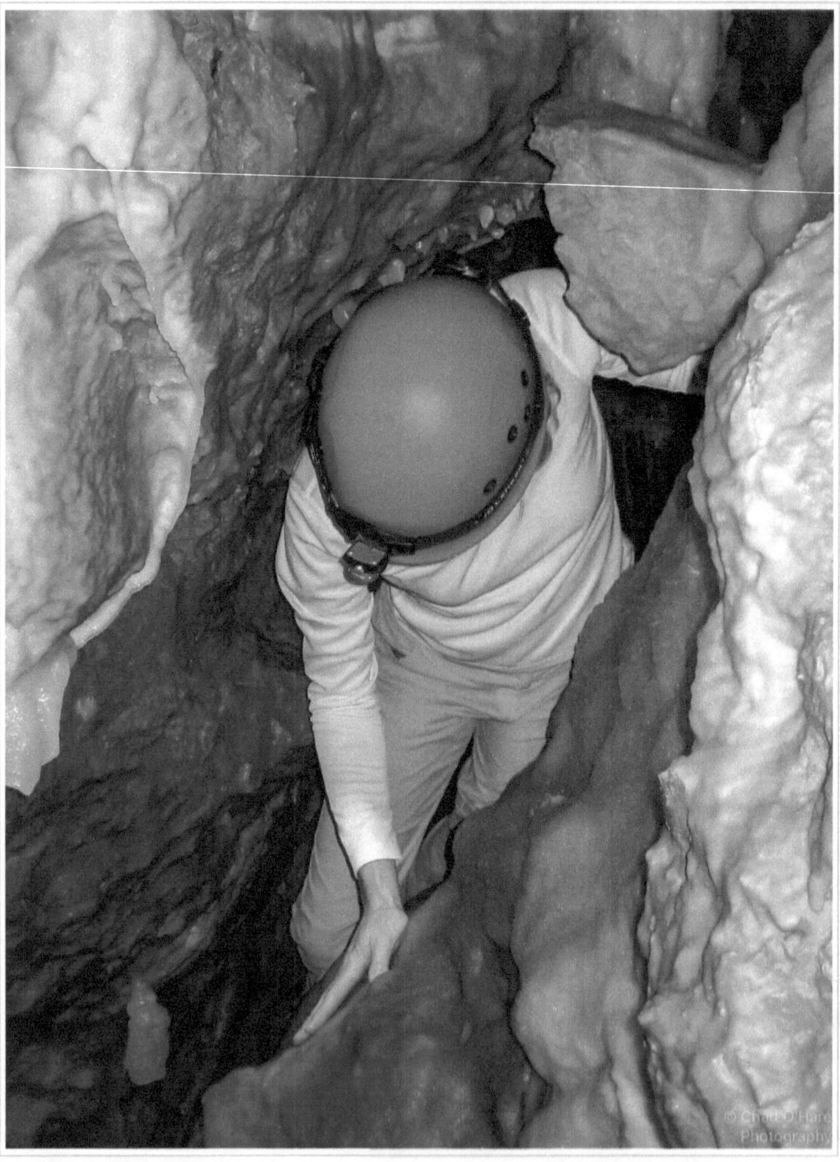

The Basics

Synopsis: Drift past corals, turtles and sharks or delve along a sunken wreck under brilliantly clear waters, likely without another dive boat in sight.

Most useful items to pack: PADI dive card and logbook

For further travel information: The Oman Dive Center, located between Qantab and Barr al Jissah, was close enough to visit on a day trip from Muscat. PADI-approved instructors offered a range of recreational dives and courses. The Oman Dive Center still operates a Facebook page, but from recent reviews on TripAdvisor.com, it appears that the center has been rebranded. The resort has undergone a refurbishment and is no longer the casual "cheap and cheerful" place to hang out as it was when we visited. It is not clear whether Oman Dive Center operates in tandem with or changed its name to Muscat Hills Resort, but PADI-approved dive courses are still offered at the Qantab location, according to both Facebook pages.

For further information on the Oman Dive Center, see facebook.com/odcqantab.

For further information on Muscat Hills Resort, see facebook.com/muscathillsresort.

A list of PADI-recommended dive sites in Oman can be found at padi.com/scuba-vacations/oman.

The Experience

The Oman Dive Center was nestled within a naturally protected inlet, perfectly situated with its own small, isolated beach. Layer upon layer of rock skirted the shoreline and encircled the beach. White cabanas were scattered to one side of the sandy area for those who wanted to stay overnight. The Oman Dive Center was fully equipped with a pool for training exercises, transfer boats and all the necessary apparatus. The instructors were PADI certified, so the location ticked all our prerequisites. My husband and I had already taken our certification course in Calgary, Canada, before moving to Oman. We had the choice of completing our open-water dive in the frigid waters of Lake Minnewanka or waiting until we arrived at the balmy Gulf of Oman. The latter option was clearly our preference.

Butterflies danced the salsa inside my stomach as we loaded up the dive boat, rechecked the oxygen tanks and reviewed our program with the instructor. The boat zipped us around the rocky heads to a nearby sheltered cove. It was the perfect location to dip fifteen feet under clear waters to a sandy bottom and test our classroom skills. After a few minutes of jostling ourselves into position, we both tipped backwards off the boat. Oman's ocean temperatures typically ranged from nineteen degrees Celsius in the winter to a lovely twenty-eight degrees in the summer. The shallower waters just off the beach could reach temperatures in the low thirties by midsummer. During our dive, the water temperature hardly varied from the air's warmth. There was no icy jolt when we plunged into the water as we had come to expect at the pool in Calgary.

After a speedy flip, my head promptly popped out of the water, and I motioned the perfunctory **okay** signal to our instructor. Tenderly dunking underwater, I apprehensively checked whether unknown creatures lurked below my fins. My nerves settled after I realized that the visibility was astoundingly clear and there were no ominous dark shadows. For a novice such as me, this was a good sign.

The dive started out as a mundane series of exercises so that we could perform the prescribed test manoeuvers to qualify for our open-water dive certificate. Then the bottom of the ocean gradually wavered. **Bloop.** I was suddenly peering at eye level with the top of the water. After an exhale and a small adjustment to my buoyancy control, down I sank. Unfortunately, my focus on the underwater sights faltered as I continued to oscillate between the vibrant fish playground below and the choppy waves above. Luckily the sandy floor underfoot was free from coral, so there was little risk that an unexpected descent could cause any damage to the seabed. And we were in reasonably shallow water, so my ears were not screaming with discomfort. However, the Oman Dive Center earned some business when I returned a few weeks later to attend their buoyancy class.

The inlets around the Oman Dive Center were perfect for beginner divers. Although I spent more time focused on my position than viewing the fish, an abundance of finned friends drifted about. The waters offered a pristine environment in which to enjoy turtles, rays and all sorts of striped fish. Experienced divers could choose from an array of options, as advanced technical dives were more common in the region than my elementary excursion.

The most popular dive site near Muscat is around the Daymaniyat Islands. These nine islands are located seventeen kilometres offshore. If you are looking for drop-offs, caves and thick coral, these islands deliver. Diverse aquatic life, including sharks, stingrays and turtles, cruises these reefs. The occasional whale shark has also been spotted. For fans of wreck dives, the Royal Navy of Oman sank the SNV *Al Munasir* a few years ago specifically for diving enthusiasts. It is located about thirty minutes from the Oman Dive Center.

For even more frontier diving, check out options around the Musandam Peninsula. We drove to Oman's most northern point on a separate trip. This section of Oman is physically separated from the rest of the country by a strip of United Arab Emirates' land. The border crossings were straightforward, so even though we had to exit Oman, enter the United Arab Emirates and then re-enter Oman, the trip was not too gruelling, and it was hands-down worthwhile. The geology along the drive was spectacular. We followed stratified rocky crevasses, dry boulder-strewn riverbeds and rough mountains, which jutted in all directions. In a few places, the landscape looked like it had been relocated from the moon. Black sheets of rock draped across plateaus. The drive was remote, passing through only a handful of tiny villages. It would have been tough to make a living in these far-flung regions, for the fields were only dried mud flats when we passed through in July. By the time we reached the coast, the road had turned into a white strip of gravel, which twisted in hairpin curves down to the water's edge.

The Musandam Peninsula is a sinewy piece of land on the cusp of the Persian Gulf. It sits in a belt of water referred to as the Strait of Hormuz. Instead of diving, we opted to cruise the waters in a dhow. Multicoloured fish came to the top of the water, almost as if we were snorkelling from the edge of the boat. The Persian Gulf's water was incredibly clear. The currents can be strong, so diving in this region is better suited for more experienced divers, which I clearly was not. Based on our local intel and the region's isolated beauty, these pristine waters are another top destination for diving in Oman.

The Basics

Synopsis: Ski down slopes across two countries with a pass that gives you access to 196 lifts.

Most useful item to pack: SPF 30+ sunscreen

For further travel information: If you are spending two or three days at Les Portes du Soleil, discounted multi-day "duo" or "trio" passes can be purchased in advance. For more information on the ski area, refer to en.portesdusoleil.com/winter.html.

The Experience

After a little over an hour's drive southeast from Geneva, our tires rolled over freshly packed snow in the parking lot at Morzine. Dark-wooded chalets lined the streets. This mountain town was one of our favourite gateways to Les Portes du Soleil ("The Doors of the Sun") ski area. We could have started from any one of twelve villages, all of which offered resorts that connected to a massive matrix of runs and lifts. On the Swiss side, Champéry was a little farther away but allowed us to start skiing at the eastern end of the range. Les Portes du Soleil is the oldest cross-border ski region on our planet. A ski pass grants access to six hundred kilometres of terrain across the Swiss Valais and France Chablais alpine regions. This giant ski hill is the only resort where I have skied across two countries in one day. We started in France, skied to Switzerland and then skied back to France, in addition to riding a gondola, cable car, chairlift and T-bar to climb the seemingly endless humps and ridges.

For some reason, skiing in Europe felt so civilized. Perhaps it was the aperitif served soon after we entered a hillside lodge for lunch, or maybe it was the spacious gondolas that shuttled us from the parking lot to the summit, tempting us with panoramic views. Ski tickets were one of the few things that were less expensive in Switzerland than in Canada. Presumably the higher concentration of ski hills across the Alps, combined with a denser population, drove the price down. Whatever the reason, I was not complaining.

The runs covered such a wide area that the hill did not feel crowded. Lift lineups rarely lasted more than five or ten minutes. Typically, we encountered the longest line waiting for the initial gondola from the parking lot to the first run. Beyond that, people scattered. There were nearly two hundred lifts, so none were overly crowded. From one ridge we could look down onto runs that led into Switzerland in one direction and France in the other. If there had not been signposts to advise skiers of the borders, it would have been impossible for me to know which slope led into which country. In both nations' towns across the range, clusters of wooden chalets lined the streets, along with patios serving up meals and apparel stores promoting the latest winter styles.

In my view, the only town that projected a truly unique appearance was Avoriaz. I was startled the first time the tall buildings came into sight as I glided around a bend. As a friend told me, the town reminded her of Gondor from the movie **Lord of the Rings**, with its towering buildings crammed across the variant terrain, even butting close to the town's rocky cliff perimeter. The structures looked like clutches of bats clinging together to form a patchwork of rooms. Avoriaz's apartments bore a completely different style than the typical two-storey peaked chalets found in other villages across the mountain.

The best part of skiing at Les Portes du Soleil was the variety of runs. The hill offered such a mélange of runs, or **pistes**, to explore that every trip was different. From Geneva, the relatively short drive made it an easy day getaway to feel totally immersed in the snowy Alps.

The Basics

Synopsis: Work up an appetite snowshoeing under the stars through the Jura Mountains' evergreen forest, and then indulge in a traditional Swiss fondue in a quaint mountain hut.

Most useful item to pack: Gaiters or waterproof pants

For further travel information: I borrowed snowshoes, or **raquettes**, from a colleague. However, many places in the villages of the Jura or in Geneva rent raquetting equipment.

Information on the fondue hut can be found at levermeilley.com.

The Col de la Givrine, where we started our snowshoeing jaunt, is located a short distance past the town of Saint-Cergue. Community-coordinated snowshoe and fondue evenings around Saint-Cergue are also arranged at st-cergue-tourisme.ch/en/winter/winterspecials/package_snow-shoes_fondue.

The Experience

One evening after work, ten of my colleagues and I drove up the Jura Mountains for an evening getaway. After following a twisty road with sharp switchbacks through the pine forest, we passed through the cute village of Saint-Cergue before carrying on a little farther up the hill. The moonlight reflected across the cotton-ball-like snow. The gentle slopes of the Jura were blanketed by a mass of evergreen trees freshly dipped in the white powder. We pulled into the parking lot at Col de la Givrine around seven o'clock. The sun had partially set. It had taken about an hour to drive from our workplace in Geneva to this winter wonderland far above the city lights. Our plan was to go snowshoeing, or raquetting, as it is referred to in the French cantons of Switzerland, for a few hours until we reached a tiny mountain chalet for a fondue dinner. We would then return by snowshoe along the same route.

When most people think of Swiss mountains, the high rocky peaks of the Alps come to mind. However, those monoliths are located to the southeast of Geneva, whereas the Jura are a range of mountains to the north of the city. **Jura** is derived from a word meaning "wooded mountain" in Gaulish and aptly describes this lush range, which is perfect for hiking in the summer and cross-country skiing or snowshoeing in the winter.[42] The Jurassic period is named for the Jura limestone that forms much of this area's bluffs. This ridge towers above the north edge of Lac Léman. On clear days, certain vantage points on the Jura's slopes offer glimpses of Geneva's iconic Jet d'Eau spurting water 140 metres into the air across the lake. During our visit, the Jet d'Eau was turned off for the night, which was fine as we were more interested in other sights.

Initially, there were a handful of people near the parking lot as we trundled off into the snowy tracks. Before long we had the forest to ourselves. We walked nine kilometres on our raquettes through wide tracks beneath the trees. Sometimes the untouched snow beckoned, and we leapt off-**piste** into deeper snow to test how well our raquettes floated atop the mounds of powder. Eventually, we curved around some trees and saw a warm glow emanating from a few windows up ahead. The hut itself looked like an old trapper's lodge. A massive bearskin covered one wall in dark brown and tawny fur, while a well-loved pair of wooden skis with the same dark brown tones hung across another wall, giving the room a rustic, homey feel. Before long, steaming bowls of various cheese mixtures arrived at our table. Bright blue flames burned from canisters of butane placed underneath the pots to ensure the fondue retained its creamy texture. After our couple of hours spent stamping through the snow, the soft bread and warm cheese oozed with satisfying heartiness. A flickering fire radiated its warm glow throughout the room, making the time pass far too quickly.

Late in the evening, we rugged up again and reclasped our snowshoes onto our now toasty-warm feet. Outside, the frosty nip in the air activated my adrenalin and must have transformed the cheesy goodness into energy, as we all kicked off at a good pace. The final two hours back to the car seemed more social than exercise.

This was one of those activities I wished I had tried earlier. Traditional mountain huts were scattered across the Jura, offering many options for similar ventures. The trailhead was a relatively short drive from the city but felt far away from the hectic pressure of daily schedules. It was the perfect way to spend an evening in the pristine mountain air with a fun-loving group of people.

The Basics

Synopsis: Paddle under stone arches and through private grottos shaded by limestone karsts.

Most useful item to pack: Pants or shorts in a quick-dry material

For further travel information: There are numerous companies in Hanoi that offer junk boat tours, including bus transport to Halong City plus all accommodation, meals and kayaks on board. Be sure to check the latest reviews of the operators. I heard many complaints that the cheaper tours also included rats and cockroaches. Plus these budget junks usually excluded kayaks, which then had to be rented separately.

The Experience

My husband and I spent three days on a tourist junk boat in Halong Bay. **Junk** refers to an ancient Chinese sailboat, which traditionally balanced up to five sails. The tourist junks that plied Halong Bay typically supported two sails, which were kept rolled up and unused from what I saw. Our junk was well kept, and our room was tidy and clean; however, the staff seemed rather frosty. On the first night, a group of twelve people sharing the boat with us celebrated a weekend away from Hanoi. They spent most of the night kicking back shots of vodka and seemed disinterested in the local beauty. By the next morning their demeanour had turned sombre, and later that afternoon they returned to solid land. For the second night, we had the entire junk to ourselves. The silence on board was almost eerie as the crew kept to themselves and seemed rather perturbed by our presence. It was hard to blame them, as it likely gets tiring continually tending to visitors. So we stayed on the upper deck, where we enjoyed sunset views over the silhouetted karsts. Compared to the experiences of other travellers who talked of junks with cockroaches and dirty bedsheets, our boat was a dream.

Halong translates to "Descending Dragons," who, according to folklore, flew into the bay and aided the Vietnamese during an ancient war. The name also provides quite a visual image for the piercing limestone karsts that shoot from the waters in the Gulf of Tonkin; one could imagine them as precious stones spit from the wide jaws of a fiery-mouthed dragon. The diversity and integrity of the limestone karsts has earned them a slot on UNESCO's World Heritage List.[43] We were interested in getting down to the water's level to experience at least a piece of this enigmatic seascape up close.

Kayaks were available on our junk to use at our leisure. From my perspective, the few hours kayaking through Bat Grotto and gliding next to the limestone cliffs was the highlight of our time in Halong Bay. With each pull of the paddle, I could feel myself drifting into a more peaceful mood among the rocky caverns. We first paddled through a cave towards a protected lagoon. The craggy cavern's ceiling had turned a soft shade of green from the moss that clung to its stony underbelly. The cave was shaded by overhanging bamboo leaves, which nearly touched the water at the exit. Out in the lagoon, foliage consumed the limestone walls, making it feel more like a humid jungle than an ocean enclave. I knew many others had kayaked into this same private space, but it felt untouched compared to the communal gathering of junks just a short distance away. It seemed a rare jewel that had retained its pristine environment.

The sides of the karst islands shot up vertically, and local residents could not build upon their shores. Instead, villages formed from floating houseboats clustered together. Bright blue seemed to be the colour of choice, besides the odd pillar painted in turquoise or yellow. Blue plastic pontoons propped houses and patios above the water, but it still must have been a wet lifestyle. Low, flat rowboats acted as both transportation and market stalls. A few outrigger fishing boats were tethered to homes, awaiting the next oyster pull or fishing run. Neighbours would have been forced to get along, as most homes bobbed right next to each other. All the houses followed a similar style: blue tarps ready to be unrolled for the next storm, tin roofs to keep the interior dry and laundry lines strung across their decks as the inhabitants tried to catch up on perpetually damp washing.

The arrival of tourists had helped a community pearl farm flourish. Hovering walkways meandered through the displays of oysters and pearls, while signs explained the various stages of the farming process, captivating foreigners unfamiliar with the technique. These once-reclusive floating villages had embraced the throngs of tourists that UNESCO's recognition had helped to entice here. Market boats continually paddled alongside the junk boats. One lady's wee rowboat barely had room for her to sit, as the entire bottom was filled with crackers and snacks for sale.

I think that the contrast between the commercial impact on the bay's traditional villages and the solitude discovered while kayaking emphasized the precarious line that tourism treads. Authenticity is craved by virtually every traveller; we long to experience exceptional places on our planet. Yet, when communities open their doors and tourism flourishes, their very uniqueness can appear contrived, and crowded tours can taint the experience. In Halong Bay, the most disappointing aspect was floating garbage, which regularly glided past our boat. Thirty years ago, before mass tourism arrived, I am quite sure the waters were pristine and the setting would have been idyllic.

The Basics

Synopsis: Row as hard as you can before the waves lift your boat and fling you into their swirling depths.

Most useful item to pack: Board shorts or quick-dry shorts

For further travel information: We visited Zimbabwe at the end of a month-long camping tour with Geckos Adventures. We started in South Africa and travelled through Namibia and Botswana before ending in Livingstone, Zimbabwe. At the time of writing, the company no longer listed this exact itinerary. Available tours can be found at geckosadventures.com.

G Adventures is a similar company, which at the time of writing ran a comparable itinerary. Further information can be found at gadventures.com.

For further information on Victoria Falls in general and on white-water rafting, refer to victoriafalls-guide.net. As always, check local guidance and recent traveller experiences for up-to-date information on any operator's safety record.

The Experience

The cardinal rule that I learned when first white-water rafting in Canada down the Fraser River's Hells Gate was not to fall out of the boat. Of all the rules the guide pressed upon our group, he told us that the most important was to hang on tight, paddle hard and whatever we did, stay inside the boat. Dangerous rocks lurked underwater. Well, this rule was turned upside down when we arrived at Victoria Falls in Zimbabwe about fifteen years later. Our guide emphatically informed us that we would indeed fall out of the boat. When this happened, we were not to panic but to simply hold our breath until our bodies inevitably popped above the water. Hearing this, I knew that this raft ride would clearly be like no other I had experienced.

The rafts set off a short distance downriver from the dramatic Victoria Falls. This waterfall is over one-and-a-half-kilometres wide. Across this expanse, the river tips over a one-hundred-metre-deep chasm. Victoria Falls is considered one of the Seven Natural Wonders of the World. When we visited, the water was not at its peak, but there was still a huge volume gushing into the narrow gorge where the Zambezi River flowed. Several crocodiles hung out along the river's shores. For those leery of cruising the water, the ravine offered a backdrop for other adventures such as bungee jumping, zip-lining or the flying fox. The plunging platform for these activities was located beside the main office for all the adventure sports. We met there for the rafting introduction session and had ample time to wander and consider other ventures. I took one look straight down the rocky bank and my stomach lurched as I remembered a small yet unpleasant thirty-foot bungee jump I once did. Rafting remained my preferred option.

As our visit coincided with the lower water levels, all the rapids were open for business. During the rainy season, the first ten rapids were closed for safety reasons. The guides seemed very well trained, and the equipment provided was in good condition. After our safety briefing, our group walked down to the river, fully kitted in helmets and life jackets. I questioned the guide to be sure that I had heard him correctly about falling out of the raft. Although we wore hard helmets, visions of much harder boulders under the surface danced in my head. He assured me with a smile that with each rapid, he would inform us in advance exactly how many seconds we **would** be underwater. Apparently, the water in the Zambezi was so deep we did not have to be overly concerned with rocks. As further support, two kayak spotters would trail our raft to help anyone who got into trouble.

The guides asked us to leave our shoes onshore so they could be taken to the endpoint for us. Someone made a joke that we should throw them into the river. A couple of the young women missed that this was a gag, and their flip-flops took the initial reconnaissance trip down the river, never to be seen again. Once in the boat, we practised our strokes on the calm waters. The first set of rapids swiftly approached, endearingly named the Boiling Pot. As promised, our guide told us that we would be beneath the water for eight seconds. I felt anxious at this point but committed to paddle hard and prove him wrong. I intensely wanted to stay inside the raft, and I wedged my feet underneath the rubber side. My strokes were strong. Before I knew what had happened, I was spinning underwater. One thought came to mind: "Count to eight." One. Two. Three. Four. ...Eight. My head popped up. I took a gulp of air. Everyone else was scattered in the choppy water, similarly stunned, but the raft was not far away. As my neurons sluggishly came back to life, my arms and legs regained their senses, and I swam over to the raft and rolled inside. The first rapid was Class IV and a shocker.

Each rapid had a name. My personal favourites were the Terminator and the Washing Machine, although the Devil's Toilet Bowl and Oblivion came in a close second. These names perfectly described the slashing water, which spun us and then spat us out. Approximately half of the nineteen rapids were Class V.

Class V is considered an expert level and is defined as follows: "Extremely long, obstructed, or very violent rapids which expose a paddler to added risk. Rapids may contain large, unavoidable waves and holes or steep, congested chutes with complex, demanding routes."[44] The first Class V rapid on the Zambezi was the Stairway to Heaven, which is like "dropping off a two-storey building and is one of the greatest river running rushes anywhere in the world."[45] Class VI rapids are rarely attempted and if so, only by experts.

Throughout all the rapids, the longest I was underwater was thirteen seconds. I was surprised how calm I remained, counting and swirling without any control over where my body was pushed. That was until we met one particularly ill-tempered rapid. I flew vertically out of the raft before being dropped under the waves. When I popped back up, I could not see my husband anywhere in the disarray around the raft. This was a chilling moment. It felt like my body had gone into a mild paralysis as I scanned the water and the word **no** reverberated in my head. Thankfully my fear was short lived. Within seconds, one of the kayakers was beside him across the river. All was well.

As we neared the nineteenth rapid, I realized that any concern about crocodiles had long vanished from my mind. There had been far too many other things to focus on. Fortunately, I never bumped into one of the armoured fellows while flailing underwater.

At the beginning of the trip, I recall thinking that the guides were lucky to snag a job that allowed them to run the rapids daily. By the end, it was clear just what a difficult role they undertook every day. One person in our group dislocated his finger, but otherwise there were no serious injuries. Both the guides and the kayak spotters were excellent and attentive.

Our world can feel like a scary place at times. At the time of this writing, Syrian communities have been pummelled by a civil war for over six years. Boko Haram continues to pillage and kidnap innocent civilians in Nigeria's northeast region at an alarming pace. North Korea's nuclear intentions have ramped up with increasingly frequent missile tests. With this seeming rise in hostility across our globe, burrowing into our zone of comfort may appear preferable to travelling to a far-flung destination.

But such a notion deserves a wee nudge. Should your itchy feet really be stifled? When I lived in Nigeria, I felt safe travelling to and from work through the often-chaotic streets of Lagos, even during the Ebola crisis of 2014. There were numerous trustworthy people I knew and respected. In my experience, turmoil does not typically impact everyone across a country. Granted, my mother may have felt uneasy from afar—it often feels safer to the one based in a region compared to someone else distantly imagining what could happen.

I recall flying into Maputo just days after the riots of 2010 had subsided. Residents living on one or two American dollars a day had revolted over the threefold rise in the price of bread. Fuel prices had also skyrocketed. Four people had been killed and many more injured during the unrest.[46] Before our arrival, my apprehension ran high. As we drove from the airport into the city centre, the streets were eerily quiet. But as we walked around the next day, people carried on with their business. Besides taking a few precautions, we felt completely safe. To be fair, the situation would have been different two days before.

Caution is smart, but fear is overrated in my view. Crime happens everywhere around our globe.

When I think of the places that have resonated with me or the locales where I have felt grounded over the years, few of them sat near my doorstep. The calming waters of the Mekong Delta in Laos or the peaceful Sultan Qaboos Grand Mosque in Oman jump to mind. These locations seemed to possess a pure identity, one woven into their very fabric. The earth and air surrounding them connected with my soul. Merely thinking of them causes my shoulders to relax and a sigh to escape my lips. These are the places that I refer to as serene scenes. Their atmosphere grounded my emotions. Their spaces transcended religious leanings but exuded a clarity of purpose and balance. So, in these times when the world can feel at odds with itself, perhaps reaching out to connect is not such a wild idea after all.

The Basics

Synopsis: Spend an hour sketching inside a Buddhist temple while a lone monk chants softly in the background, or listen while hundreds of monks recite a mantra in unison.

Most useful item to pack: Sketchbook or camera

For further travel information: Our visit was part of a longer tour through Bhutan. All travel in Bhutan is governed by the Tourism Council of Bhutan. Further information can be found at tourism.gov.bt/plan.

Visitors must use an approved tour company. I would highly recommend Rainbow Tours & Treks, as the quality of the guides, accommodation and overall coordination were outstanding. Refer to rainbowbhutan.com for more information.

The Experience

Guru Rinpoche, one of Bhutan's most revered deities, was legendary in the small village of Kurjey. This village was located in the Bumthang district of central Bhutan. We wanted to experience his story for ourselves. Midmorning we arrived at a hill with a short walkway framed by stupas painted white and topped with golden crests. Stupas are sacred bell-shaped monuments that reveal the path to Enlightenment.[47] The occasional stupa had been painted an emerald colour to match the forest that encircled the Kurjey Lhakhang Temple complex. At the entrance, a white banner marked the One Hundred Thousand Mantras ceremony. Its greeting was written mostly in the native Dzongkha text. A monk draped in bright orange robes was hunched over a wooden railing, and he smiled as we walked past. It seemed he had drawn the short straw and had to man the gate while all his friends were gathered in the temple.

A low rumble echoed from the buildings. Slow, methodical chanting was blended into a melodious rhythm. It had an enchanting effect. We climbed four levels of stairs that led to the temple from which the music was emanating. Rows of crimson-cloaked monks sat cross-legged on the floor, calmly chanting the mantra. Those on the outer edges of the group motioned for us to come inside. The mantra purred steadily. A bell gonged. I was mesmerized by the soothing vibes that radiated in the room. These monks spent hours repeating the same chant, comfortable to just be there, together. After some time, we slipped out of the room and returned to the sunlight.

Across the yard, I found a vacant temple with an enormous golden Buddha statue poised inside. A single monk sat in the rear of the temple softly chanting. He smiled and continued his hymn as I entered. Sticks of incense burned at the

front of the temple below the Buddha's feet. The light smoky scent was calming. For the next hour, I sat on the wooden-plank floor and attempted to capture the statue in my sketchbook. The soft mantra continued and time seemed to float away as I sketched and erased and then drew some more. I heard a rustling sound. A young monk padded up behind me in bare feet. He did not say a word, but I could feel his presence. Afterwards, my husband told me that about five young boys had tiptoed into the temple and crouched behind me, watching silently as I sketched. The tranquil atmosphere in the temple felt like no other place I had experienced. Similarly, the entire complex exuded a feeling of acceptance and tolerance.

The ambience transformed as the monks finished their chanting and left the temple. The majestic flow of their maroon cloaks seemed to bring a sense of purity to the white brick walls bordering the open staircase. Perhaps it was the zigzag shape of the stairs, but their slow procession in front of the alabaster wall fringed with moss and mould seemed to signal a change. The monks gathered around the lawn in front of the complex. Most of the younger monks hung out in pairs, huddled together and giggling, while a few stood aside by themselves looking pensively out in the distance.

Elderly folks from the village arrived. Some walked slowly around a large square stupa on the side of the main grassy area. They held prayer beads tightly between their fingers and softly chanted. Others chatted in small groups, catching up on their family news. Both men and women wore long handwoven panels of cloth wrapped in various styles. The weather was cool, and they covered themselves in many layers, some with a scarf hanging loosely around their neck. The group eventually congregated on the stone slabs, which acted as an outdoor foyer to the temple complex. The elderly villagers sat in a row, all cross-legged, still grasping their prayer beads. A few gently swung a golden hand-held prayer wheel as they waited.

Monks carried out insulated buckets of rice and scooped large servings for everyone seated on the ground. By this point, many of the younger monks had sat down to form their own line. Shortly after the rice was served, adolescent monks brought around a silver bucket filled with a lemon-coloured saucy dish. It too was ladled into waiting bowls that were held out eagerly. Three healthy-looking dogs roamed around the periphery of the group, wagging their tails. As with any family gathering, once the food was served, talking subsided as people turned their attention to the delicious dishes.

While most people ate, we explored another room of the temple complex. A few monks sat inside a dimly lit alcove, which had become the pottery shack. They shaped miniature stupas out of clay and stacked these icons along a low shelf to dry. Everyone seemed relaxed, and they chattered among themselves, in no particular hurry. I suspected that this was a favoured task. When we walked back into the sunlight, I felt as if I had absorbed a droplet of Kurjey's surreal essence. This was certainly a special place built upon years of tradition.

Centuries ago, the adored Guru Rinpoche was first invited to Bhutan on this very hillside. Feuding kingships and illness among the local nobility had caused strife across the community. They needed divine help. The guru arrived and immediately began to meditate inside a nearby cave. He meditated for months, and his concentration was so intense that an impression of his body and a handprint were imprinted on the cavern's rock. After coming out of the cave, Guru Rinpoche employed nonviolent shock tactics along with his not-so-subtle supernatural powers. He transformed himself into eight manifestations, who all began to dance in the meadow. He then grabbed dancing partners by turning the king's daughter into five maidens, each holding a golden pitcher. The brilliant vessels reflected the sunlight into dazzling streaks. Such a sight demanded attention; the bickering kings were enraptured. At this critical point, the guru turned himself into a Garuda, a bird-like deity, and the duelling kings soon succumbed to his display of power. Harmony was returned to the valley. A cypress tree grows on what is said to be the very spot where Rinpoche pounded his staff to mark the kings' agreement of peace.[48]

Overall, Bhutan is one of my favourite countries to visit, even if the government-imposed day rate is rather steep. The Bhutanese have managed to preserve a culture rooted in Buddhist beliefs, an unmistakable artistic style and an overarching sense of caring and fun. The day we spent with the monks and elderly villagers at Kurjey epitomized a feeling of balance. Everything seemed right in the world, and everyone was accepted and cared for, just as they were.

The Basics

Synopsis: Lounge on your private patio overlooking the Mekong Delta while sipping a glass of liquefied mango before renting a bicycle and pedalling across the island to try to glimpse the reclusive Irrawaddy dolphin.

Most useful items to pack: Walking sandals and an engrossing novel

For further travel information: We stayed at the incredibly friendly, family-run Sengahloune Resort in a private bungalow with a palm-fringed patio overlooking the Mekong Delta. The restaurant's **laab gai** and mango juice were some of the best that I tasted in Laos. For more information, refer to sengahlouneresort.com.

The Experience

In the far southern reaches of Laos, four thousand islands poke through the vast Mekong Delta's murky waters. The Si Phan Don islands are named after a former prime minister of Laos, General Khamtai Siphandon, who has retained a personal residence on one of the larger islands. Otherwise, most of the islands are home to just rocks and palm trees, undisrupted by human settlement. After riding a shuttle bus from the mainland city of Pakse and then hopping on a small ferry, we set foot on the tiny island of Don Khon. Its centre included one main street: a dry dirt road lined by thatch buildings and a fence built from moderately straight bamboo poles. Although it was the rainy season, the storms came in spurts, leaving most of the daytime period dry. When we arrived, the weather was pleasant, so we took our time walking down the street to check out the available accommodation options.

Nearly every place was empty at this time of year. After we had looked at several rooms across town, the traditional wood and rattan bungalows at the Sengahloune Resort were our top choice. We negotiated a price of less than thirty American dollars per night. It was the low season in 2010, and the rates were particularly good. Our stay on Don Khon was off to a promising start with an impeccably clean and spacious room with air conditioning, a hot-water shower, comfortable queen beds and a private patio. Considering electricity had been wired onto the island only a few years before this, the room's amenities were impressive.

The cappuccino-coloured waters of the Mekong drifted a few feet from our patio's railing. Palm branches swayed gently over the roof's edge. I grabbed Paul Theroux's **Ghost Train to the Eastern Star: On the Tracks of the Great**

Railway Bazaar from my pack and nestled into one of the wicker chairs that rested on the patio. Just upstream, an old cement railway bridge with multiple arches connected Don Khon to Don Det. Nowadays the bridge is used by pedestrians and occasional bicycles, but not by trains. Rusted remnants of the narrow-gauge railway lay scattered across the island, unused since around the time of the Second World War. An abandoned engine car sat on the grass near town, its oxidized engine covered in partially corroded bolts and dormant pipes.

Theroux's book was fascinating, but I was easily distracted by life on the river. We could see a lot of activity from our little patio. Low boats travelled back and forth, most carrying fishermen as they flung their nets. On one occasion, the challenges of living on a remote island became expressly clear. A long wooden boat puttered upstream, propelled by a new black engine. Any traces of paint on the boat's sides had long since worn thin. This was a functional craft, not concerned by its lack of aesthetic appeal. Three men in bright T-shirts rested against one side under the shade of a makeshift roof. A faded piece of canvas had been draped across half of the roof's rafters. Empty boxes leaned against the opposite side. As the vessel approached the shore, an unexpected bulky, box-like shape came into view. A large deep freezer sat precariously balanced on an angle, wedged between the edges of the boat and the roof boards. The heavy appliance dominated the boat's bow. I was surprised that the vessel had not tipped end over end. No one seemed concerned. A young boy balanced on the bow's tip as he scouted their landing point. Over the four days we stayed on Don Khon, we saw a variety of furniture and construction materials ingeniously strapped onto these relatively small boats and shuttled between islands.

On another occasion, with my coffee cup balanced on the top railing and my feet comfortably propped on the middle bar, I surveyed the slow-moving water. Downstream, a young Laotian stood thigh deep in the water, wearing only a pair of dark green shorts. A piece of string was tied around his left wrist. He hurled the line out into the water and slowly recoiled it. The small weighted net at the end usually returned empty. Across the river, another lone fisherman balanced in his small fishing boat. His net looked somewhat, tangled and he attempted to sort through the strings and loops, holding some sections adeptly between his teeth. Magically, he launched it out in a smooth oval over the cloudy waters. I turned back to my book for a while. Later, as I glanced up, a shiny flicker caught my eye. One of the fishermen had captured a prize, even if it was a wee one. The youngest fisherman I saw was probably seven years old, but he balanced his little carved boat perfectly on his own. He appeared completely at ease in his bright blue skivvies while his boat floated close to the reeds. People here grew up in boats and seemed just as comfortable piloting their long skiffs as they did walking on land.

Occasionally we pulled ourselves away from our idyllic patio to explore the tiny island. Bicycles could be rented along the main strip. My allotted bright pink bike had a matching front basket. As we rode, its clean frame was quickly covered in an abstract muddy design. The rims were splattered from the grooved pathways that had become immersed in puddles from the morning's rain. We passed a decrepit colonial home, long deserted, its white cement having turned grey and black from the mould that had engulfed the building. Patches of siding were so dark they looked as if they had been in a fire. Some of the tile shingles had cracked while others had fallen off entirely.

Farther along, we rode up to the Li Phi Falls ("Spirit Trap Falls"). Local superstitions told of troublesome souls captured there. The normally calm waters turned aggressive as they passed between narrow boulders and sharp rocks. Gushing foam whirled around and was hurled between twists and dropped down vertical shoots in a relatively slim space. The island's typical silence was replaced by a dull roar. Fishermen loved this enclosed area and had loosely constructed wooden traps to capture fish, although to us they looked more like piles of bamboo poles tied together to construct partial bridges. Some were connected to one another while others crossed overhead. It all looked quite precarious. People were known to have fallen into this quagmire with dire consequences.

Early one rainless morning, we hopped on our bikes once again. They had one gear, which was sufficient for the island's flat terrain. At least today, we pedalled across dry, hard-packed-dirt trails, and my bike graciously retained its pristine pink for the duration. Our destination was at the far end of the island, a little community named Ban Hang Khon. We arrived by six o'clock, and a few locals were already hanging out under the shade. Eventually we tracked down the boatman we had spoken to the previous day, and we set off together. We hoped to spot a rare and endangered Irrawaddy freshwater dolphin. Ten Irrawaddies were known to inhabit these waters. Sadly, their numbers have dwindled from approximately thirty in the early 1990s. For much of the time, the boatman tethered his wooden rig to a rocky outcrop—if one was generous, it could be considered an island. We perched atop its highest vantage point in an ultimately futile attempt to see an Irrawaddy surface. Minutes ticked by. An hour passed without even a flicker of a tail or the tip of a nose. It became clear that we would not be lucky today. Our guide concluded that the critters must be in Cambodian waters, merely two hundred metres away. Similar islands and cocoa-coloured waters beckoned but were uncrossable due to border controls and inconvenient visa requirements. We did not entertain the thought of going through this administrivia for such a quick flit. Our unsuccessful venture seemed to accentuate the acute difficulties facing this scarce species.

Whenever anyone asks about visiting Laos, I advise them to consider the Si Phan Don islands. This archipelago offered a range of accommodation, delicious authentic food and a glimpse into serene island life. Don Khon had a laid-back vibe and was an easy place to spend a few days, which could have been extended without difficulty. Part of the pleasure was due to our comfortable little cabana, where we quickly felt at home. Our stay oozed with friendly comfort wrapped in a blissful atmosphere.

The Basics

Synopsis: Leap down an eighty-five-metre sand dune, and then explore an ashen clay pit peppered with petrified tree skeletons.

Most useful item to pack: Hiking sandals

For further travel information: Our afternoon at Sossusvlei was part of a month-long camping tour with Geckos Adventures. For more information, refer to geckosadventures.com.

For information on the Sossusvlei sand dunes, petrified forest, accommodation and other useful information, refer to sossusvlei.org.

The Experience

The sand slipped, grain by grain, sucking my feet back down towards the base of the giant dune. Even though the surroundings looked as if we had landed on another planet, the force of gravity confirmed otherwise. I leaned ahead and lifted my leg again, slowly pulling it up and forward to try to minimize backwards slippage. As I gradually gained headway up the sand, the panorama opened. Rolling mounds of sand spread out across the land, reminding me of the piles of cumin and saffron that filled baskets at Gujarati spice markets. The iron oxide had turned the sand a deep ochre colour, which caught the sun's rays in subtly different nuances throughout the day. The sand at Sossusvlei was over five million years old, carried inland on winds from the Namibian coast, which lay approximately sixty kilometres westward.

Dune 45 rose eighty-five metres and was the only dune that visitors were allowed to climb. When we walked its rim, it seemed enormous, yet it was a mere baby next to some of the mounds in the range. The largest loomed over three hundred metres in height. At the top of Dune 45's ridge, my slow ascent switched over the course of one step. Instinctive impulses spun through my head as I swapped directions: "Lunge. Slide. Quick, rotate a leg and get your foot out." Within seconds, I was in a full run with longer strides than I had thought possible as the sand carried my feet with each step. It felt more like gliding than running. My only word of caution is to close your mouth if you tumble. The sand welcomes you with its soft embrace but mischievously hunts for any unsuspecting cranny to dive inside.

It was 2006, and my husband and I were traversing from Namibia through four of Africa's southern countries as part of an overland tour. Sossusvlei seemed like a world of its own, unlike anywhere else in Africa. In Afrikaans, the name means "dead-end marsh," referring to where the dunes prevent the Tsauchab River from continuing to flow along its natural riverbed. However, as time passed the river no longer reached this far-west position, and the expanse remains bone dry. The area lies in Namibia's central-western region, inland from the Atlantic Ocean. Every few years the rains are abnormally heavy, and the typically dry pan at the dunes' base transforms into a reflective lake. This was one of those years, but much of the water had evaporated by the time we walked the valley. The next flooding came in 2011.[49] At the peak of the floods, images of the salmon-coloured dunes appeared inverted in the glassy lake.

While we visited, the parched pan was crusty and dry. The contrast was peculiar between the bright orange sand dunes and the cracked white basin. From above, the view reminded me of an orange Le Creuset enamel saucepan with fried egg whites left overnight to harden and flake. Once inside the pan, our view shifted from the silty floor to the striking skeletons of trees. These wizened remnants crouched in mangled positions, without any trace of their leaves. They were nine hundred years old. Life had long since departed, but the shells withstood time, lacking the necessary ingredient to decompose. Not only is water life-giving, but it is also essential for the decay process.

Standing beside these ancient brutes, we saw that old sorrows had become enhanced. A striated pattern of weathered creases was chiselled along their branches, only deviating to avoid a stubborn knot. Cracks had split once formidable trunks so that they were tipped onto their heads and left to balance on thin stubs. Some petrified giants had collapsed completely, leaving only a desiccated strip of serrated bark. Surprisingly, at the edge of the pan we came across a tiny pond, not much bigger than a large puddle. This was the only residue from the earlier flooding. A soft breeze rippled its surface, blurring the dune's reflection. Green bushes sprouted along its edges, clawing at any chance to survive in such a harsh environment.

As we walked through the lower valley of the dunes, our guide spotted tiny pinprick tracks. They belonged to the darkling beetle. This ingenious critter balances upside down in the wee hours of the morning to catch a dew droplet inside specialized grooves on its body. These canals then funnel the water directly into the beetle's mouth. Despite the presence of the pond, the bugs continued their balancing act. Perhaps they persevered out of habit, or maybe they needed to preserve the strength in their front appendages for the inevitable times of drought.

The local guide's passion for Sossusvlei made this experience truly special. She was Japanese but had been living in Namibia for years. Her deep care for the environment and the creatures that fought to survive in this unique place shone through in her descriptions of their daily struggles. Nature had adapted in strange ways to stay alive in this severe landscape. As we walked through the valley and dunes, we learned to appreciate the vitality that lay hidden beneath its surface. Balance had been achieved, even if it was a delicate one.

The Basics

Synopsis: Absorb the tranquility exuded by the cool creamy marble in every niche of this sanctuary while warm smiles welcome you to explore.

Most useful items to pack: Head scarves for women; long sleeves and pants for everyone

For further travel information: The mosque is open to non-Muslim visitors from 8:30 to 11:30 a.m., every day except Friday. Dress should be modest with arms and legs covered. Women should also bring a head scarf. For further information, refer to omantourism.gov.om, and click through the options under the "Experiences," "Culture" and "Religious Sites" tabs.

The Experience

If you ask Omanis about the Sultan Qaboos Grand Mosque—more frequently referred to simply as the Grand Mosque—their faces will light up, and they will encourage you to visit. National pride wrapped in humble modesty seemed to emanate from this impressive structure. Its theme centred around Islam's role in scientific and intellectual knowledge, illustrated by the fact that it held equal capacity for worshippers in the prayer halls and for reference books on its library shelves—twenty thousand of each. The mosque's design displayed many fine touches that epitomized the devotion put into the building. A dazzling chandelier of Swarovski crystal extended fourteen metres in length and hung inside the main prayer hall. It lit up a 4,200-square-metre hand-knotted Persian rug. A group of Iranian women had spent twenty-seven months tying 1.7 billion tiny knots to create this masterpiece. Both the chandelier and carpet were the largest in the world at one time until a neighbouring country eagerly crafted a larger specimen. Nevertheless, they were spectacular.

Corridors enclosed the Grand Mosque like a protective wall embracing its sanctuary. Each stretch of corridor ran approximately 240 metres in length and included a string of compartments, each showcasing a different Islamic artistic style. These spaces were not only for visual appeal, but were also used as ablution rooms. Water sprung from tiled fountains for pre-worship cleansing. As a non-worshipper, I was struck by the detailed designs on the tiles. One niche included tiny golden stripes in a wavy pattern around alabaster-coloured marble. The dome was decorated in peacock-blue tiles with yellow-and-orange leafy swirls. A little farther along the corridor, a design of minuscule inlaid marble slices was arranged like delicate flowers. Farther yet, the Ottoman-themed section brought alive the lotus flower of paradise. A garden was fashioned from the wee tiles; lotuses, tulips, roses, carnations and bunches of grapes covered the walls and were thought to dispel grief and sorrow. In other sections, tall windows had been inset with an intricate screen made of marble. Light permeated the screen, but cool shade still pervaded the alcove. Some ceilings were dressed in wood panelling carved with geometric motifs, while elsewhere tiles coated both the walls and ceilings.

The women's prayer hall held up to 750 worshippers. Its interior was smaller than the main prayer hall but retained an exquisite quality. Multiple chandeliers hung from a carved wooden ceiling, and the walls were made of etched marble. Verses from the Koran were inscribed into the marble facade along the upper level, while geometric patterns adorned the lower walls. Every inch of the doors had been etched, and they were each topped with a stained-glass arch. Although the entire complex was decorated in this elaborate style, the light-coloured marble balanced the intricacy with a soothing tranquility.

A shared feeling of harmonious calm seemed to radiate from the corridors and soft carpets. I did not feel an ounce of hostility aimed at me, as a non-Muslim exploring an Islamic sanctum. In fact, specific beliefs seemed irrelevant, as this space was a place of tolerance and love. The light turquoise-and-white tones in the main prayer hall created an ambience that felt full of peace. As we walked around the complex, I felt as if I had just received a heartfelt hug from my grandmother, without judgement or expectation. I enjoyed this place more every time I visited. It was truly a masterpiece of serenity.

The Basics

Synopsis: Pass green-shuttered homes and historic bubbling water fountains before running between rows of Gamay grapes dangling from lush vines.

Most useful item to pack: Saucony running shoes, my personal favourite brand

For further travel information: A mélange of paved trails cut through the vineyards to connect villages along Lac Léman. Further information for the Anières to Hermance portion plus a possible extension to the route described below can be found at wanderland.ch/en/routes/route-0105.html.

The Experience

When we lived in Switzerland, my preferred way to decompress was to run along the trail system on the south side of Lac Léman, east of Geneva. In the early morning, the trails were nearly always empty. Shadowy trees and silhouetted rows of grapevines offered an idyllic path to run along. During the autumn, sun glistened off a collage of yellow, green and red leaves while plump purple grapes hung waiting to be plucked. On longer runs with my husband, we sometimes stopped at a village patisserie for a pain aux raisins that supplied a much-needed jab of energy. Its buttery layers may not have been overly healthy, but the treat certainly made for a satisfying outing.

The Canton of Geneva's countryside offered a mosaic of routes, but my favourite section connected the town of Collonge-Bellerive to Hermance. This route started on Chemin du Milieu, which soon changed into Chemin Armand-Dufaux and hugged the lakeshore from Collonge-Bellerive to Corsier Port. This residential section contained stately mansions with manicured gardens beside modern modular houses, all shaded beneath rambling old trees. The atmosphere exuded calm composure. Gated driveways were often marked by tall cement pillars covered in a soft fuzz. The muggy air felt invigorating as I moved along the shaded sidewalk. Occasionally, the hedges parted to reveal views of the lake, where sailboats often floated past. My next target was the public beach, Plage de la Nymphe, which was usually deserted. Broad leafy trees shaded grassy picnic areas almost too perfectly positioned. On weekends, the occasional family lounged along the shore. From where I ran along the sidewalk, I could not hear their voices, so it felt like I was watching a silent film from 1910.

The road wrapped around a tight bend at Corsier Port. The Chantier Naval de Corsier Port, an old, shuttered shipyard and a marina still in use, provided an interesting distraction.[50] Sailboats rested on their stands under the storage shed's protective roof, while luckier vessels were moored in the harbour awaiting their next outing. A left turn at this corner led onto Quai de Corsier. Knobby old trees were staggered between the grassy bank and the lane. A decrepit rowboat leaned in its customary position, nearly sliding into the lake but somehow keeping a grip on the land. I always wondered who had left such a cute boat to decay along an otherwise flawlessly tidy bank. The water lapped its soft lullaby while ducks intermittently popped above water after a hungry dive. An occasional swan drifted by, lost in his own world. This was one of my favourite sections. The road then turned inland, narrowed and switched to Chemin du Nant-d'Aisy. Tall shrubs lined the route and led to a small bridge that crossed a trickle of a creek. Humidity was thick here, heightening the scent of pine and moss.

Soon after I reached the sidewalk along Route d'Hermance, I jutted right onto a road that angled into the town of Anières. Rue Centrale was its main street. A former barn, surrounded by flowerpots overflowing with blooms, had been transformed into the cute Épicerie Fine, an Italian specialty grocer. Farther along, an antique water pump filled a similarly ancient cement tub with pure water. On a platform overhead, an old piece of farm equipment displayed its reconditioned brilliance. Streets were lined with stucco houses overgrown in vines that had wound around the wooden shutters and scaled the walls. Such rustic aesthetics brought a feeling of authenticity to the town. Although the village was small, two family-run wineries kept active blending their locally grown grapes. Their business was fitting, as the entire community was surrounded by rows and rows of grapevines.

As the buildings faded, I turned left onto Route de Chevrens at a roundabout. This road rarely had any vehicles to dodge. In places, lavender sprouted from a divider that separated the bike route from the car lane. Horses often sauntered to the fence, watching from behind their long lashes as if they were cheering me on my run. Fields of sunflowers beamed a mass of yellow smiles. After crossing through yet another quintessentially charming Swiss town, the path zigzagged around a working farm onto the slender Chemin des Bouchats. Farmers typically used this lane to drive their tractors between fields, but it was usually clear. A small apple orchard grew alongside, its trees bursting with bright little spheres begging to be picked. The route eventually dipped downhill and curved left into the town of Hermance.

Hermance is the last Swiss town on the south side of the lake. To travel farther, a tiny border crossing grants access to and from France. Running along Hermance's twisty streets felt like stepping back in time, as they date from the thirteenth century. My turnaround point was an old stone tower, the last vestige of a castle that had once overlooked the village. Arrow slits pierced the tower's otherwise perfectly smooth facade.

There was no one magical element along this route that made it so special. It seemed to balance a string of tiny sparks of loveliness in perfect equilibrium. The lake's water was pure and transparent, plants flourished and people embraced the land. Somehow, after spending time along these trails, my sense of fortitude felt replenished and my mind ran clear. Running here became addictive.

Big animals bring big swigs of adrenalin. I recollect sitting inside a Land Rover in Southern Malawi when a solitary male elephant decided to charge us. All the cells in my body felt momentarily stunned, unable to move beyond flicking my eyelids wide open. Our guide then calmly introduced us to the subtle communiqué between the moody elephant and our vehicle. The initial sign that the adolescent male was growing perturbed was his flaring ears. The elephant then trumpeted and flung his trunk, a final warning for us to back off. As we held our ground, he lunged in a mock charge. Our guide revved the vehicle's engine in response but held our ground. Startled, the adolescent paused. He retreated slightly while glaring at our obstinance. The risk of simply driving away from such a situation is that the elephant would perceive this as fleeing—a win for the elephant. Elephants are smart animals. They could learn to attack vehicles as a reliable mode of defence when they feel distressed if drivers do not deter such signs of hostility. This is not the mentality that game parks want to inspire.

Moments later, the elephant charged again, this time more aggressively. I tensed my shoulders and may have held my breath for a few seconds. It was scary watching a beast bigger than our four-wheel drive rush straight for us. Dust blew up from his feet as he barrelled down on our vehicle. Once again, our guide revved the engine but louder this time, while also creeping towards the elephant in an equal show of defiance. The angry elephant halted with a wet snort of disgust. We sat a while longer. Eventually our guide nonchalantly drove past the cranky bachelor, sending the message that we would leave but in our own time. The elephant trailed us for a while, making one final sprint as if to make a point that we were not welcome in his domain.

The opportunity to view wild animals in their own environment is full of the unexpected. I have encountered some electrifying situations when creatures have crept close to my personal space. These moments are hard to forget. As a general rule, animals do not attack humans unless they feel threatened. They tend to disdain surprises, not unlike some people. So keeping this fundamental guideline in mind can lead to a better response when you are presented with such an encounter. The hardest part may be to control your nerves. Knee-jerk outbursts will certainly not help the situation.

After all, animals follow their instincts. Survival reigns. I find it fascinating that this same tendency gives animals the uncanny ability to coexist in relative harmony. Different species inherently gravitate towards different food sources. This unconscious choice has created a sustainable ecosystem. The carnivorous food chain is the most obvious example of this coordination. Its linear progression leads the hunter to become the hunted.

Similarly, yet less notoriously, herbivores have developed their own system. Each species has developed a specific taste for certain plant types. Elephants go after rough, high-placed trees. Giraffes prefer the leaves of shrubs. Zebras pick tall grasses, while the tiny dik-dik antelope stick with low grass.[51] Nearly every animal has been allocated a particular plant as its preferred meal, as explained in the **National Geographic** article referenced in the footnote. This allows all animals a chance to eat without desiccating any one plant species.

The Basics

Synopsis: Tuck inside your tent while hippos frolic in the camp's swimming pool and elephants sample the foliage.

Most useful item to pack: Non-crinkly sleeping bag

For further travel information: We tented in the campsite, but more luxurious accommodation options were available. An upscale Mvuu Lodge offering swish permanent tents was also located nearby. Refer to cawsmw.com/index.php/lodges/mvuu-camp.

The Experience

The Mvuu Camp was set inside Liwonde National Park in Southern Malawi. They offer chalets, but we chose a more rustic option and pitched our tent in their campsite. When exploring our new digs, we noticed copious plops of elephant dung sprinkled on the ground, mostly dried, from previous days' ramblings. The tenting area was integrated into the park's natural setting, free of any protective fence. Our guide told us that elephants did not typically visit during the day but came at night when we would be tucked inside our tent and safely out of sight.

He continued to sedately explain that hippos had an affinity for late-night bathing in the camp's swimming pool, which was regrettably positioned at the entrance to the washroom facility. I missed having an ensuite already. The stars were twinkling when we zipped up our tent flap that first night. Its military-style canvas had initially felt sturdy, but as the sun set, it seemed a flimsy barrier. Normally, paraffin candles were burned on poles secured in front of the tents. Their flickering flames magically dispelled hungry visitors otherwise tempted by the camp's foliage. However, it was our unlucky day. The camp's paraffin supply was dismally low, quashing any chance of receiving such a blazing deterrent.

The temperature had cooled, so I snuggled tightly inside my sleeping bag and pulled the top layer close around my chin. We fell asleep to hippo grunts as they frolicked in the river about one hundred metres away. Around one in the morning, we were both awoken by a twig cracking. **Crack. Ping.** The last snap was less than a metre from our tent. The next noise came from directly above our tent. **Crunch. Chomp. Munch.** A hippo would not eat branches so high, for they tended to graze on grass. This was a much larger creature, one that was able to extend its long reach towards its chosen sapling. For a massive animal, elephants could tread surprisingly softly. The sounds when it approached were no louder than those made by a small child stepping on a branch.

Remembering our guide's advice earlier in the day, we did not dare make a move or sound. If an elephant is frightened, its most likely response is to run and trample anything in its way. I squeezed my husband in a bear hug, not aware of how hard I was actually clenching. I do not know exactly how much time passed, probably thirty minutes. We lay still. I felt my heart thumping and was conscious of every breath. Every muscle in my shoulders had tensed. Each twitch seemed amplified. I barely inhaled and scarcely exhaled. Finally, a branch cracked farther away and then a second snapped beyond that. We remained silent for another few minutes, holding still. As the minutes passed, we gained confidence that the elephant had, in fact, left. We were okay. I was struck by how important it is to give wildlife the respect they deserve. The elephant had no intention of causing us harm—we just needed to allow her space and time. My respect for the wild was elevated after such a close encounter of an otherwise mundane activity.

On another occasion, our guide told us a story from about twenty years before, when he used to work as a ranger in this very park. He was driving a four-wheel drive with two British tourists along the park's trails. They spotted a herd of elephants and slowed to watch. The matriarch, however, was not impressed by the vehicle's intrusion. She flared her ears before thrusting them back against her neck. The old gal kicked her feet on the ground in dismay. It was no act. The elephant charged, ramming her tusks straight through the grill of the vehicle. The tip of the elephant's tusk ripped through the metal, nearly spearing the brake pedal. This startled the old lady, for she now had a rather large hunk of metal hanging below her trunk. She instinctively shook her head. The vehicle shifted and the matriarch stepped back, disengaging herself from the situation. The engine luckily revved to life.

A stirring scene then transpired. As the matriarch prepared to lunge once more, two other female elephants stepped forward and restrained their mother. The ladies manoeuvered their tusks to hold back their angry elder. They must have felt that the vehicle and its occupants were not worth fighting over. This extra time allowed our guide to reverse from immediate danger while still holding his ground somewhat, so as not to leave the impression that vehicles would run away in fright. A photo taken soon after the incident of our guide with his punctured vehicle was published in the Liwonde National Park's coffee-table book, which was on display at the camp's main reception area. I found this story to be a powerful illustration of nature's fear and compassion.

The Basics

Synopsis: Trek through the Virunga Mountains and spend an hour in awe watching a mountain gorilla family as they forage among the bamboo.

Most useful items to pack: Waterproof jacket and water-resistant hiking boots

For further travel information: Group sizes are small. Visitors must purchase a permit, which sets a daily limit on the number of people who can trek to see the gorilla families. There are also guidelines regarding proximity, length of visit and acceptable protocol when near the animals.

The national park website has a load of information to help you plan your trip. It offers insights to better appreciate the mountain gorillas, including trekking etiquette and background on the various gorilla families in Volcanoes National Park. See volcanoesrwanda.org.

The Experience

After we had tramped through dewy bamboo and across hilly landscapes covered with thick ferns, the guides asked our group of eight people to stop speaking. We then quietly ducked under the brush into a grassy meadow. Maybe ten metres from us, three mountain gorillas squatted on their back legs casually chewing shafts of grass. They were shorter than me, but their build was much wider, with noticeably stronger shoulders and biceps. These female gorillas seemed at ease with our arrival. It was almost as if they nodded a greeting for us to take a seat and partake in some tender shoots, the local specialty. Behind a rather large fern and half-hidden by foliage, a mother cradled her little baby, who relaxed with his eyes three-quarters closed. Back in the grassy area, a large female spotted a delectable clump across the meadow. She leaned on her fists as she sauntered forward slowly and deliberately. She swiped a prize stalk before resting back on her haunches to enjoy her snack. The animals seemed to be savouring their extended brunch.

Higher up and somewhat separated from the ladies, a lone gorilla perched, tearing a bamboo shoot between his teeth. His eyes scanned the area, seemingly unfazed by our company. He was the only adult male of the group, the silverback. His charcoal-coloured hair was damp from the morning's dew. A distinctive silvery white glow, roughly in the shape of a diamond, spanned his back. About fifteen minutes later, we had a truly up-close experience. The silverback had wandered into a cluster of bamboo and then something caught his eye. That something lay just beyond where our group was hunkered. We all held our position, not moving or looking him directly in the eye. In an instant, the male tipped over onto his shoulders and leapt with impressive speed. His right arm brushed the jacket sleeve of one of our group members. Everyone was stunned for a few seconds before we broke into a nervous chuckle as we absorbed how close we had come to this massive primate. He meant no harm, but his enormous power was indisputable.

The Basics

Synopsis: Hike through the savannah with armed guides, and keep your eyes wide open for what may be concealed behind the next bush.

Most useful item to pack: Comfy hiking shoes

For further travel information: The gorgeous Lukimbi Safari Lodge offers full-board chalet-style accommodation in southern Kruger National Park. They also operate an equally fantastic sister lodge, Idube Game Reserve in the Sabi Sands Reserve, which is described later in this chapter. Road transfers between the airport and either lodge can be arranged by the lodge. For more information, refer to lukimbi.com.

The Experience

In South Africa's eastern frontiers, game reserves speckle the landscape. These safe spaces support sustainable communities for wildlife and locals alike. There is often a close relationship between neighbouring villages and the parks. In 2013, my husband, mother-in-law and I spent a few days in the Sabi Sands Reserve and in Kruger National Park. Both safari lodges we stayed at included morning and afternoon game drives. So when the guides at Lukimbi Safari Lodge offered us the opportunity to step away from the open-vehicle game drive and walk the dusty savannah, our curiosity was piqued. We decided that for our second afternoon, my husband and I would swap the game drive for a two-hour bush walk. Over lunch, we savoured an extra mug of hearty coffee to energize us for our impending walk.

After a short drive from the lodge, we stepped out of the vehicle onto low, tangled scrub near a barely-there gurgling creek. Off we tramped, peering closely through the branches in an attempt to see what lay ahead. Not more than a few minutes into our walk, the guide heard rustling across the creek bed. We inched forward ever so quietly. A large grey body came into view. Then the mass twitched its relatively puny tail, swatting at flies that teased its rump. We held still. Within minutes, three additional brutes came into view. We stood transfixed as four stunning white rhinoceroses shuffled in the grass, munching lazily to feed their massive bodies, an endless job. They stood thirty metres from us. Their heads hung low to the ground, weighted down by a pointed horn propped above their nose. A second smaller horn grew slightly higher from the centre of their face. Rhino horns have a similar composition to our fingernails or the hooves of horses. The rhinos' skin was thick, essential to protect them from annoying thorns and the burning rays of the sun. Rhinos are not the friendliest of animals and are easily scared—a good thing given that an unfortunate number of humans are out to slice off their horns and leave them for dead. For this reason, we edged backwards, out of sight, and carried on with our hike.

What a start to the trek. Our adrenalin had perked up with this first sighting, more so than the lunchtime coffee had induced. As we ambled along, the guides explained various facts about the local birds and plants that we came across. As dusk was approaching, the main lodge came into view. One of the staff members stood on the deck. She waved to us particularly emphatically; however, her message was unclear. We all continued to watch our surroundings extremely carefully. Soon enough, the puzzle was solved. Directly ahead of us, dusty haunches poked out from behind a bush. These rather wizened and scarred buttocks belonged to an old water buffalo. He had been squeezed out of his herd by younger, more virile buffalos. Because he was lacking the protection of the group, life had turned hard for this old guy. The situation had made him rather cranky and therefore quite dangerous. So far, he had kept his back to us and had not caught our scent. We swiftly reversed our steps and took a wide arc around him towards the lodge. Low shrubs and long grass obliterated the terrain. This offered us cover but also obscured the buffalo's location from our view. One of the guides held his gun ready in case the beast suddenly came rushing through the vegetation. Luckily, we remained incognito to the cantankerous chap.

Once safely back at the lodge, we watched the water buffalo scrounge among the grass across the narrow river that ran between him and us. His coat had lost much of its normally wispy black hair. The skin encircling his eyes was bleached white and looked cracked and grooved. He must have seen a lot throughout his life. We felt safe from our higher vantage point as guards monitored the lodge and boulders barricaded the residential area from access. Nevertheless, we were mindful of our surroundings. After all, we had chosen to partake in an intimate wildlife experience.

The Basics

Synopsis: Travel in open-air vehicles through the reserve with a good chance of viewing all the Big Five[52] and many more incredible animals.

Most useful item to pack: Camera with a good zoom lens

For further travel information: The Idube Game Reserve is an all-inclusive lodge within the Sabi Sands Reserve, which is on the periphery of the well-known Greater Kruger National Park. To reach this lodge, we took a charter flight from Johannesburg's Tambo International Airport to Kruger Mpumalanga International Airport near Nelspruit. We had prearranged a transfer through Idube Game Reserve to travel the remaining distance. Their driver picked us up at the airport and drove us to the lodge. For more information on the Idube Game Reserve, refer to idube.com.

For more information on the Sabi Sands Reserve, refer to sabi-sands.com.

The Experience

The Idube Game Reserve consisted of a cluster of elevated bungalows within the Sabi Sands Reserve. The bungalows were connected by a raised walkway, which led to a central dining area. Tastefully decorated suites had private patios overlooking the surrounding savannah. The staff's impassioned personalities guaranteed a memorable experience. We stayed at Idube for three days before heading to its sister lodge, Lukimbi Game Reserve, as described in the previous section.

Our first game drive took place at dusk. After driving for a few minutes, a flash of movement caught our attention. We came across a young leopard with his mother. The cub was tearing into a freshly caught impala. After only a couple of minutes, a hyena burst through the bushes and rudely interrupted the little one. In a blink, the wee cub scrambled up the nearest tree as the hyena snarled a few warning grunts. Within seconds, the intruder had dragged the carcass out of sight. The mother leopard was no match for a hyena and retreated behind the trees until he left. She then returned to the base of the tree where her cub had climbed, sniffed the ground where the impala had laid and waited for her young one to drop down. The cub tentatively crawled down the tree before dashing to his mother. She cuddled and reassured him that everything was still all right in their world. All this excitement occurred within the first fifteen minutes of our drive.

I think this drama caught us by surprise more than the wary leopards. During our stay, we ran across this little fellow a few more times. He entertained us with an unending game of play-hunting while his mother was off stalking their next meal. The cub often balanced on fallen trees, which gave him better visibility, but was equally amused by crouching in the tall yellow grass. From down low, his coat offered the perfect camouflage. Clearly, the cub's mother had taught her youngster well.

I was amazed by the concentration of wildlife in the Sabi Sands Reserve. The reserve's thick forest, abundance of water and diversity of plants and animals allowed wildlife to prosper within its protective boundaries. Herds of zebras, families of rhinos, tall giraffes and prowling lions roamed in abundance. During one drive, we saw lion sisters lounging along a sandy bank of the river. Eight little cubs ran along the shore, barely visible as their colouring blended into the sand. The sisters watched as the little ones scurried around. Soon after heading inland from the river, we found a third lioness following some vehicle tracks. The driver stopped to watch. Farther along the same set of tracks, a leopard sniffed the bushes, oblivious to what lay ahead. We remained silent. Eventually, the two animals came within a few metres of one another. The lion lunged. We heard the chase continue in the bushes into which the leopard had ducked. Our vehicle slowly wound along the pathways as we attempted to figure out where the two cats had disappeared. We finally spotted the leopard high in a tree, where she had wedged herself between two branches. As we drove closer, her predicament became clear. The lion was circling the base of the tree. Surveying the area, the ranger saw yet another leopard stuck in a tree about a hundred metres away. The guide concluded this lioness must be another sister, a protective aunt. She dutifully kept the leopards far from her vulnerable nieces and nephews. After about thirty minutes of watching this story unravel, we left the animals to resolve their dispute on their own time.

While my husband and I went out on another game drive, my mother-in-law decided to relax in her chalet. Hearing a banging noise at her front entrance, she peeked through a side window. There stood three full-grown elephants, just two metres away. She rightfully remained safely inside. The animals were more interested in a few succulent plants growing on the opposite side of the raised walkway that led to her door. One of the elephants was determined to munch on the lovely leaves for his afternoon snack. He attempted to cross the boardwalk, but his weight proved too much for the wooden boards and they collapsed under his heavy feet. He was not a happy elephant, but after some delicate manoeuvering, he eventually detangled himself from the mess. All three elephants then hastily retreated to the other side of my mother-in-law's chalet, where her plunge pool offered some tantalizing water. A long slurp helped to calm their nerves.

The staff at Idube came quickly after hearing the ruckus. Smashed wooden planks with jagged splinters pointing in all directions remained as evidence of the incident. Such disruptions were part of a typical day when living in a game park. You never knew what surprise the animals might bring.

The Basics

Synopsis: Be welcomed by wildlife as you drive through a game park flush with big game, only to show the animals the same hospitality in return when back at camp.

Most useful item to pack: A spare bar of dish soap

For further travel information: The Track and Trail River Camp offers a variety of accommodations from luxury chalets to campsites. Each campsite has a private barbecue island with running water and a light pole. During our stay, the shared ablution block was kept very clean and was usually vacant. For further information, refer to trackandtrail-rivercamp.com.

The Experience

After an exhausting ten-hour drive from Malawi's Viphya Plateau, we arrived at South Luangwa National Park in Zambia's southeastern corner. With a dizzying array of animals, it proved to be a phenomenal game park. The following stories took place after our game drives had wrapped up and we were relaxing back in camp. Because of the element of surprise, these were some of the most memorable moments of our stay.

The initial incident occurred during our first night. We had comfortably fallen asleep inside our canvas tent, which we had pitched beneath a thatched roof held up by four poles. This open-sided structure supposedly deterred animals. After our previous encounter with an elephant feasting above our tent, we happily opted for this cover.

Sometime in the middle of the night, my husband and I both awoke suddenly. We looked around, not sure what had startled us. We then heard a low snort a few metres away. This was followed by the sound of grass being pulled. Then a faint chewing sound grated over and over. Another sniff, but nearer. Whatever had come for an evening snack was approaching our tent. Soundlessly, I raised my head to peer outside the mesh window. The moonlight shone brightly and lit up the campground's grassy field. There stood a rotund hippopotamus blissfully grazing. Her head was as big as a garbage barrel and her body nearly comparable in size to the Land Rover in which we had arrived. After about ten minutes, she toddled around to the front of our tent. We watched her through the tent's mesh door as she stood grazing about a metre away. A battle raged inside my head between nervous fear and wondrous admiration for the animal. Being so close to an enormous wild creature, separated only by a piece of canvas, was captivating. In due course, the healthy hippo sauntered farther away and finally out of sight. Gradually, our sleepiness returned.

On our second evening, the sun set as we zipped our tent flap closed. A few campers remained outside, enjoying an extended dinner. They were soon interrupted by three social elephants that emerged from the bushes and sauntered towards their campsite. Surely all neighbours were welcome to join the festivities. As the folks backed away, the elephants sniffed the table and poked at the vehicles with their trunks. While we watched from inside our tent, a camp manager arrived to encourage the elephants on their way. The animals danced around, trying to evade the manager's efforts. They ultimately wandered on, or so we thought. A few minutes later, a lone elephant stepped out from the bushes that grew near the ablution facilities. He stood about fifteen metres from our tent and seemed thoroughly unappreciative of being scuttled away from his dinner party. We kept quiet and watched the excitement unfold. After a few minutes, the young elephant rushed forward, heading directly for our tent. Unmoving, we tensed. He bellowed and, thankfully, veered around our thatch cover at the last second. In the meantime, our guide crept into his Land Rover and pursued the angry elephant at a distance to ensure that he indeed continued on his way.

Our last close encounter with the residents of this game park proved less dramatic. While washing up from the evening meal, I stepped away from our private campsite sink to check for any remaining dishes. At that moment, an inquisitive vervet monkey swung down from the tree above the sink. With a quick swipe, he grabbed the enticing green bar of dish soap that sat exposed on the corner of the sink. This audacious monkey likely presumed that it was a juicy leaf or succulent piece of mysterious fruit—a misleading first impression. It did not take long before the soap was thrown back to the ground. From the look of the teeth marks decorating the discarded bar, the soap had clearly failed his taste test.

On the morning we left this charismatic campsite, a couple of local giraffes decided to introduce themselves. On their long legs they practically floated across the grass as they smirked down upon us wee humans. It was an odd scene as we drove out. Even tents perched high on top of camper vans could not escape the giraffes' inquisitive reach.

The Basics

Synopsis: Hop aboard a game drive, or unwind in camp and let the wildlife come to you.

Most useful items to pack: Biodegradable shampoo and soap

For further travel information: The Mvuu Lodge offers various accommodation options, including luxury safari tents, self-catering tents and campsites. The campground and lodges are located along the Zambezi River, near the Lower Zambezi National Park. We stayed in one of their uber-deluxe campsites, which included a private open-air shower and toilet area and an unexpected and reliable WiFi signal. For further information, refer to mvuulodge.com.

Malawi's Liwonde National Park also has a lodge called Mvuu Lodge, as described in a previous section; however, it is completely unrelated. **Mvuu** means "hippopotamus," so it is a frequently used term across the region.

The Experience

The Lower Zambezi National Park is located east of Zambia's capital city, Lusaka. We had driven for two days from the South Luangwa National Park to reach this spot. Miombo woodlands shaded the attractive campground. We quickly realized that this location was not only preferred by campers, but it also doubled as the elephants' favoured lunch scene. As we turned into our designated campsite, two large elephants were helping themselves to a fair number of juicy branches. Wet patches interspersed with clumps of mud still clung to their skin from their morning bath in the nearby Zambezi River. They were not fazed in the least by our arrival. Instead, they continued to tug on selected branches and tenderly stuff the pieces into their mouths. Their trunks seemed to dodge thorns and inedible plants with ease, proving their expertise at the delicate process.

We stayed in the vehicle for a few minutes before the two elephants shifted off our site and onto the adjacent grass. Our guide felt comfortable with their presence but advised us to stay at least five metres from them. Undoubtedly, we were preoccupied with their rather close proximity while we tentatively pitched our tent. They seemed unconcerned and eventually meandered farther away. Their daily visits turned into one of the highlights of our stay. Where else can you hang out in your backyard with such a magnificent animal?

The bathrooms at this campsite were particularly pleasant. Curvy cement walls created private spaces for the toilet and shower. There was no roof to block the view as you lathered up. Usually a family of vervet monkeys swung on the overhead tree branches, scouring our campsite for any tempting bits to steal. Watching their mischievous faces, darting bright eyes and pursed lips always made me laugh. My morning shower turned into a comical scene as a vervet monkey flitted across branches high above. The cheeky monkey was not gutsy enough to pop down low and steal my shampoo, but nonetheless his morning frolic kick-started my day.

One evening after we had settled into our sleeping bags, my husband felt something push his foot. His toes reached the end of the tent, and he had been instinctively pressing outward. Oddly, something gently pushed back. This was disturbing as only bushes lay outside—and the wild. Crouched on the ground was what looked like a large house cat but with an extremely long tail. He was happily playing footsie with my husband through the canvas. The next morning, we enquired at the lodge; however, this was no trickster pet. We were told the critter was likely a civet cat, known to be fond of nocturnal activities.

CHAPTER NINE: UNFORGETTABLE ACCOMMODATIONS

As a devout **Lonely Planet** fan, I rely on their guidance for many of my travels. However, it pains me to concede that their success can also be to their detriment on the accommodation front. Specific endorsements can be fleeting as new competition improves the options on offer. Sadly, some hotel management may simply slack off once their establishment is published in a **Lonely Planet** guidebook. For this reason, I always cross-check hotel reviews on TripAdvisor. com or Booking.com, which are my personal favourites for the latest viewpoints. Overall ratings provide a guideline, but they may be skewed by the general curve of rankings and can blur specific annoyances. I suggest you get into the details and read the lower ranked reviews to gain insight into a place's quirks. Then you can judge whether the complaints are relevant to your personal travel tastes or are unimportant quibbles.

The following sections describe standout places that far surpassed my expectations. I find that friendly staff can have a massive impact on how well I enjoy a place. Setting and the activities offered can also elevate locations to my top picks. Cleanliness is a fundamental quality for me; a lack knocks the hotel out of consideration. Throughout the following sections, I explain why a particular place achieved perfection, at least from my perspective.

These stories are based on my personal experience, so they may not reflect the current situation or other travellers' views. I am describing these places of my own free will and have not received any compensation for these comments, as with all of the places mentioned in this book.

The Basics

Synopsis: Recline in individually decorated chic rooms, partake in an afternoon espresso in the lounge and savour Chef Emir's delectable creations.

Most useful item to pack: Comfy pyjamas

For further travel information: Visit the hotel website at bohemiahotelboutique.com.

The Experience

My husband and I spent a month studying Spanish in the wine-rich region of Mendoza. Our first apartment, which we had coordinated in advance, turned out to be dismally dirty and uninviting. Disappointed, we wandered along nearby streets considering our options. We stumbled upon the suave Bohemia Hotel. I fully expected that their rate would be too steep for a month's stay. However, timing was on our side. The low season's spare capacity played into our favour, and we agreed upon a fair price for an extended stay. Walking through the hotel, our steps lightened as we eyed the gleaming espresso machine sitting on the counter in the breakfast-cum-lounge area. The Bohemia Hotel gave a completely opposite impression than did the apartment we had reserved. Towels were plush. The bathroom sparkled. New bright throw pillows and crisp sheets topped a splendidly comfortable king-sized bed in our spacious room. I convinced myself that Bohemia's bold colour palette would inspire my creativity, a distinct advantage going into four weeks of intensive Spanish lessons.

Although the decor was cool and sublime, the staff were warm and welcoming. After all, it was a family-run hotel. The son, Emir, had recently returned from working as a sous-chef in New York. He had turned his dream of running his own hotel into a brilliant reality here in Mendoza. At the time we stayed, the restaurant had not yet opened. In its absence, Chef Emir tailored meals on request for us. His attentive technique resulted in some spectacular dishes. He would devise a plate depending on what was fresh at the market that day. I enjoyed a particularly delectable peppered steak with grilled vegetables for my birthday dinner. He rounded it out with a softly spiced baked apple, a scoop of ice cream and, of course, a bottle of local earthy Malbec. Emir's care and attention were catching. Everyone working at the hotel was immensely helpful and kind. The reception staff even encouraged us to practise our new Spanish phrases with them. Their patience never seemed to fade.

The Basics

Synopsis: Relax in this solar-powered, naturally constructed ecolodge's full-board chalets amid pristine jungle along a calm river.

Most useful item to pack: DEET mosquito spray

For further travel information: Catch a longboat to the remote Rainbow Lodge along the shores of the Tatai River, where you can kayak, hike or just chill. The lodge can advise you on transport to reach Tatai Village and help with your onward longboat connection. For further information, refer to rainbowlodgecambodia.com.

The Experience

Our thatched-roof cabana was nestled under the shade of lush palm trees. High ceilings and fans kept the temperature comfortable. Terracotta tiles kept the floor cool, while screened windows allowed for ample air circulation. Private balconies were equipped with hammocks and lounge chairs. It was difficult to choose between lazing with a book, paddling upstream or exploring the forest trails. During the day, the lodge facilitated excursions around the area. Kayaks were offered at no extra charge. Hiking paths extended from the main lodge, and anyone craving a cool dip could jump in the river that flowed past the chalets. An array of guided walks, river cruises and cultural tours were available upon request for an extra fee. Packed lunches, snacks or other personal touches were offered to ensure visitors were well looked after during any outing.

Early one morning we pulled ourselves from the oh-so-comfortable bed and trudged down to the jetty. The kayaks shimmered in the morning sun, inviting us to jump inside. They delicately sliced through the Tatai River waters, which were porcelain smooth at that early hour. Images reflected the finest of details, from spiky grasses to fluttering leaves. When we reached our destined waterfall, I decided that the kayak ride was more appealing than the cascading flow. The paddle back to the lodge was just as intoxicating. After our morning exercise, I felt no guilt over chilling with a book on our balcony for the remainder of the day.

The remote Rainbow Lodge in Cambodia's South Cardamom Protected Reserve offered a model of sustainable tourism embedded in the local community. Guest comfort was ensured with hot-water showers, fresh Khmer or

Western meals and delightful cabanas. Check out the "Green Roots" section of the lodge's website for the lowdown on their conservation efforts. They comprehensively address solar and hydro power, food and human waste management, water filtration systems and ties with local suppliers. Between the activities, helpful staff and ecologically friendly footprint, it was truly a worthwhile retreat for a few days.

The Basics

Synopsis: Submerge yourself in traditional Cambodian life with the help of a remote village whose residents have united to offer a coordinated package of homestay, daily activities and local cuisine.

Most useful item to pack: Rain cover for backpack

For further travel information: Hail a cargo vessel near the bridge in Andoung Tuek to travel upriver to the community of Chi Phat. This town has transformed itself into an extensive ecotourism initiative. Homestay accommodation is allocated among families in the village using a rotational scheme. Facilities are basic. Expect bucket showers and pit toilets. For more information, refer to chi-phat.org.

The Experience

From Rainbow Lodge, the swish minimalist ecolodge described in the previous section, we switched up the style of our next accommodation for a simpler concept. The entrepreneurial village of Chi Phat overcame its difficult-to-reach location and basic infrastructure by offering visitors a chance to experience true Cambodian village life. Its business plan proved popular. During our stay, most homestays were fully booked by intrepid travellers keen to experience the "real" Cambodia. We may not have found Egyptian cotton towels or hot showers, but the array of activities and the unprecedented community approach outweighed any perceived discomfort.

The journey to Chi Phat started from the nearly imperceptible village of Andoung Tuek, where a couple of market stands and two nondescript cafés sat a few metres off National Highway 48, and random structures dotted the road leading to the Preak Piphot River. A steel bridge and muddy embankment marked our next transport point, but we had to wait a few hours. As more rain threatened, we walked back up the highway to the more promising of the two cafés. Its rows of tables inside a windowed room belied the image of a reputable establishment. Once inside, we saw a lone employee lolling in a hammock, completely unaware of our potential business. Despite our mild attempt to awaken the lady, she remained comatose. The kitchen appeared vacant.

Across the road, outdoor tables were partially protected by a tin roof, and this quickly became our venue of choice. At least there was movement at this less formal establishment. The staff turned out to be incredibly friendly and prepared a decent plate of fried rice. An hour passed quickly as we chatted with our new hosts and watched local life carry on. The rain continued to pelt down in waves. Mini-streams picked up rubbish or anything that rested along the roadside and carried it along the walking path. Most people stayed under cover and, like us, watched the rain. Women lounged in brightly coloured pyjamas while men stood shirtless below roof overhangs. Only a couple of roosters stepped out into the onslaught to poke around for a potential treat.

During a lull in the storm, we grabbed our packs, which were already wrapped in their protective rain cover. With a quick prayer that the cargo vessel would operate that day, we hustled to the bridge. There she floated, a bulky hunk of steel piled with goods that had been covered in plastic sheets. A small raised platform was tucked behind the engine for passengers to sit on. There were no chairs, only space to crouch. The surly captain remained sour even after we paid the desig-nated price of two dollars and fifty cents. Perhaps it was his demeanour, but the entire trip seemed rather gloomy. Thunder pounded, raindrops ricocheted off the plastic covers, the engine growled and the other passengers withdrew inside their hoods. After two hours of such pleasure, we were relieved to see the "Chi Phat Community" sign come into view. The Chi Phat website now advises that boat fees have increased fourfold since our visit in 2010. They also recommend earplugs for the ride. I suggest you heed their advice.

After disembarking from the barge and gathering our packs, all guests were directed to Chi Phat's Community Office. We swung our backpacks over our shoulders and walked up the main street. It was a wide reddish dirt road. Grey tin-roofed wooden homes sat a few metres off the road. An occasional green tarp was stretched across tables to add extra shade or rain cover, depending on the weather's mood. Dogs scampered along the road while chickens ran sporadically. Most homes were elevated on stilts. I could not be sure if this was due to the risk of floods or to provide the perfect place to hang a hammock. These recliners had become an essential part of Cambodian life, perfect for rocking babies, taking shaded afternoon naps or just hanging out with family members.

We were assigned to sleep at the Chiva Guesthouse. The family had construct-ed a three-bedroom building on stilts across a three-metre dirt walkway from their home. The walls and floor were made of wood planks, offering generous air flow through cracks and gaps between the boards. This also allowed random bugs to come and go. A palm-sized brown spider seemed quite at home but sprinted out when we prodded it gently. It may have returned later but shrewdly kept out of sight. A mosquito net in fairly good condition hung from the ceiling and fit around the mattresses, which lay on the floor. We also had a fan in our room to add some movement to the hot, muggy air—at least when electricity was available, from 6:00 to 10:00 p.m. The family generally kept to themselves, but were friendly enough.

The town offered excursions to a variety of destinations, either by boat or bike or on foot. During our boat ride to Stung Proat, grey monkeys flitted in the palms close to shore. Their whitish beards fluttered as they leapt from tree to tree. Black-and-white birds with vast wingspans also flew overhead, and curved beaches intercepted thick rainforest as we sailed past. On our return to Chi Phat, we savoured some of the best iced coffees in Cambodia, served in the town's minimalist café.

This village had come together to create an organized opportunity to show foreigners their utopia in all its simple splendour. I did not see any other town in Cambodia that had embraced this concept in the same manner. From looking at their website more recently, it seems that they have increased the excursions available and have continued to evolve their unique cultural experience. It was well worth enduring the basic lodging and rather uncomfortable transport to get there. Consider this destination if you are searching for a genuine slice of Cambodia's village life.

The Basics

Synopsis: Indulge in artistic cottages raised on stilts, overlooking a manicured garden, tiered rice paddies and tantalizing jungle.

Most useful item to pack: Comfortable walking or hiking shoes

For further travel information: To reserve your own private bungalow, designed in traditional Indonesian glamour, refer to melantingcottages.com.

Most visitors hire a private vehicle to reach the town of Munduk in northern Bali, which would be the most direct and likely the simplest mode. However, we hopped on a Perama shuttle bus in Denpasar and travelled north to Pancasari. This northern bus station was reputably the hub for onward transport across Bali's northern region. Although we had read that onward buses could be caught in Pancasari to travel to Munduk, when we arrived there were none. The station was deserted save for a vegetable market in dire need of customers. The parking lot was also empty except for a couple of guys reclined on their motorcycles.

They watched as we asked the only other people we could find about getting to Munduk. One of the bike drivers then approached us with a proposition. We negotiated a reasonable fee for him and his buddy to double us on the back seat of their motorcycles. This would take us the final forty-five minutes through what turned out to be a varied landscape of coffee plantations and mountain ridges. The views were gorgeous. Each driver managed to balance one of our big packs in front of his body while we each sat behind a driver with our small day pack. The bikes were certainly loaded down, but the drivers drove impressively steady-handed. Their services must have been needed on a frequent basis, as they even had spare helmets on hand for us to wear.

The Experience

While my husband and I were walking on the outskirts of the town of Munduk, a sign for the new Melanting Cottages caught our attention. I find that new hotels lack brand recognition and strive to win business, often by offering better value and fresher rooms than the competition. As the underdog, they are fighting to prove themselves. As we approached Melanting's reception area, orange-tiled roofs came into view. Closer still, we noticed a web of pathways connecting bungalows amid an oasis of flowers, palm trees, shrubbery and neatly trimmed grass. Intricately carved panels decorated darkly stained wood bungalows. Each unit was raised on stilts and had a private patio. At the foot of each cabin's entrance, serene statues etched from whitish limestone portrayed a closed-eye, slyly smiling person with a crooked head. Inside the bungalow, matching lamps were carved from similar limestone. They lit a four-poster bed draped in bright white mosquito netting, a stunning contrast to the dark siding. The cabin's ultimate feature was its patio. It offered a perfect location to observe terraced rice paddies framed by palms and clove trees.

I relished the cooler temperatures compared to the lower beach regions of Bali. Morning walks through misty rice fields and thick jungle became our favourite pastime while in Munduk. We passed clove pickers balanced high in the trees. They climbed makeshift ladders made from a tall pole with five-inch rods affixed perpendicularly to create intermittent steps. After wedging their poles securely against a tree, the pickers scampered up holding a large canvas sack on one arm. One cheerful picker with a wide grin chatted and showed us a perfect cluster of clove flowers that he had just plucked. The pink blooms had not yet dried to the familiar chocolate brown stubs that I normally associated with the spice. Their switch from flower to flavouring became evident along Munduk's streets. A sight more frequent than cars were tarps covered with a layer of cloves left to dry along the roadside. Residents would intermittently rake the harvest to rotate the buds and allow for consistent evaporation. The wooden rakes were stubby and made of solid wood. They were usually wielded by someone walking atop the tiny cloves in flip-flops, making me wonder about any subsequent cleansing process, which surely existed. With the help of the sun's gentle rays, the buds eventually transformed from their initial cream and pink to a dark chestnut tone. As we walked along the streets, random whiffs of this exquisite spice made the town seem like a baker's paradise.

On the walk to the Melanting Waterfall, we passed even-more-remote villages accessible only from the same walking path. The forest along this route was diverse; a mélange of clove, vanilla, hibiscus, poinsettia, bougainvillea and coconut palms turned the hillsides into an artistic masterpiece. Everyone's face broke into a smile as we walked past, and these encounters often turned into inquisitive chats. Many people were keen to practise their English skills and shared helpful local insight about the walking trail. On one of the lower rice paddy walks, local guidance turned out to be essential advice as our map failed to mark a critical turn. The return to our bungalow hideaway after these friendly walks confirmed that this mountain village was indeed a tiny oasis. The grounds were beautifully maintained and the staff incredibly friendly. Although such care is common in Bali, this hotel seemed to have perfected the tranquil mountain vibe.

The Basics

Synopsis: Pamper yourself at Morocco's version of rustic chic, and indulge in a sumptuous home-cooked breakfast.

Most useful item to pack: Binoculars to scan Marrakesh's skyline from the rooftop lounge

For further travel information: From recent research, it appears that Riad W no longer operates under this name, as it did when we stayed. However, from comments on TripAdvisor.com and Booking.com, I understand that the name has been changed to Riad UP. In photos on their website, this establishment looks similar in structure, but it appears to have been renovated since our stay. I cannot confirm whether the same management runs the hotel, but further information can be found at riadup.com.

The Experience

After a two-week tour through Morocco, my husband and I spent a leisurely two days in the lovely city of Marrakesh. With backpacks comfortably balanced on our hips, we said our goodbyes to the tour group. The Riad W was located a five-minute walk from the Jemaa el-Fnaa Square. As depicted on the map, we turned left off the main Rue Riad Zitoun Jdid onto a narrow street. From here, the map and reality appeared to deviate. The dead-end lanes and twisty alleys seemed more like an amusement maze than the clear trail we had expected to follow. An elderly gentleman sat beside the road, watching the day's activities transpire. We inquired whether he knew of Riad W's whereabouts. He pointed us farther along and around a bend. I was not sure if he really did know or just wanted us to move along. Eventually, we came to a massive carved wooden door. A tiny marker indicated that we had, in fact, landed on Riad W's doorstep. The dull cement walls rose two storeys, hiding what might lie within. This was the style in Marrakesh: high protective walls that looked less than inviting from the outside. But as we stepped inside, it was like entering a different world. We never knew what we would find behind the barrier.

Our room in Riad W was decorated in a Moroccan contemporary style. The bed was on a raised cement platform. A red-and-orange stained-glass light hung overhead. Leather cushions created a seating area to the left of the bed. The bathroom was reached through a traditional Moroccan wooden door, split into upper and lower sections. The colours were a warm mixture of stained wood, worn brown leather and creamy tones. Outside our room, a few stairs led to the rooftop. From here, neighbouring roofs, tips of palm trees and otherwise concealed lounge areas could be seen. It felt almost as if we were spying on the real Marrakesh, that hidden persona behind its imposing cement walls.

The central area of the building was open to the sky, so the sun shone in and created a private garden inside the hotel. On the lower level, a small L-shaped pool gurgled. Half of it extended into the central area and was warmed by the sun's rays. A cushioned seating area offered guests space to lounge, while a large canvas painted by a local artist brightened the space.

Riad W's breakfast was exquisite. Traditional Moroccan plates filled a long wooden table. Homemade jams, freshly grilled crêpes, slices of homemade date loaf, bowls of fruit, freshly squeezed juice and a silver flask of hearty coffee brought the table alive. Mornings may have been the best part of this hotel, but they had stiff competition from the sublime room.

The Basics

Synopsis: Wake up to breakfast served on your private beach, hike to a nearby community and chat with the village chief and, above all, experience Nkwichi Lodge's masterful balance of creating a traveller's retreat while sustainably developing local communities.

Most useful items to pack: Sun hat and walking shoes

For further travel information: We flew to Mozambique's north-western town of Lichinga, the capital city of Niassa Province. Alternative modes of travel include private vehicle, charter plane or the intermittent and often-delayed train from Nampula. From Lichinga, we had prearranged the remaining transportation through Nkwichi Lodge. The first leg was via a four-wheel-drive vehicle to the lakeside town of Cobue. As our driver sped down the road, I wondered if he was practising for the Dakar Rally. The vehicle became airborne as it ricocheted off frequent potholes, and goats dodged off the road to escape his blaring horn. Nkwichi's website indicates that this section is a four-hour drive, but we arrived in a mere three hours.

At the waterfront in Cobue, a motorboat transferred us the final twelve kilometres south along Lake Niassa's shoreline to arrive at the pristine Nkwichi Lodge. Take note, the names Lake Niassa and Lake Malawi are used interchangeably. For more information, refer to nkwichi.com.

The Experience

Nkwichi Lodge definitively ticked the luxury box for savvy travellers. At every meal, we had the choice of eating at a number of locations along beaches and inlets or on the patio of the main lodge. My personal favourite was the private sandy enclosure in front of our chalet, referred to as Venus Beach. Social vervet monkeys swung down to join us at one of the other tree-encircled beach locations. One young guy stared at us innocently before he swiftly reached down and stole a slice of freshly baked banana bread. After that episode, we upped our defensive tactics. After all, the meals were aromatic and savoury but not intended for cheeky monkeys.

We stayed in one of seven handcrafted bungalows constructed of local materials by nearby community staff. They were quite extraordinarily styled. Thatched roofs shaded the interior and patio but allowed large gaps for airflow. Wooden slatted screens acted as movable walls along the water-facing side. Our outdoor bathroom mimicked a spa. Its stone floor was surrounded by trees, shrubbery and wooden poles strung together to create a wall of privacy. Steps dipped down into a large curved tub. A couple of metres behind the tub rested a mirror and vanity made of matching stone. In the opposite corner, an equally lovely **au naturel** shower was concealed by thick trees and a short stone wall. For those less keen on the outdoor experience, an ensuite offered a convenient indoor alternative.

Although we technically stayed lakeside, Lake Malawi looked more like an ocean, as its distant shore melded into the horizon. The lake is the third largest in Africa and home to one thousand different species of fish. Of these, approximately 350 species are unique to Lake Malawi, found nowhere else worldwide. These vibrantly coloured swimmers are referred to as **cichlids** or **mbuna**.[53] Forget the murky lake full of reeds from your childhood summer camp. Snorkelling in Lake Malawi is said to be clear and impressive—just be sure to avoid stagnant water. The bilharzia parasite has been found in the lake, although while we stayed at Nkwichi Lodge, staff told us that the waters around the lodge were free of this infectious worm. Snorkelling gear was available from the lodge, as were kayaks, paddle-boards and, unexpectedly, Canadian-made canoes. Nkwichi's management surely had impressive supply-chain skills to get such bulky items across the globe to these remote shores.

Instead, we opted for land sports. Nkwichi's staff, who were from the neighbouring communities, took us along local pathways that passed through their hometowns. We started one four-hour walk by following the shoreline, which offered a light breeze to marginally dissipate the blazing heat. We spotted fishermen inspecting the traps they had set on the previous day. Onshore, their earlier prize catches were spread out to dry under the sun's rays. The men could earn a small profit by selling these dehydrated fillets at the popular market in Lichinga. Farther along the trail, children played. They fled at the sight of us, yelling, **"Mzungu, mzungu!"** ("White person, white person!"). After we called out, **"Wah, wah,"** which meant "hello" in their local dialect, they seemed to relax. One child even chirped back with a friendly hello in English and proceeded to follow us, albeit at a slight distance. We carried on along the sandy path. At a mound of boulders near the water's edge, six slightly older children attempted to fish. The eldest girl, aged about eight, seemed the most adept at managing the long wooden pole with a plastic bucket strapped around her shoulders. One of the younger boys seemed more interested in two fist-sized pods covered in a velvety exterior. They had fallen off an indigenous tree but looked more like music shakers than fruit.

By the time we arrived at the nearby village of Mbueca, the breeze had vanished completely, and as a result, a sweaty film clung to our skin. Much like in other northern Mozambique towns, homes were constructed of mud walls and topped with a thatched roof. One man, who turned out to be the village chief, was building an extension for his kitchen. His jovial smile and frequent laughter made it easy to understand his popularity among the villagers. The chief welcomed us to explore the dusty streets of his town. We chatted for a while, and he joked that perhaps his next project should be to build a bar; that way he could sell beverages to parched travellers such as us.

A short distance away, a cluster of houses nestled beneath some trees. In the yard, cassava roots had bleached white and lay drying on a wooden table built specifically for this purpose. Cassava was a popular root, used to make a starchy side dish to accompany virtually every meal. These residences belonged to our guide's family. He graciously invited us to see the interior of his home, where the temperature was surprisingly cool compared to the sweltering heat outside. Somehow the mud walls and thatched roof acted as a simple yet effective air conditioner. The dirt floors were swept clean. Carved wooden furniture created a functional space, and decorative touches hung from the walls. Between the lake views, the cool breezes and a congenial atmosphere, we gained a refreshing perspective of what it might be like to live in a mud house.

During another day's walk, we passed baboons that looked like little trouble-makers. They stopped whatever they were doing while we walked by and continued to stare until we were out of sight. When we returned along the same path, the mischievous primates had retreated without a trace of their antics. Our destination was the town of Cobue, the same village we had briefly passed through en route to Nkwichi Lodge. Its most striking feature was the remains of a Catholic church that was nearly destroyed during Mozambique's civil war. The roof was missing. Pockmarks from shelling had chipped the cathedral's faded artwork. I recall a poignant painting of a dove flying towards the sun against a faded blue background, painted directly onto a cement wall. Gunfire had left scars across the surface, and blackish mould tarnished its finish. In my view, these flaws added a sentimental touch. The depiction conveyed hope twisted by conflict and brought tears to my eyes as I looked around the empty interior of the chapel. On the day that this church was destroyed, a local couple had hoped to be married. The groom-to-be was killed and many of the wedding guests were injured during the carnage. It was a heartbreaking place, a reminder of the anguish and destruction inflicted on the country for sixteen long years. My appreciation grew for Nkwichi's dedication to enable and support the surrounding communities.

Nkwichi Lodge was not simply a charity that funded ad hoc projects. It was part of the Manda Wilderness Area, a privately initiated conservation program that had partnered with fifteen surrounding communities. The current count has risen to sixteen communities, according to the organization's website. Their ideology supports responsible tourism through enabling sustainable agriculture, creating employment opportunities, encouraging education and protecting local flora and fauna. We visited a sponsored hospital and school; they were both basic but functional. Residents from these communities filled positions throughout Nkwichi Lodge's operation, including management, kitchen staff, guides, transport drivers and other necessary roles. The restaurant's food was purchased from local farmers who engaged in sustainable practices, as taught by the Manda Wilderness Area. The success of the entire business was interwoven with the health and development of the local communities. For me, this level of care, combined with the impeccable quality of the experience, made Nkwichi Lodge a very special place, well worth its all-inclusive day rate.

The Basics

Synopsis: Float along the lazy river below palm trees, and indulge in delicious Arabian cuisine.

Most useful items to pack: Bathing suit and sunscreen

For further travel information: The Shangri-La Barr al Jissah Resort & Spa can be reached by driving about twenty minutes from Mutrah, old Muscat. For more information, refer to shangri-la.com/muscat/barral-jissahresort.

The Experience

The Shangri-La Barr al Jissah Resort & Spa (which I will refer to as simply "Shangri-La") was designed as if it were a string of traditional Omani towns. Three styles of hotels and an even greater selection of restaurants formed the resort. The white-and-cream buildings of the Al Waha and Al Bandar hotels spread across the beachfront, rising no higher than three storeys. These two hotels were similarly styled, with geometric edging that outlined their rooftops. Al Waha translates to "The Oasis" and was intended for families, while Al Bandar means "The Town" and provided the focal point for the resort. Arches framed the doors, and balcony alcoves were inconspicuously tucked into the walls. Palm trees speckled the entire grounds, while water channels flowed between swimming pools and throughout the resort. The channels had been fashioned after the Omani **falaj** system, an irrigation method that has been used to transport groundwater since AD 500. Atop a bluff to the east of the beach was the distinctive pink Al Husn; fashioned after Arabic royal palaces, it was the most exclusive of the three hotels.

We stayed at the Al Bandar for two nights as a weekend getaway while living in Muscat. During the forty-minute drive from our home to the hotel, we crossed the edges of Mutrah and cut inland towards Wadi al Kabir, a wide dry riverbed that had developed into a suburb of its own. A **jebel** range rose on either side to create a striated ridge that towered over the low rectangular buildings. White-washed houses hugged the base of the mountains until the point where it became too steep to build. We cruised through the iconic roundabout with its giant orange frankincense burner decorating the centre. Before long, the structures faded and we were alone with the jagged jebels, interspersed with dry flat stretches. By the time we turned off the main road towards Shangri-La, the city felt a distant web of activity compared to the current tranquility. The azure-blue ocean looked like a dot of colour that quickly spread and enveloped the sandy cliffs ahead. Around the last bend, we spotted a beach naturally enclosed by rocky outcrops that offered protection at either side. Spread below, the Shangri-La lay like a tiny town, true to its intended image.

We filled our afternoon by floating along the waterway that meandered around the resort, which was dubbed the "lazy river." Its water served the dual purpose of keeping us both cool and entertained. After swirling about in the pool and cruising on the waterway, we felt it was time for a drink. A slushy lemon-mint beverage was my go-to nonalcoholic beverage. I have tasted this mixture done well only in the United Arab Emirates and Oman. The mint leaves must be ground to a pulp and blended with just the right amount of fresh lemon juice, crushed ice and a squirt of sugar water. Once our liquids had been sufficiently replenished, it was time to check out the beach. Most beachgoers lounged under the white sun umbrellas, leaving the remainder of the golden sands empty except for the odd scuttling crab. As we walked, only the waves lapping against the sand and the occasional cry from a gull could be heard. Shangri-La's private cove and mountainous backdrop created a secluded ambience, the perfect weekend getaway or longer-term retreat. If visiting the resort as part of a longer trip to Oman, I recommend taking an excursion to the city, at least for a morning. Mutrah's **souq** has some gorgeous handicrafts for sale and interesting stalls to peruse. An authentic fish market lies near the souq. If you tire of the beach and solitude, there are also many accessible day trips. Refer to Chapter Four and Chapter Six regarding the Nizwa Fort and diving in Oman.

The Basics

Synopsis: Wrap up in a fluffy white robe after hiking in the Jungfrau region, and savour the chef's delicately layered croissants with a perfectly prepared cappuccino over breakfast.

Most useful item to pack: Map of the surrounding hiking trails

For further travel information: We hiked from Grindelwald to Wengen. The clifftop town of Wengen can also be accessed via train from Lauterbrunnen or via cable car from Grindelwald. The Wengen town website provides excellent information on how to reach this car-free village: wengen.ch/en.

For more information on Hotel Caprice, refer to caprice-wengen.ch.

For more information about all car-free towns in Switzerland, refer to myswitzerland.com/en-ca/carfree-destinations.html.

The Experience

My husband and I were hiking in the Grindelwald region of central Switzerland when we decided to spend a night in Wengen. Check out Chapter Three for a full run-down of our hiking escapades. Wengen is one of a handful of car-free towns in the Lauterbrunnen valley. **Lauterbrunnen** means "many fountains" and refers to the seventy-two waterfalls decorating the rocky cliff below the town. Wengen sits on the edge of the valley's eastern cliff, and two other car-free towns, Winteregg and Mürren, lie on the western side. Cable cars shuttle people to Winteregg and Mürren, while a train chugs up the ever-so-slightly gentler slope to Wengen.

In the winter, Wengen was a skiing mecca, while in the summer months, when we visited, the region was a hiking haven. The pretty town sat across a ridge, west of Grindelwald and in the shadow of the imposing Jungfrau Mountain. Our view from the Caprice Hotel's windows caught it all. Glacier-frosted mountain peaks framed grassy highlands spreading below. Across the valley, sharp cliffs cut down to the main highway. The town's fortuitous location beckoned outdoor enthusiasts. Most buildings were hotels, restaurants, souvenir shops or mountain chalets. None were located very far from the central train station.

The town seemed oddly quiet. Occasionally an electric bus whirred past, hauling tourists' luggage between the train station and their chosen hotel. These vehicles were no louder than a whisper. Few private vehicles appeared to exist. All the ones we saw displayed their respective hotel's logo on the door. Presumably, Swiss regulations have kept the town truly exhaust-free and, as an added bonus, free from noise pollution.

At the time we visited, Hotel Caprice stood out for its airy modern decor. The entire hotel appeared well thought out. As hikers, we carried only a small day pack for our stay, so the full array of luxurious toiletries, plush housecoats and cozy slippers made the end of a hard day quite pleasant. Staff were extremely warm and helpful. They seemed at ease with guests entering the contemporary reception and lounge area dusty and sweaty after a day's hike. The restaurant was nearly better than the hotel itself. Meals were presented with an artistic flare. The croissants at breakfast were some of the lightest and flakiest that I had ever tasted. At the time we were there, the chef had returned to his hometown in France but had left a full stock of frozen croissant dough, which had been rolled into perfectly shaped crescents. When baked fresh each morning, the little puffs tasted as if someone had awoken far too early to make the dough. We combined these delectable mouthfuls with sliced meats, the customary Swiss-German break-fast, to sustain our return hike to Grindelwald later that day. Well, perhaps we only reached our full energy levels after tipping back a third hit of strong coffee.

The Basics

Synopsis: Chill with a book on your private brick veranda shaded by palm trees, or pop down to the beachside restaurant for an iced coffee.

Most useful items to pack: Sandals and a good novel

For further travel information: The island of Phu Quoc in southern Vietnam has a huge range of hotels. Lien Hiep Thanh Resort is a basic bungalow-styled hotel situated at the south end of Long Beach, away from the town centre. We enjoyed the simplicity and friendliness of its standout budget cabanas. For more information, refer to lienhi-epthanhresort.com.

The Experience

Lien Hiep Thanh Resort is a family-run budget hotel located along Long Beach on Phu Quoc Island in southern Vietnam. The owners were over-the-top friendly, and the bungalows were spic and span clean. Their restaurant on the beach offered fresh, light and tasty dishes, including an array of grilled local fish and seafood. The traditional Vietnamese iced coffees served with indulgent sweetened condensed milk induced a smile to my face—oh so delicious. Overall, the attention to detail was the extreme opposite from where we had stayed the first night of this trip. Our journey to get to the lovely Lien Hiep Thanh Resort played a large role in why we never wanted to leave.

In the summer of 2010, my husband and I were making what we expected to be a simple overland trip from Kampot, in southern Cambodia, to the island of Phu Quoc, in Vietnam. We had obtained the prerequisite Vietnamese tourist visas from the embassy in Sihanoukville. This surfer town was a two-hour shuttle ride from where we were staying in Kampot. The embassy staff duly checked our passports, certified our paperwork and stamped a visa on a blank passport page within an incredible five-minute turnaround period. Back in Kampot, we then coordinated our overland transport to Phu Quoc with one of many travel agencies that offered the equivalent service. We used the same agency that had provided our shuttle to Sihanoukville, as we had a certain level of confidence in their services. The plan was straightforward. We would catch a minibus from Kampot to the Cambodian border town of Prek Chak-Xa Xia, and then motorcycles would double each of us with our backpacks to the Vietnamese border town of Ha Tien. After clearing customs, we intended to travel straight to the ferry terminal and catch a hydrofoil to Phu Quoc. We should be enjoying an iced Vietnamese coffee on the beach by ten in the morning, according to the plan.

The morning started out well. We even welcomed a familiar face as the same driver from our visa-run drove the initial leg. His manic driving style had not softened. The vehicle somehow managed to dodge the masses of bicycles, cows, dogs and motos that haphazardly meandered in and out of the semidesignated lane. Ignoring our comments that we were not in a rush, the driver even passed other shuttle buses in his haste to get us to the border. Once there, exiting Cambodian customs went smoothly. A few minutes later, we stood at the Vietnamese border control hut. The Vietnamese customs officer keenly processed our paperwork. Counterintuitively, he ticked off every disease listed, assuring us that a checked box indicated that we did **not** suffer from the indicated ailment. The official then requested a one-dollar unofficial "fee" from each of us unless we could present our vaccination certificates. Unfortunately for him, we had our cards and avoided making a one-dollar donation for his morning coffee. As promised, our two motos were waiting, and we crossed into Vietnam. At this point, we were still on target to catch the 8:00 a.m. hydrofoil.

Seven months before, Vietnam had passed a law that required a helmet to be worn when riding a motorcycle. Our drivers handed us their spare helmets. Thinking they had built some level of trust, they then suggested that we should change money at the border. It might have been early, but we were not going to fall for their ploy. From our experience, border crossings are the absolute worst places to exchange currency because of the lousy exchange rate. They then attempted to explain that the ATMs would not function on the island. The two schemers wanted to stop en route for us to withdraw cash. We graciously declined. These drivers had earned themselves a couple of red flags before we had even departed for the ferry terminal.

We first drove past grubby food market stalls, typical of border regions worldwide. The landscape then cleared to reveal saturated rice paddies shaded by towering limestone karsts. A short time later, office towers and apartment blocks came into view, and we entered the recently developed port town of Ha Tien. Market stalls had popped up to take advantage of the new law, selling helmets in every design imaginable, including ones featuring a stripe of the fashionable faux-Burberry's beige, black and red plaid down their centres. An overwhelming majority of riders showcased this design.

Our drivers curved through the city streets, across a bridge and down a deserted lane and eventually pulled into a run-down, abandoned jetty. This scene was nothing like the terminal we had expected. The lack of officials, passengers or even a proper ticket booth made us very uneasy. A rough-looking middle-aged man crawled out from beneath the shade of an umbrella. He sauntered over and explained, in an all-too-practised spiel, that the boat needed two or three days of repair work. While spouting his rehearsed lines, the man pointed to a decrepit ship that bore no resemblance to the hydrofoil ferry for which we had already purchased tickets. The only other nearby boats were shabby fishing vessels. Our helpful moto drivers suggested that we purchase a ride from them to travel to the neighbouring town of Rach Gia, two and a half hours away. From there, we could purchase yet another ticket for an alternative boat to Phu Quoc. Their kindness underwhelmed us.

At that point, we insisted that the moto drivers take us to a bona fide ferry ticket office. The supposed ticket man put on a mild tirade as if he were deeply insulted by our disbelief. Finally, we left the ancient harbour with its rickety catfish boats and went to a ticket booth in the centre of town. The custodian inside this newer kiosk informed us that the ferry was not running that day due to bad weather. We looked up at the clear blue sky and out across calm waters, distrusting this new piece of information. As we were at least in Ha Tien's centre, we decided to disengage from our scheming drivers. After some persuasion, they reimbursed the amount that we had paid for the mystery ferry tickets and left.

We checked with two other tour companies, who both confirmed that the ferry had not run due to poor weather. They also verified that the modern ticket booth that we had visited in central Ha Tien was, in fact, authentic. By this point, we conceded to stay in Ha Tien for the night and checked into a newish-looking hotel with friendly staff. For the remainder of the day, we undertook some additional reconnaissance and tested a nearby restaurant. The afternoon progressed largely uneventfully. The next morning, we met the reception staff by six thirty. The young man manning the desk called the ferry office and confirmed that the hydrofoil was indeed running, but he was told that all tickets were sold out. What?! Because we have learned to probe the first response, we headed straight to the ferry ticket office ourselves. We explained a simplified version of our situation and our previous attempt to sail the day before. Five minutes later, we left the office carrying two tickets for second-row seats on the 8:00 a.m. hydrofoil.

Sure enough, by ten o'clock we had arrived on the island of Phu Quoc, only twenty-four hours later than originally envisioned. The sun was shining and the island's ATM machines functioned just fine. Life was in order once again. Near the end of Long Beach, we checked into a bungalow that seemed pleasant at first. However, it proved rather disappointing. Wires poked out of the room's electrical sockets, the shower sputtered with dismally low pressure and, worst of all, the staff were indifferent at best. The next morning, we walked next door to check out the Lien Hiep Thanh Resort. Its bungalows led down to the beachfront and initially looked similar to those we had just left. But then we met the staff. The difference was dramatic. Everyone we met was warm and welcoming. For twenty-five American dollars, we had a sparkling clean bungalow, proper electrical outlets, a forceful shower and the cutest patio with lounge chairs, all nestled under palm trees. We quickly checked out of our first night's accommodation and settled into our new home. I think that our smiles remained on our faces all day after the effort it took to reach this idyllic hideaway. After five days, we still dreaded leaving our serene retreat.

Thank you for reading my book. If you enjoyed it, won't you please take a moment to leave me a review at your favourite online book retailer?

Thanks!

Nancy O'Hare

For twenty years, Nancy O'Hare coupled her love of diverse cultures with a career in finance; she has been based in Nigeria, Oman, Switzerland, Australia and Canada—plus completed a couple of short stints in Qatar and Ecuador. Between work assignments, O'Hare and her husband have taken multiple around-the-world trips for months at a time, covering all seven continents. They gravitate towards hidden gems tucked away from the crowds and aimed to see the essence of a place.

Connect with Nancy O'Hare:

Facebook:

www.facebook.com/ByNancyO/

Twitter:

twitter.com/DustInMyPack

Blog:

www.bynancyohare.com

ENDNOTES

1   http://www.arcticantarcticcollection.com/ship/antarcticDream/4900023.htm

2   http://www.whitsundays-australia.com/whitsundays-history.html

3   https://www.awesomewhitsundays.com/about-whitehaven-beach

4   http://whc.unesco.org/en/list/1432

5   https://www.okavangodelta.com/

6   https://www.okavangodelta.com/general-information/wildlife/

7   http://animals.nationalgeographic.com/animals/wild/shows-deadly-60/fun-facts

8   https://www.usgs.gov/news/earthview-glaciers-worldwide-are-retreating-one-defies-trend

9   http://www.bbc.com/news/world-middle-east-38084391

10 http://whc.unesco.org/en/list/181

11 **Flat white** is a term used in Australia for an espresso with swirled frothed milk, similar to a latte, yet not quite the same.

12 In 2015, Bhutan earned a score of 0.756 on its Gross National Happiness Index. Transparent reporting can be found at the aptly named Gross National Happiness website at www.grossnationalhappiness.com.

13 http://www.summitpost.org/villarrica-volcano/151480

14 http://www.bbc.com/news/world-latin-america-31708312

15 reuters.com/news/picture/sleeping-volcano-awakens?articleId=UKRTSDQ6Q

16 http://whc.unesco.org/en/list/971

17 http://earthquake-report.com/2012/09/09/volcano-activity-of-september-9-2012-san-cristobal-eruption-update-nicaragua-very-nice-etna-video/

18 http://travelguidenicaragua.com/en/destination/norte/jinotega/reserva-natural-datanli-el-diablo/

19 http://whc.unesco.org/en/list/1224

20 http://www.cambodia.org/Preah_Vihear/?history=A+Khmer+Heritage

21 http://whc.unesco.org/en/list/242

22 http://www.bbc.com/culture/story/20150223-uncovering-caves-full-of-treasure

23 https://www.youtube.com/watch?v=VI4q4ShXNYw

24 http://whc.unesco.org/en/list/481

25 http://whc.unesco.org/en/list/433

26 http://www.mozambique.co.za/About_Mozambique-travel/mozambique-info.html

27 http://www.historymuseum.ca/cmc/exhibitions/civil/maya/mmc01eng.shtml

28 http://www.history.com/topics/maya

29 Coatimundis are mammals that look like a cross between raccoons and anteaters. They have pointy pliable snouts and fuzzy brown bodies, but they run like warthogs with their tails pointed straight up.

30 http://whc.unesco.org/en/list/64

31 http://maya.nmai.si.edu/calendar/calendar-system

32 http://whc.unesco.org/en/list/129

33 http://www.visitpetra.jo/Pages/viewpage.aspx?pageID=124

34 http://www.calvin.edu/petra/about/nabataeans.php

35 http://whc.unesco.org/en/list/444

36 http://www.ephesus.us/ephesus/theatre.htm

37 http://www.ucalgarycelebrates.ca/arabian-desert-surrenders-queen-shebas-secrets

38 http://whc.unesco.org/en/list/385

39 https://joshberer.wordpress.com/2009/10/05/the-qamariya/

40 http://stradbrokeisland.com/

41 https://taronga.org.au/conservation/conservation-science-research/australian-shark-attack-file/2016

42 https://www.britannica.com/place/Jura-Mountains

43 http://whc.unesco.org/en/list/672

44 http://www.c-w-r.com/information/classification.html

45 http://www.zambezirafting.com/livingstone-zambia/
zambezi-river-rapid-guide.html

46 http://www.bbc.com/news/world-africa-11150063

47 http://www.kurukulla.org/stupa-project-what-is-a-stupa-kurukulla-tibetan-
buddhist.php

48 http://www.bhutanculturalatlas.org/606/culture/sites-structures/monasteries-
temples/kurje-lhakhang/

49 https://sossusvlei.com/en/emergence-of-sossusvlei/

50 http://corsier-port.com/en/

51 http://phenomena.nationalgeographic.com/2015/06/01/how-do-african-grasslands-
support-so-many-plant-eaters/

52 The Big Five animals include the lion, elephant, black rhinoceros, Cape buffalo
and leopard.

53 http://whc.unesco.org/en/list/289

Abdulaali, W. 2012. "Echoes of a Legendary Queen: Contemporary Women Writers Revise and Recreate Sheba/Bilqǎs." **Harvard Divinity Bulletin**, 40 (3 and 4).

Carter, T., L. Dunston, V. Jealous, and R. Chau. 2009. **Australia Travel Guide.** Singapore: Lonely Planet.

Mayhew, B., R. Kelly, and J. V. Bellezza. 2009. **Tibet Travel Guide,** Singapore: Lonely Planet.

McCarthy, C. 2009. **Trekking in the Patagonian Andes,** 4th ed. Singapore: Lonely Planet.

Slobig, Z. 2014. "The Brain Aquatic." **Psychology Today** (July/August): 30-31.

www.ingramcontent.com/pod-product-compliance
Lightning Source LLC
Chambersburg PA
CBHW032012050726

47590CB00006B/2139